Management for Professionals

The Springer series "Management for Professionals" comprises high-level business and management books for executives, MBA students, and practice-oriented business researchers. The topics cover all themes relevant to businesses and the business ecosystem. The authors are experienced business professionals and renowned professors who combine scientific backgrounds, best practices, and entrepreneurial vision to provide powerful insights into achieving business excellence.

The Series is SCOPUS-indexed.

Uwe Wolff

Disinformation Attacks On Businesses

The Dark Business of Fake News & Co. and How to Combat it

Springer

Uwe Wolff
Lectures, Seminars
NAIMA Strategic Legal Services GmbH
Berlin, Berlin, Germany

ISSN 2192-8096 ISSN 2192-810X (electronic)
Management for Professionals
ISBN 978-3-658-51406-8 ISBN 978-3-658-51407-5 (eBook)
https://doi.org/10.1007/978-3-658-51407-5

This book is a translation of the original German edition "Desinformationsangriffe auf Unternehmen abwehren" by Uwe Wolff, published by Springer Fachmedien Wiesbaden GmbH in 2024. The translation was done with the help of an artificial intelligence machine translation tool. A subsequent human revision was done primarily in terms of content, so that the book will read stylistically differently from a conventional translation. Springer Nature works continuously to further the development of tools for the production of books and on the related technologies to support the authors.

This Springer imprint is published by the registered company Springer Fachmedien Wiesbaden GmbH, part of Springer Nature.
The registered company address is: Abraham-Lincoln-Str. 46, 65189 Wiesbaden, Germany

The issue for many people isn't exactly a denial of truth as such. It's more a growing weariness over the process of finding the truth at all.
And that weariness leads more and more people to abandon the idea that the truth is knowable.
– Sean Illing,
Flood the zone with shit:
How misinformation overwhelmed our democracy on vox.com

Foreword by Dr August Hanning

As former president of the Federal Intelligence Service (BND), I have witnessed firsthand the growing threat posed by disinformation attacks targeting companies and businesses. These attacks are carried out by professionals motivated by various factors such as financial gain, competitive advantage, or ideological convictions.

Disinformation attacks have long since moved beyond the political–military sphere. They now represent a significant threat to companies and businesses of all sizes and sectors. It is therefore crucial that business leaders and executives take this threat seriously and prioritize the implementation of strategies to mitigate the risks arising from such attacks.

The damage caused by these attacks can be severe, ranging from financial losses and reputational harm to business disruption. It is therefore essential that companies and businesses are aware of this growing threat and take proactive measures to defend themselves.

National intelligence services have recognized the danger that disinformation attacks pose to the economy. They have made this issue a focus and are working to support companies in their efforts to defend against such attacks. The aim is now to raise corporate awareness of the threat and to provide them with the necessary tools to counter disinformation attacks.

Uwe Wolff, the author of this book, is an experienced expert in the field of strategic legal communication and has himself fought and won several "battles" against deliberately orchestrated disinformation attacks. His book offers, for the first time, a comprehensive overview of disinformation attacks on companies and businesses, including the perpetrators, their motives, and the methods they employ. It also provides practical advice and guidance on how to defend against such attacks.

This book serves as a valuable resource for business leaders and executives seeking to protect their organizations from this growing threat.

Former President of the German Federal Intelligence Service (BND)
Berlin, Germany
August Hanning

Preface

For over 20 years, I have worked in the field of strategic legal communication, a communications discipline I first encountered in the United States and subsequently introduced to Europe under the term Litigation PR after my return from the United States to Germany in 2002. The service portfolio of our company, NAÏMA Strategic Legal Services GmbH, has since expanded to include crisis communication, reputation management, and now also disinformation crisis management.

Working in this field means that, among other things, we act on behalf of our clients (mainly companies or high-net-worth individuals), in cooperation with media lawyers, to counter unfavorable or even false reporting and to communicate accordingly. Not infrequently, during legal disputes, it became apparent that journalists had fallen for false or fabricated information supplied to them by interested parties. These planted pieces of disinformation appeared so enticing to the journalists that they neglected the journalistic caution and diligence required prior to publication. Eliminating such damaging information for our clients has been, and remains, part of our daily work.

As someone with a keen interest in politics, I could not fail to notice how perceptions of truth and facts have changed in recent years. Trump's election campaigns (Part I and Part II), Brexit, Bolsonaro in Brazil, right-wing populist parties in Germany, France, and Italy, and Russian disinformation campaigns in Europe and Africa provided the backdrop for a period described as "post-factual," which would ultimately culminate in the coronavirus crisis.

State actors (Russia and China), political actors (right-wing populists), and private actors exploited this extraordinary situation, each driven by different motives, to attack the manufacturers of COVID vaccines. This caught my attention. Could it be that what we had previously associated with the political sphere—namely fake news and deliberately spread disinformation—was now crossing over into the economic sphere?

Reliable information and stable communication channels are the lifeblood of our modern economy. Could it be that this foundation of free societies is now increasingly exposed to disinformation attacks, unleashing their enormous destructive potential and causing devastating economic consequences?

I wanted to find answers to these questions and began my research. At that time, the database was still thin, and there was barely any understanding of what might distinguish disinformation attacks from cyberattacks.

Nevertheless, the deeper I delved into the subject, the clearer my understanding became: companies are facing an epic threat. It took 2 years before I had gathered enough material to write my book, which was published in Germany by Springer Gabler under the title "Defending Companies Against Disinformation Attacks" in April 2024.

The topic attracted considerable interest. The media reported on it. My publisher, Springer Nature (the American parent company of the German publisher), offered me the opportunity to publish the book in English due to the high level of interest and to revise and update its content. This was urgently needed, as developments and research in the field of disinformation were constantly providing new approaches—as were the techniques and tools used by attackers.

Now, 2 years later, the situation has changed once again. The issue of "disinformation attacks on companies" has now reached the boardrooms. There, it is gradually being recognized that the number of disinformation attacks on companies and institutions is rising sharply. The damage caused by such attacks can be enormous. The World Economic Forum (WEF) has identified disinformation as one of the major challenges of our time. The figures calculated in Davos are alarming: the consequences of disinformation attacks on companies are now resulting in market losses amounting to billions. Artificial intelligence, which produces particularly insidious products such as deepfakes and intelligent bots, is accelerating disinformation campaigns. Losses from negative review campaigns in commerce and industry alone are estimated at around 152 billion US dollars, according to one study.

It is a fact that most CEOs believe disinformation attacks are something that only occur in the political sphere or are akin to cyberattacks. The reality, however, is that disinformation attacks on companies are real and occur far more frequently than we have previously realized.

These attacks can take many forms, from spreading false rumors about a company to creating a negative and damaging narrative that damages its reputation, full-scale campaigns aimed at harming a company's market value, or competitors seeking to prevent a company from expanding or to drive a rival's product or service out of the market. Such attacks affect not only the targeted company but also markets, supply chains, and jobs associated with the company.

As a communications expert with over 20 years of experience in strategic legal communications, crisis communications, and reputation management, I have encountered a variety of cases involving disinformation attacks on companies. Often, it was traditional media where perpetrators used journalists to place false information.

This changed dramatically over the past 10 years, both strategically and technologically, as well as in terms of content. Perpetrators no longer need traditional media for their attacks. At best, these serve as amplifiers or refiners for disinformation campaigns already underway in the digital sphere. The gatekeeper function, of which traditional media are so proud, is increasingly eroding under the pressure of media companies' profit targets, modernization, the speed of online media and social media, shrinking newsrooms, and acute shortages of budget and time.

Influencers, whether real or synthetic, now play a dominant role in many people's lives.

Journalists have become more susceptible in this environment to disinformation campaigns in which they—usually unwittingly—play a role. This vulnerability is exacerbated by the rise of advocacy journalism and activist journalism. Such journalists, who should be fulfilling their gatekeeper function, open the floodgates with their one-sidedness to information from NGOs and activist groups that is often unchecked, highly distorted, one-sided, and difficult to verify—groups which, incidentally, can themselves be part of a devious disinformation attack. In my book, I address this pernicious symbiotic relationship between journalists and NGOs, providing examples.

This book is not a blanket criticism of traditional media and their representatives. Rather, I wish to highlight how vulnerable the traditional media sector has become. Over the years, we have seen numerous cases in which journalists were clearly instrumentalized for a disinformation attack. In almost all cases, the journalists vehemently denied this, just as they indignantly rejected the suggestion that they could ever be used for a disinformation campaign. This vain, ignorant, and lacking self-criticism attitude leads to a complete failure of journalists' personal gatekeeper function. Firmly believing they cannot be manipulated, they abandon all caution against disinformation.

Vanity, overconfidence, and ignorance were the key to the "gate" that suddenly stood wide open for malicious communicators. If journalists—regardless of the medium—do not remind themselves every single day that they can be instrumentalized by skilled disinformers, they—usually unwittingly—become accomplices of disinformers.

Today, disinformers no longer even need to enter the newsrooms of traditional media. With today's tools, they can orchestrate campaigns on social media from their kitchen tables that are so effective they do not escape the attention of traditional media. Once a topic becomes "big" enough, many newsrooms feel they can no longer ignore it. They pick up the story. This was the case with the notorious Paris bedbug hysteria in the summer of 2023, which dealt a severe and costly blow to the Paris tourism sector. Behind it was Russia with a professional disinformation campaign targeting France. However, the bedbug hysteria also demonstrated that today, each of us has access to digital tools capable of causing immense and destructive harm to a company, an organization, or an entire industrial sector. And no, this is not about hacking or cyberattacks; rather, it concerns the deliberate use of false and damaging information as part of a digital campaign. It is about images; it is about words as weapons in the battle over the now numerous "truths" of an increasingly polarized and fragmented society.

The research for this book was, in a way, fascinating. But it was also unsettling. The deeper I delved into the subject, the more I learned about the perpetrators and their motives, and I realized that disinformation attacks had long since moved beyond the political sphere and opened a new battleground in the business world. I also discovered that we are already in the midst of this battle, albeit a highly asymmetrical one.

I learned a great deal at the outstanding conferences of the NATO Strategic Communication Centre of Excellence (NATO StratCom COE) in Riga, Latvia. Here, disinformation experts from academia, politics, the military, and communications meet annually. The discussions focus on the future of disinformation, new tools, their impact on people, and how the overarching topic of artificial intelligence is completely reshaping the field and multiplying the risks.

Disinformation attacks thrive in a polarized society, a situation brought about by politics and social media corporations. A study by the Pew Research Center in the United States found that political polarization is a key factor in the spread of disinformation. People who strongly identify with a political party are more likely to share content that supports their beliefs, even if it is false. This dynamic can also be observed in the business world, where employees or customers may be highly loyal to a particular brand or company.

When I began investigating the masterminds behind disinformation attacks on companies, I found that they are not always easy to identify. This is inherent to the issue, as they do not wish to be recognized. Nevertheless, it was possible to distill the different motives of these groups. These individuals or groups have various motives, such as gaining market share, competing for talent, rivalry in product sectors, or pursuing an ideological agenda. They may also be individuals or state actors, as we have seen in the cases of Russia, China, Iran, and now, to some extent, the United States.

During my research, I not only sifted through countless studies but also spoke with experts working for NATO StratCom, with representatives of intelligence services, and with the former board member of the German Wikimedia Association, which supports Wikipedia. I interviewed media lawyers who have experience with disinformation attacks, even from times when the term itself did not yet exist. I spoke with the Berlin-based scientist Martin Grothe, who, together with his team and sophisticated software, monitors the digital space to identify potential activist perpetrators. I spoke with the American performance artist Joey Skaggs, the king of media hoaxes, who has been outwitting the media and journalists for over 50 years because he knows them better than they know themselves. I spoke with Mark Turnage, CEO of the Colorado-based company DarkOwl, whose analysts monitor the darknet for corporate risks and have encountered disinformation mercenaries—contract killers in matters of reputation. I spoke with Jack Devine, a former senior CIA veteran who now advises companies. He described to me how cases of disinformation attacks on companies are increasing significantly. I also spoke with journalists, politicians, criminal investigators, crisis managers, and entrepreneurs. The latter often declined to speak with me, as they were unwilling to discuss disinformation attacks on their companies. And I have discussed with prominent media lawyers in the UK, the USA, and Germany what specific role lawyers should play in defending against disinformation attacks.

Through my research, I embarked on a journey into an unknown land, whose belligerent inhabitants draw from a vast arsenal of weapons and descend upon companies to plunder or destroy them. On my journey, I encountered digital warlords who care only for their own interests and have no regard for their victims or the damage they cause. But I also met courageous individuals who strive to disarm or neutralize these digital warlords. Above all, I encountered people for whom the topic of “disinformation attacks on companies” was entirely new.

Dear readers, I invite you to join me on this illuminating journey through a little-explored digital wilderness. You are holding the guidebook in your hands.

Berlin, Germany Uwe Wolff
January 2026

Acknowledgments

This book is the work of many people. It is the work of those who supported me during its creation, who encouraged me, and who showed great patience. It is also the product of people who lent me their valuable time. Only those who have written a book during their independent professional lives know how difficult it can be to find the necessary time and to maintain motivation.

For this reason, my deepest gratitude goes to my family: The person who was by far my greatest support in this project is my wonderful and amazing wife, **Nadine**, who always had my back, continually motivated me, spurred me on, and kept me afloat with her radiant optimism. She and our daughter **Rosalie** gave me the time I needed. My son **Vincent** supported me in my research and unearthed small gems that shine throughout the book's text. He proved to be an invaluable help, and I must now fear that I will recruit him for further book projects in the future. My "grown-up" children, **Sophie** and **Julian**, have already accompanied me through two book projects and supported me. They motivated and supported me in their own special way, and their love and presence cannot be put into words. Unfortunately, I cannot guarantee them that this will be my last book project. Thank you for your support, your tolerance, and simply for being there. Love you!

A heartfelt thank you goes to **Martin Jenewein**, with whom I developed the idea for this book. Originally, we intended to write the book together, but unfortunately, his time became too limited. Nevertheless, Martin's input is evident throughout this book.

Many thanks also to **my colleagues at NAÏMA Strategic Legal Services**, who patiently—and at times with exasperated eye-rolling—endured my constant stress levels. My friend **Cornel Faltin** made his house in the Bavarian Alps available to me, where I was finally able to complete a large part of the book. Without Cornel, I would probably still be working on the manuscript today. A heartfelt "thank you" goes out to **August Hanning**, the former president of the German Federal Intelligence Service (BND), who spontaneously agreed to write the foreword for this book.

My deepest thanks go to **Melanie Riley** and **Louise Beeson** of **Bell Yard** in London, who supported me with their input and connected me with the country's leading media lawyers. Sincere thanks also go to Brussels, Belgium, to **Caroline Sapriel** of **CS&A**, the experienced, internationally active crisis manager who gave me a wonderful interview for my book. **Andrew Frank**, founder and president of **KARV** in New York, introduced me to the legendary CIA agent **Jack Devine**, who shared with me his experiences of disinformation campaigns during the Cold War, as well as his current work as an adviser to companies under attack. Martin, Mel, Louise, Caroline, Andrew, and I are all part of the **Crisis & Litigation Communicators' Alliance (CLCA)** in London, an international organization of experts in our field, bringing together the best of the best in this specialized profession to collaborate, and which continues to grow. I am proud to serve as one of the co-directors of this outstanding organization.

A heartfelt thank you goes out to my publisher **Springer Gabler in Germany**, who granted me countless extensions for submitting the manuscript and ultimately encouraged an international and revised edition of the book. Thank you for your patience.

Berlin, January 2026

Competing Interests The author has no competing interests to declare that are relevant to the content of this manuscript.

Contents

About the Author

Uwe Wolff is a communications consultant and founder and managing director of NAÏMA Strategic Legal Services GmbH in Berlin.

In 2002, he introduced Litigation-PR (strategic legal communications) from the USA to Europe and established it successfully. Uwe Wolff has advised on many high-profile and media-sensitive cases both nationally and internationally and is regarded as the consultant with the longest and most profound experience in Litigation PR.

Over his more than 20 years as a consultant, he has repeatedly been involved in countering deliberately orchestrated disinformation campaigns against companies, witnessing how such attacks have evolved in recent years and the threats they now pose to the entire business sector.

Uwe Wolff abandoned his law studies in favor of journalism, working for various daily newspapers before moving to New York in 1991 for 10 years to establish the US correspondent office for a prominent news magazine. He reported from North, Central, and South America, the Caribbean, and Africa. Fascinated by the interplay between lawyers, prosecutors, and the media, Uwe Wolff became acquainted with Harvard professor and star defense attorney Alan M. Dershowitz, who represented, among others, O. J. Simpson and Mike Tyson. With him, he discussed the influence of public opinion on the judiciary and the reputation of clients.

Uwe Wolff is the author of several books, book chapters, and specialist articles, including the German-language standard work on Litigation-PR, "Im Namen der Öffentlichkeit" ("In the Name of the Public"), and "Medienarbeit für Rechtsanwälte" ("Media Relations for Lawyers"). He regularly gives lectures and presentations on the subject. He trained with NATO as a Crisis and Disaster Response Manager (CDRM) and is co-director of the London-based international Crisis and Litigation Communicators' Alliance (CLCA).

Part I

The Rise of the Information Warriors

1 The Hazim Nada Case

Dies irae, dies illa
Day of wrath, day of sins (Latin: opening of a medieval hymn about the Last Judgment)

In March 2023, the American magazine "New Yorker" published an article entitled "The Dirty Secrets of a Smear Campaign" by David D. Kirkpatrick. It provides a perfect example of the devastating impact a disinformation campaign can have on a company.

At the beginning of the story in 2017, Hazim Nada was 34 years old and living as a successful entrepreneur in Como, northern Italy. Nada, an American by birth with a Syrian mother and an Egyptian father, had studied physics at Cambridge and completed a doctorate in applied mathematics at Imperial College London. After his academic career, he built a company that grew rapidly within a few years: LORD Energy—an acronym for "Liquid or Dry"—specialized in the transport of crude oil and bulk goods and reported a turnover of 2 billion US dollars.

Nada himself lived in a beautiful house on Lake Como (Italy), right next door to George Clooney. It was on his terrace—not George Clooney's—that the Nespresso commercials were filmed. Hazim Nada simply had the better view. Business was good. He was married, and the couple was expecting a child. One could say life was treating him well.

But in the summer of 2017, he received a suspicious text message that gave him an uneasy feeling. It came from his mobile phone provider, asking whether he had been satisfied with the services he had requested. What Hazim Nada did not know at the time was that someone had apparently tried to obtain a copy of his incoming and outgoing calls under his name (The New Yorker 2023). In fact, this text message turned out to be a harbinger of what awaited him, his family, and his company in the coming months.

Hazim Nada claims that he has nothing to do with politics and little to do with religion. In any case, he is not a particularly devout Muslim. But suddenly, obscure media reports began to appear, linking him and his company to the radical Islamic

U. Wolff, *Disinformation Attacks On Businesses*, Management for Professionals,
https://doi.org/10.1007/978-3-658-51407-5_1

Muslim Brotherhood. Various online platforms even claimed that Hazim Nada was financing Islamist terrorists. The company name LORD Energy was cited as evidence that he was on a divine mission. The attackers turned "L-quid OR D-ry" into the religious term "Lord." Hazim Nada was desperate. The accusations were completely unfounded, yet he increasingly became the focus of media attention. What Nada did not realize at the time was that he had become caught in the geopolitical crossfire between the rival countries United Arab Emirates and Qatar.

1.1 The Nightmare Becomes Reality

It was a time when the United Arab Emirates, together with Saudi Arabia and other neighboring countries, was attempting to politically isolate Qatar. The Emirates, the Saudis, other Gulf states, and Egypt accused the Qataris of financing the Muslim Brotherhood—with the aim of seizing power in various Arab states. This led to the further accusation that the Qataris were funding Islamist terrorists.

According to research by the "New Yorker," representatives of the United Arab Emirates hired the Swiss businessman and private detective Mario Brero, president of "Alp Services" in Geneva. Brero was well-versed in the fields of disinformation and smear campaigns—an expertise that was evidently highly valued by some of his clients. This was revealed by information from a hacker group that penetrated deep into the "Alp Services" system. The documents extracted by the hacker group from Brero's company computer proved that the United Arab Emirates paid millions for the disinformation campaign against Hazim Nada.

1.2 Help from Hackers

The story took a surprising turn when the data stolen by the hacker group from the "Alp Services" computer was offered to Nada for purchase. Up to that point, the events had remained completely obscure to Nada. He assumed he had fallen victim to an attack by a competing company. However, the documents, emails, photos, and other materials obtained by the hackers pointed to the true instigator of the disinformation attack on his company: Sheikh Mohammed bin Zayed, ruler of the United Arab Emirates and one of the richest people in the world. The data also revealed the role of Mario Brero as the organizer of the campaign and the millions in fees he received for the Sheikh's commission. Hazim Nada, on the other hand, was left around 100 million US dollars poorer and became the victim of perhaps the most extreme, effective, and fact-free disinformation campaign ever successfully waged against a company.

The case of Hazim Nada's LORD Energy demonstrates that any company can potentially fall victim to a disinformation attack. The company itself does not even have to be the primary target; it may simply serve as a convenient steppingstone toward an entirely different objective. In this instance, LORD Energy and its bankruptcy were merely collateral damage to portray Qatar as a supporter of terrorism.

As we will see throughout this book, both the perpetrators and their motives are highly diverse. The tools, intensity, and duration of their attacks depend on the financial resources available to fund a multi-instrumental disinformation orchestra, conducted by a persistent yet sensitive director.

One thing is clear: the case of Hazim Nada is neither the first of its kind nor will it be the last. We are only at the beginning of a disinformation war that is set to impact our economy with tremendous force.

Reference

Kirkpatrick, D. D. (2023, March 27). The dirty secrets of a smear campaign. *The New Yorker*. Accessed at: https://www.newyorker.com/magazine/2023/04/03/the-dirty-secrets-of-a-smear-campaign

The Impact Is Drawing Closer

2

In the previous chapter, we saw how an uninvolved company became a geopolitical casualty. The operation was financed by a wealthy state and executed by a lone smear campaign specialist in Switzerland.

The situation was different in the case of the city of Paris in the summer of 2023. A social media influencer was staying there and spent the night in a hotel. She discovered a bedbug in her bed, photographed it, and posted the image on her social media channel.

What followed was a well-orchestrated and highly successful disinformation campaign by a state actor, whose agents seized upon the young woman's bedbug story for their own nefarious purposes. They propelled the tiny bedbug to great notoriety.

The outraged hotel guest's photo of the bedbug was shared across various social media platforms. Other individuals, claiming to have had similarly poor and unhygienic experiences in Paris, joined in. Coordinated bots amplified the outrage, spreading the topic ever further and blowing it out of all proportion. The issue grew so large that traditional media outlets picked it up, abandoning their usual gatekeeping role.

This led to a veritable bedbug hysteria in Paris. Television stations showed pest controllers in protective suits treating cinema seats and underground train seats with insecticides. The images and reports from French media, combined with social media, reached neighboring European countries, whose media also reported on the alleged bedbug infestation. The result: tourists cancelled their trips to Paris en masse, along with their hotel and restaurant reservations—the Paris tourism sector suffered massive losses in the summer of 2023.

It took months for the French government to uncover who had orchestrated the bedbug disinformation campaign. One disinformation agent overreached and claimed that Ukrainian refugees had brought the bedbugs to Paris. At this point, French authorities began to suspect who was behind it: Russia and its state-sponsored disinformation cohorts (Reuters, 2024).

U. Wolff, *Disinformation Attacks On Businesses*, Management for Professionals,
https://doi.org/10.1007/978-3-658-51407-5_2

But why did they target France? Why Paris? First, French President Emmanuel Macron had positioned himself as a staunch opponent of Russian President Vladimir Putin and supporter of Ukraine. Second, the Olympic Games were scheduled to take place in Paris in 2024. However, due to the invasion of Ukraine and subsequent sanctions, Russia was not permitted to participate under its national flag. The Russians apparently sought retribution against Paris in their own way, inflicting significant damage on the tourism sector.

In recent years, the number of disinformation attacks on companies, organizations, and the economic sector has increased. It is now clear: the wave of disinformation is spilling over from the political sphere into the economic sector, with companies as its primary focus. Whether individual bad actors, organized crime, NGOs, states, short sellers, activists, or competitors with varying motivations—they are all adopting disinformation techniques and methods from the political arena, employing the same structures and dissemination strategies as politically motivated disinformation campaigns.

The increase in disinformation attacks on companies is closely linked to the growing importance of social media and other online platforms in the business world. These platforms offer companies opportunities to engage with customers and obtain relevant data. What the advocates of social media praise as a tool for customer retention and marketing has, for some companies, proven to be nothing but toxic. In fact, corporate social media channels create new risks by facilitating the rapid spread of false information, which can have significant impacts on a company's reputation and financial results. An existing corporate social media channel, especially if not strictly moderated, should fundamentally be regarded as a potential entry point for a disinformation campaign.

At present, it remains difficult to obtain reliable figures on disinformation attacks against companies in the USA, the UK, or Germany. Anyone searching for studies on disinformation attacks targeting companies in the USA will have to search for a long time. Generally, references to the issue can be found in reports by major auditing firms, which only touch on the subject in passing. Unfortunately, disinformation attacks on companies are, with few exceptions, lumped together with cyber and IT risks. Business leaders, industry associations, and politicians are still struggling to consider disinformation attacks outside the political sphere and to recognize the real dangers they pose to the economy. Yet there are some very clear examples, which will be discussed later in this book.

The conflation of cyberattacks and disinformation attacks on companies demonstrates that the nature and scope of disinformation attacks have not yet been even remotely understood. Auditors and cyber experts find it difficult to grasp the complexity of a communicative attack.

Yet it is not so difficult to understand: while in a cyberattack, the attackers manipulate the central nervous system at the very core of the company and operate from within, disinformation attackers come from outside and target the company through various media channels using false narratives. Their aim is to destroy the trust of those essential to the company (customers, employees, banks, suppliers, and policymakers). Unlike cyberattacks, disinformation attacks are harder to detect because they begin insidiously and quietly, gradually building up in the public digital space.

In my lectures, I illustrated the difference between disinformation and cyberattacks as follows:

In a **cyberattack**, hackers penetrate a company's IT systems. In this way, they can block the company's access to its own IT and demand a ransom for restoring access. Alternatively, hackers may infiltrate the company's IT and steal important documents, emails, and records, which they may then pass on or sell.

In a **disinformation attack**, the attackers infiltrate the minds of consumers, suppliers, shareholders, insurers, employees, and others with powerful, toxic narratives (see Hazim Nada or the bedbug hysteria in Paris), which they disseminate and amplify via social media, thereby influencing the perceptions of the company and damaging its reputation. In effect, they reprogram a company's stakeholders and shareholders, altering their trust in the company.

During my research for this book, I attempted to find studies on disinformation attacks against companies. My research covered both English- and German-speaking regions (the author of this book is German). There may be studies in other languages, but I am not currently aware of any.

For the USA, there are no comprehensive statistics from industry or law enforcement on purely communicative disinformation attacks against companies. However, initial estimates of the damage are available. For example, "Audit Committee Quarterly Extra—Fake Futures" (2025) estimates the global economic cost of fake news at between 70 and 80 billion US dollars annually—and rising (Audit Committee Quarterly, 2025).

For Germany, too, we do not have reliable figures on the number of companies already targeted. However, the "Munich Security Report 2025" (Munich Security Report, 2025) and KPMG/Audit Committee Quarterly now count disinformation among the greatest economic risks. German companies estimate the annual reputational or stock market damage caused by disinformation campaigns to be in the hundreds of millions. Here, too, there is often a lack of clear statistics distinguishing between cyber and disinformation attacks.

In fact, I did find a useful study commissioned by the German "ASW Bundesverband", an association for the protection of German companies. The study dates from 2019 but remains highly informative. I will cite this study several times throughout the book. Entitled "Disinformation—Situation, Forecast and Defense", it sheds at least some light on the poorly illuminated statistics of disinformation attacks. In a survey conducted by the authors, even the otherwise reticent German companies opened up. The study concludes:

> The interviews conducted as part of this study, Expert interviews and the online survey conducted for the study indicate that companies intend to assign significantly higher priority to protection against disinformation attacks than they have done so far. (…) Almost 90% of the companies surveyed are convinced that disinformation attacks will require significantly increased attention in the near future. (…) Disinformation is becoming one of the central threats of the 21st century for German companies.

The situation in the USA is as follows: In 2020, the American security institute Ponemon Institute conducted a survey on disinformation attacks and their impact on companies. The survey included responses from 700 IT and security experts from various industries across the USA.

The essence of the survey:

- 81% of the companies surveyed stated that they had fallen victim to a disinformation attack in 2019.
- The most common types of disinformation attacks were false rumors or lies (67%), followed by manipulated or fake news (63%) and fake social media accounts (59%).
- The main impacts of disinformation attacks on companies were reputational damage (89%), loss of customer trust (87%), and loss of revenue (62%).
- The average cost of a disinformation attack for a company was $1.7 million.
- Only 29% of the companies surveyed had a formal strategy for detecting and responding to disinformation attacks.

I have spoken with former representatives of police and intelligence services in the USA, UK, and Germany about whether they have observed an increase in disinformation attacks. All of them now work as security consultants for companies. I quote Frank-Martin Heise, former head of the Hamburg State Criminal Police Office, the second largest state criminal police office in Germany. Frank-Martin Heise is now CEO of the business intelligence company Intafors in Hamburg. He answered my question about the increase in disinformation attacks unequivocally in the affirmative and added: "What makes this so attractive for perpetrators is that disinformation campaigns sometimes require only minimal to moderate effort, yet the intended effect of harming the company can escalate very quickly."

2.1 The Mercenaries of Disinformation

Disinformation attacks are inherently asymmetric, meaning they are inexpensive to produce and can be rapidly disseminated on a large scale. In contrast, the costs of defense and the resulting damage to the company are generally much higher.

Until a few years ago, conducting an effective disinformation campaign required considerable effort, logistics, and personnel, and above all, it was expensive. However, with the tools available today, costs and effort can be kept relatively low, especially if one engages the right service providers.

In a 2021 report, the "New York Times" provided deep insights into the world of mercenaries for lies and disinformation:

"Private firms operating at the intersection of traditional marketing and the shadowy world of geopolitical influence are selling services that were previously the domain of intelligence agencies." (New York Times, 2021). According to the New York Times, the business of "Disinformation-as-a-Service" (DaaS) has developed into a veritable boom industry. The US think tank "Brookings Institute" shares this view:

> Political actors are increasingly outsourcing their disinformation work to third-party PR and marketing firms and are using AI-generated profile pictures. (Brookings Institute, 2021)

The auditors at "PWC USA" have researched the prices for disinformation services. These are surprisingly low:

> Disinformation campaigns are asymmetric in nature, meaning they are inexpensive to create and distribute at scale. DaaS providers now charge clients from hundreds of dollars to hundreds of thousands of dollars for highly customizable packages. Here's a sample of costs: $15–$45 to create a 1,000-character article; $65 to contact a media source directly to spread material; $100 for 10 comments to post on a given article or news story; $350–$550 per month for social media marketing; and $1,500 for search engine optimization services to promote social media posts and articles over a 10- to 15-day period. (PWC USA, 2021)

Mark Turnage from the security company Dark Owl in Colorado, which scans the dark web for threats on behalf of large companies, told me that it can be even cheaper. Spoiler: Disinformation attacks are already being offered by malicious service providers for a three-figure sum (see my interview with Mark Turnage).

It may seem surprising that so-called bad actors, who otherwise remain in the shadows, pay third-party companies to disseminate false information. The risk that the client of such a disinformation campaign will be exposed through the service provider they have hired is high. However, this risk is offset by an invaluable advantage for the information warriors: they have the possibility to deny any involvement in the dissemination of false information. As long as the service provider remains silent and no data is leaked, there is no evidence of any commission for a disinformation campaign.

And what happens if things do go wrong and the whole affair is exposed? In that case, the service provider is made the scapegoat and becomes the sacrificial pawn. In the case of Hazim Nada, the actual client offered their full support in any legal disputes that Hazim Nada might initiate against Brero of "Alp". The New Yorker (2023) describes it as follows:

> Nada can expect a vigorous counterattack. Among the hacked files was a recording of a phone call with Matar about how to handle an e-mail from Nada threatening legal action. "Ignore it," Matar told Brero. The U.A.E. was ready for war. 'We're fully, fully a hundred per cent behind you,' Matar said. 'Whatever it takes.' (The New Yorker, 2023)

But before we delve deeper into disinformation attacks on companies, let us first consider some historical background on disinformation and clarify the relevant terminology. After all, not everything labeled as disinformation is actually disinformation.

References

Audit Committee Quarterly. (2025). Fake futures or the end of reality. Retrieved from: https://audit-committee-institute.de/media/aci-qextra-2025-Fake-Futures.pdf

Fisher, M. (2021). Disinformation for hire, a shadow industry is quietly booming. Retrieved from: https://www.nytimes.com/2021/07/25/world/europe/disinformation-social-media.html

Goldstein, J. A., & Grossmann, S. (2021). How disinformation has evolved in 2020. Brookings Institute, Tech Stream Online. Retrieved from: https://www.brookings.edu/techstream/how-disinformation-evolved-in-2020/

Kirkpatrick, D. D. (2023). The dirty secret of a smear campaign. Retrieved from: https://www.newyorker.com/magazine/2023/04/03/the-dirty-secrets-of-a-smear-campaign

Munich Security Report 2025. (2025). Disinformation among the greatest risks for Germany // Mehring: 'We must not become spectators within our own democracy.' Retrieved from: https://www.stmd.bayern.de/munich-security-report-2025-desinformation-unter-den-groessten-risiken-fuer-deutschland-mehring-wir-duerfen-nicht-zu-zuschauern-innerhalb-unserer-eigenen-demokratie-wer/

PWC USA. (2021). Disinformation attacks have arrived in the corporate sector. Are you ready? Retrieved from: https://www.pwc.com/us/en/techeffect/cybersecurity/corporate-sector-disinformation.html

Reuters. (2024). Russian 'disinformation' hyped Paris bedbug scare, French minister says. Retrieved from: https://www.reuters.com/world/europe/russian-disinformation-hyped-paris-bedbug-scare-french-minister-says-2024-03-01/

How Words Can Ignite the World

3

3.1 Disinformation in History

Rumors, conspiracy theories, false claims, or outright disinformation—words and misinformation have often laid the groundwork for crises, wars, and genocides. Examples of this can be traced back to the earliest recorded history of humankind. Certainly, some warlords saw no need to justify an attack on another country—they simply invaded.

Other warlords did in fact go to the trouble of linking their assault on another country with a premeditated disinformation campaign or a propaganda offensive. The most recent example is Russia's invasion of Ukraine. At the outset, Putin claimed the country was ruled by dangerous neo-Nazis who had to be destroyed to liberate the brother nation of Ukraine. So, he sent in his troops and attacked the neighboring country, to which he had already annexed territory. The only problem was that the Russian disinformation campaign in Ukraine collided with reality: Ukrainians did not want to be liberated by the Russians and instead bravely resisted the occupiers.

Time and again, those in power have fabricated false justifications for war or genocide to incite their own population against another. This can already be found in the Bible: Alleged divine commands provided the basis for various genocides described and justified in the Old Testament. Ever since humans could wield a club as a weapon, belief in gods, nationalism, constructed identities, political systems, physical characteristics, tribal affiliations, faith and religion, and even, in the case of the Trojan Wars, a woman, have all served as pretexts for humanity's wars.

Here are just a few examples from the endless list that bear witness to the power of words and the targeted use of disinformation and propaganda as a prelude to war and genocide throughout human history.

Second World War (1939–1945) The Nazi regime in Germany used propaganda and disinformation to justify the invasion of Poland in 1939 and subsequent military

U. Wolff, *Disinformation Attacks On Businesses*, Management for Professionals,
https://doi.org/10.1007/978-3-658-51407-5_3

aggression in Europe. Nazi propaganda portrayed Germany as the victim of aggression by neighboring countries (Poland) and used false information to demonize Jews and other minorities. Adolf Hitler made no secret of how he would use propaganda to launch the war: "The outbreak of the conflict will be brought about by suitable propaganda. The credibility does not matter; in victory lies the right." On 10 August 1939, the Nazis ordered an attack on the German radio station at Gleiwitz on the Polish border. It was intended to appear as if the station had been attacked by Poland. This event is considered the beginning of the Second World War.

The Gulf of Tonkin Incident (1964) The alleged attack by North Vietnamese patrol boats on two US Navy destroyers was used by the US government as justification for the Vietnam War. Later investigations revealed, however, that the attack may never have taken place and that the US government had fabricated the incident to justify military action in Vietnam.

US Invasion of Grenada (1983) Grenada's left-wing government under Prime Minister Maurice Bishop nationalized several businesses and focused primarily on social reforms. The USA, under President Ronald Reagan, saw this as a communist-influenced movement and launched a disinformation campaign against the government of the small Caribbean island to justify an invasion in violation of international law. The US government portrayed Grenada as a close ally of the Soviet Union and Cuba. Reports were published about the construction of a Soviet submarine base in southern Grenada, until, in 1983, a correspondent from the "Washington Post" visited the site and reported that the construction of a submarine base was entirely impossible due to the shallow waters. In February 1983, the US Department of Defense circulated reports of Soviet arms deliveries. No evidence for these claims was ever produced, yet the US military invaded Grenada. After 4 days, the fighting ended and the government in Grenada was overthrown.

The First Gulf War under George H. W. Bush (1991) After Iraq's invasion of the oil-rich state of Kuwait, an ally of the USA, the US government sought to convince its own population and the world of the necessity of a military response by the USA and its allies. To this end, the cruelty of the Iraqi dictator Saddam Hussein and his soldiers was to be highlighted to increase international willingness to mobilize. The stage for this was to be the US Congress, to secure approval for the first Gulf War under US President George H. W. Bush.

> The PR strategists (the American PR agency "Hill & Knowlton") created Nayirah, a 15-year-old Kuwaiti girl who allegedly worked in a hospital in Kuwait City. With a trembling voice and in tears, she reported on camera how Iraqi soldiers tore babies from incubators, took the incubators away, and left the infants to die on the cold hospital floor (C-Span 1990). The world was appalled by such cruelty on the part of the Iraqis. The media went into overdrive, and politicians expressed outrage. US President Bush quoted the girl's statement. The delegates of the United Nations shook their heads and voted for war against Iraq, which ultimately cost more than 100,000 lives. It later emerged that Nayirah's testimony was nothing but a blatant lie. Moreover, the supposed hospital volunteer was the daughter

of Sheikh Saud Nasir Al-Sabah, the former Kuwaiti ambassador to the USA. The Kuwaiti government-in-exile had paid Hill & Knowlton to enable the recapture of their country. The media's belated attempts to speak to the girl and verify her statement came to nothing in the sands of the Kuwaiti desert (Wolff, 2002).

Kosovo War (1998–1999) The Kosovo War was fueled by disinformation on both sides of the conflict. Serbian media portrayed Kosovo Albanians as terrorists and criminals, while Kosovo Albanian media depicted Serbs as aggressors and oppressors. This disinformation contributed to fueling tensions between the two groups and ultimately led to the outbreak of war.

The Second Iraq War under George W. Bush (2003) The US-led invasion of Iraq was based on the false claim that Iraq possessed weapons of mass destruction. This deliberate deception was largely fueled by assertions from the US government, which relied on the dubious informant "Curveball" and was later proven to be untrue. The intelligence used to support these claims was subsequently shown to be false and fabricated. As a result, the Iraq War was widely criticized.

Annexation of Crimea (2014) In 2014, Russia annexed the Ukrainian region of Crimea. The annexation was accompanied by a disinformation campaign in which Russian media portrayed the event as a "reunification" with Russia and claimed that Ukrainian nationalists were threatening the safety of ethnic Russians in Crimea. This disinformation served to justify Russia's actions and contributed to heightened tensions between Russia and Ukraine.

Disinformation and Genocide Genocides are driven by a combination of factors, including ethnic and religious tensions, power struggles, and the desire for control and dominance. In many cases, these factors have been exploited by political leaders to justify violence and genocide. In most instances, disinformation campaigns paved the way for violence. Here are some examples.

Kristallnacht (1938) The assassination on 7 November 1938 of Ernst vom Rath, a counsellor at the German embassy in Paris, by the 17-year-old Polish Jew Herschel Grynszpan, served as the pretext for a pogrom ordered and directed against Jews. Over two nights, on Nazi orders, Jews were systematically murdered, disenfranchised, and deported; their businesses destroyed, and their homes looted. This marked the beginning of the largest genocide in human history.

Rwandan Genocide (1994) The Rwandan genocide was partly fueled by propaganda and disinformation spread by the Hutu government. The Hutu regime used the media (especially radio) to disseminate lies about the Tutsi minority, portraying them as a threat to the Hutu majority. This disinformation campaign helped incite violence against the Tutsi, ultimately leading to genocide. The violence lasted 100 days and resulted in the deaths of an estimated 800,000 to 1 million people.

Bosnian Genocide (1992–1995) The Bosnian genocide was the systematic extermination of Bosniak Muslims and Croats by the Bosnian Serb army during the Bosnian War. It is estimated that up to 100,000 people were killed during this period. The genocide was triggered by nationalist and religious tensions between the different groups. The Srebrenica genocide was a massacre of more than 8000 Bosniak men and boys by Bosnian Serb forces during the Bosnian War. The victims were taken from the UN-protected enclave of Srebrenica and killed over several days.

3.2 Trump, Johnson, Orban, and the Spin Dictators: The Modern Political Faces of Disinformation

Fake news and disinformation have also played a significant role in recent political history, particularly regarding the presidency of Donald Trump, the leadership of Vladimir Putin, and the Brexit referendum in the United Kingdom under Prime Minister Boris Johnson. It appears that with every populist leader, disinformation and fake news accompany them, both bringing them to power and keeping them there.

Disinformation is a key component of authoritarian rule, used to achieve its objectives. Disinformation helps autocrats remain in office, discredits the opposition, suppresses uncomfortable truths, or gives them the "right" spin.

In recent years, we have witnessed politicians getting away with the most brazen lies, even in supposedly functioning democracies with free elections and a diverse, effective, and critical media landscape. Just 15 years ago, a blatant lie would have meant the political end for a politician.

During his first presidency, Donald Trump conducted politics via Twitter. Through his account, he spread misinformation and attacked his opponents. He targeted the media, labeled them as "fake news," and promoted his own version of events, no matter how outrageous. Trump was supported in this by his adviser Kellyanne Conway, who justified his lies as "alternative facts". Here are just a few examples of misinformation spread by Trump:

- Claims of widespread electoral fraud in the 2020 US presidential election, which were not supported by evidence, led to an enraged mob of Trump supporters storming the Capitol.
- The promotion of unproven treatments for COVID-19, such as hydroxychloroquine or bleach.
- The propagation of conspiracy theories, such as the claim that Barack Obama was not born in the USA.
- The assertion that the media were covering up terrorist attacks.
- The claim that the crowd at his inauguration was larger than it was.

The Washington Post counted the lies during Trump's first term as president and arrived at the astonishing figure of 30,573 lies or false statements over his 4-year presidency. Remarkably, he lied and distorted the truth increasingly each year, apparently realizing that he could get away with it (Washington Post, 2021).

During his 2024 presidential campaign, he continued with his lies and false claims. Among them:

- He claimed that presidential candidate Kamala Harris was not Black.
- He claimed that he had completed the wall with Mexico during his presidency.
- He claimed that his lost second presidential election in 2020 was "stolen" and the election results were rigged.

The list could go on indefinitely. Particularly tragic were the consequences of the claim made by Donald Trump's team and his vice-presidential candidate, J.D. Vance, that Haitian immigrants in the small town of Springfield, Ohio, were eating cats and dogs. There was no evidence for this racist and false allegation. As a result, the town of Springfield had to contend with a wave of bomb threats and a further influx of Trump-supporting YouTubers and bloggers who descended on Springfield to report on the supposed massacre of cats and dogs.

The remarkable thing is, that despite all the obvious lies and falsehoods, Trump's supporters continued—and continue—to stand by him.

A similar pattern can be seen with another populist, the Briton Boris Johnson, who had already attracted attention for lying during his time as a journalist in Brussels. Johnson presented himself as a champion of Brexit and spread false information about "those in Brussels," the cost of EU membership for the British, and that his compatriots would be significantly better off economically after Brexit.

During the campaign for the Brexit referendum, both sides of the debate used false information and disinformation. Some examples of false information from Boris Johnson include:

- The claim that the United Kingdom would save £350 million per week by leaving the EU, for which there was no evidence.
- The assertion that Turkey was on the verge of joining the EU, which was not true.
- The dissemination of conspiracy theories, such as the claim that the EU was planning to create a European superstate.
- The spread of false information about immigration, including the claim that leaving the EU would reduce the number of immigrants in the United Kingdom. In fact, Brexit led to a reduction in the number of immigration applications and work permits, with devastating consequences for, among others, the health and agricultural sectors.

And here too, as in the USA, all this took place within a functioning, albeit highly polarized, democracy, with free elections and a free press.

Spin Dictators

The situation is different with the so-called spin dictators. With this term, the authors of the book of the same name, Sergei Guriev and Daniel Treisman, describe a new type of authoritarian leader. Spin dictators stand in contrast to the fear dictators, such as Stalin, Hitler, Saddam Hussein, Mao Tse-tung, and many other terrifying figures of the twentieth century, who oppressed their people with bloody force, allowed no free press, and used massive propaganda apparatuses and perfidious disinformation to hammer their existence, power, and wars into the minds of the people.

The modern spin dictator pursues a different approach. "They are not old-school tyrants who have simply picked up a few new tricks. They have developed their own coherent approach. The key elements—media manipulation, the creation of popularity, the pretense of democracy, the limitation of public violence, and openness to the world—complement each other to create a model of unfree governance that is spreading" (Guriev & Treisman, 2022, p. 13). Spin dictators are certainly not the first of the autocrats to manipulate information. In contrast to the Fear Dictators, they do not seek total control over opinion and the media. They do it more skillfully: "… less Maoist agitprop, more Madison Avenue" (Guriev & Treisman, 2022).

Their priority is to bring the most important media under their control, as demonstrated successfully by Putin in Russia, Orbán in Hungary, and Nazarbayev in Kazakhstan. In this way, Spin Dictators can shape public opinion through their mouthpieces. Spin Dictators such as Putin or the Chinese leader Xi Jinping command vast troll factories, which they use to steer discourse on social media.

They leave the low-reach media, such as intellectual magazines, to their critics. This allows them to maintain the façade of press freedom. "Spin Dictators manipulate information to boost their popularity among the broad population, and with this popularity they secure political control. Thus, while pretending to be democratic, they disguise their violent repression and integrate their countries with others" (Guriev & Treisman, 2022, p. 18). At this point, I would like to add that there can certainly be overlaps between a Fear Dictator and a Spin Dictator, as we see in the case of Xi Jinping, who oppresses his people with violence, repression, and brutality, while at the same time promoting the "People's Republic of China."

Disinformation and propaganda reached new dimensions under Vladimir Putin. Through his notorious troll factories in St. Petersburg, he spreads lies, fake news, conspiracy theories, and propaganda to influence political events in other countries, including the 2016 US presidential election, which was won by Russia's preferred candidate, Donald Trump.

Some examples of Russian disinformation:

- The dissemination of conspiracy theories about the 2016 US presidential election, suggesting that the outcome was predetermined and that Hillary Clinton was responsible for various crimes
- The use of social media to spread and amplify divisive messages, often targeting vulnerable communities

- The promotion of alternative media that portray Russia in a positive light and downplay the actions of the Russian government
- The deployment of hackers to steal and publish sensitive information, such as the email accounts of Clinton campaign staff
- The financial and propaganda support of right-wing parties such as the AfD in Germany and Le Pen in France
- Influence on election campaigns in Romania, Bulgaria, and African countries

Another prominent example of Russian disinformation in connection with the war in Ukraine was presented by Russian television channel "Channel One" in the summer of 2014. It was a report about a 14-year-old boy from the occupied Donbas region who was allegedly crucified by Ukrainians.

Furthermore, the Ukrainians were said to have tied the boy's mother to a tank and dragged her to her death. Both victims were supposedly members of the Russian minority. Channel One featured a woman who had fled from Donbas to Russia, who tearfully recounted the event. The audience was left shocked and agitated by this report.

Fact-checkers from "EU vs. Disinfo," the European East StratCom Task Force, investigated the case and concluded, "However, it was a complete fabrication. The 'eyewitness' turned out to be a Russian actress living in Moscow, not a local refugee. There was no boy, no crucifixion, no mother, and no Ukrainian tank. Nothing. Just pure theater and a creative, if shamelessly manipulative, journalist from Channel One who supported this manipulation and invented a story. But by the time the fact-checkers exposed this forgery, millions of Russians had already seen it on Channel One or shared it on other platforms" (EUvsDisInfo, 2023).

The fact that China and Russia can also direct their troll factories at companies, to attack them or their products, became evident during the coronavirus pandemic. The attacks targeted Western vaccine manufacturers in order to present their own vaccines, "Sputnik," "Sinopharm," and "Sinovac," as superior to Western vaccines.

After this brief excursion into history and the political sphere—the origin of disinformation—we should, for further understanding, clarify the terminology that is related to disinformation and fake news.

References

C-Span. (1990). Nayirah. Retrieved from: https://www.c-span.org/video/?c4496761/nayirah

EUvsDisInfo. (2023). Lighting fire to emotions with lies. Retrieved from: https://euvsdisinfo.eu/lighting-fire-to-emotions-with-lies/

Guriev, S., & Treisman, D. (2022). *Spin dictators—The changing face of tyranny in the 21st century*. Princeton University Press.

Washington Post. (2021). Trump's false or misleading claims total 30,573 over 4 years. Retrieved from: https://www.washingtonpost.com/politics/2021/01/24/trumps-false-or-misleading-claims-total-30573-over-four-years/

Wolff, U. (2002). The mercenaries of the lie. t-online.de. (no longer available online).

4 Terminology: How Do We Define the Definitions?

False information, misinformation, disinformation, rumors, propaganda, lies, half-truths, and conspiracy theories—and above all, the buzzword "fake" news—hovers above all of them. The terminology appears confusing, and the individual terms are imprecisely defined.

When addressing disinformation attacks on companies, we must first define the term "disinformation" and consider it in the context of related concepts.

One example is the related term "fake news." Jon Roozenbeek (Cambridge Social Decision-Making Lab) and Sander van der Linden (Department of Psychology, University of Cambridge) point out in their NATO Stratcom report "Inoculation Theory and Misinformation" (Roozenbeek & van der Linden, 2021) that the term "fake news" has two sides: there is the harmless side, which plays with satirical distortion of news, as seen on satirical news sites like "The Daily Brine" or "The Onion" in the USA.

On the other hand, there is the less harmless side of fake news. These are actual news items whose author removes them from their relevant context and subsequently presents them in a misleading manner.

"Fake news" has now become a buzzword, ironically hurled even at those who try to combat fake news: the media. At his campaign rallies, Donald Trump repeatedly insults media representatives as "fake news." The authors of the book "Fake News—A Roadmap" from NATO Stratcom (Strategic Communication) write in their foreword: "The term 'fake news' has become the default catchphrase for truth-seekers wishing to label inaccurate reporting, truth-obscurers spreading malevolent assertions, or the unprepared who simply want to close down uncomfortable discussion. The shorthand expression 'Fake News' may fit neatly into tweeted messages, but willing amplifiers have spread it across all media, traditional and social, without necessarily giving it a meaningful definition" (Althuis & Haiden, 2018).

To clearly delineate the term "fake news" and not declare it a catch-all for any piece of information that certain people dislike, it is necessary to precisely define and distinguish related terms.

U. Wolff, *Disinformation Attacks On Businesses*, Management for Professionals,
https://doi.org/10.1007/978-3-658-51407-5_4

Thus, fake news could be defined as a news item—whether a newspaper article, a radio or TV segment, or a tweet—that has been demonstrably and deliberately falsified to mislead readers. However, this would roughly correspond to the definition of disinformation, whose essence is also to deceive and mislead news consumers through manipulated messages.

The authors of the Fake News Roadmap note that the term "fake news" underwent a transformation in the second half of 2016, shifting from a term used mainly in academic contexts to one embedded in popular culture. Fake news evolved from a descriptive term to an insult and buzzword (Althuis & Haiden, 2018).

The authors at the "Shorenstein Center Harvard" produced a report on behalf of the Council of Europe on the topic of "Information Disorder" produced. They refer to "information pollution" when pointing to the kaleidoscope of "polluted messages" (Wardle & Derakhshan, 2017).

In English-speaking contexts, the formula of mis-, dis-, and malinformation is often used (see Fig. 4.1):

- Misinformation occurs when false information is disseminated—often unintentionally—without the intention of causing harm on the part of the distributor.
- Disinformation refers to the deliberate creation and dissemination of false information with the intent to cause harm.
- Malinformation describes situations where genuine information is taken out of context or distorted and shared with the intention to cause harm or mislead.

In addition, there are now several highly reliable and widely accepted definitions for these individual terms:

1. **Fake News** are intentionally fabricated or misleading pieces of information presented as news. This involves the dissemination of deliberate falsehoods or

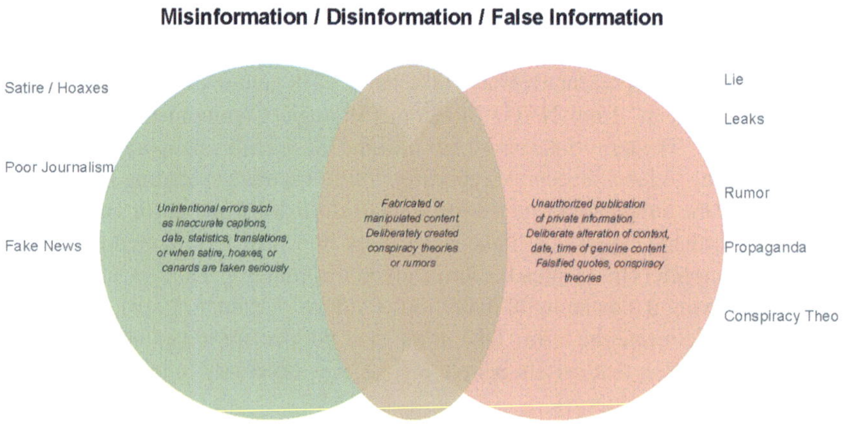

Fig. 4.1 Information spheres

disinformation aimed at influencing or manipulating public opinion or political decisions. They are designed to resemble genuine news articles and are often spread via social media or other online channels to generate clicks, views, or advertising revenue. Fake news may be created for political or financial gain, or simply for entertainment purposes (satire).

2. **Disinformation** is the intentional dissemination of false or misleading information to achieve a specific objective, such as deceiving people or manipulating their opinions. It is frequently employed by governments, political groups, or other organizations to influence public opinion or achieve particular goals. Disinformation can be spread through a variety of channels, including social media, propaganda campaigns, or fake news websites. Example: A government deliberately spreads false information to achieve its political aims, for instance, by claiming that a political opponent has committed a crime, even though this is untrue.
3. **Malinformation/Misinformation** refers to the dissemination of false information that is not done intentionally or with malicious intent. It may arise from insufficient information or misinterpretation. This often involves inaccurate or misleading information that is spread unintentionally. In contrast to disinformation, which is deliberately misleading, misinformation is often the result of error, misinterpretation, ignorance, or incomplete information. Misinformation can spread rapidly via social media and other online platforms, leading to confusion, panic, or other unintended consequences. Example: Someone mistakenly shares on social media the claim that certain foods cause cancer, without knowing that this is not scientifically substantiated.
4. A **lie** is a deliberate false statement made with the intention to deceive. Lies may be used for various reasons, such as to gain some form of advantage, to protect oneself, or to avoid punishment. Unlike fake news or misinformation, which may be spread unintentionally, lies are always intentional and typically involve a conscious effort to mislead others. Example: A politician claims in a speech never to have made a particular statement, even though there is video evidence to the contrary.
5. **Rumor**: An unverified, often sensationalized story or piece of information that spreads rapidly and is often based on emotions and prejudice. Example: There is a rumor circulating that a particular restaurant is unhygienic, even though there is no evidence for this and health authorities regularly inspect the restaurant.
6. **Conspiracy Theory:** An unproven explanation for an event or situation that claims there is a secret conspiracy at work behind the scenes to achieve certain objectives. Example: A group of people believes that a secret organization controls the world economy and makes all major decisions without the public being aware of it.
7. **"Pranks"/Media Hoaxes** are fabricated news stories and other forms of deliberate deception, primarily intended to mislead the media. The aim is to exploit the vulnerability, bias, and prejudices of the media or media consumers and to expose them to the public. These pranks are often intended to be humorous or

satirical. Media pranks with malicious intent, such as spreading false information or discrediting individuals or organizations, are simply forgeries or hoaxes that the media fall for (see Chap. 7 on Joey Skaggs).

8. **Propaganda:** Propaganda is the dissemination of information, ideas, or opinions, usually via media channels, with the intention of influencing or manipulating public opinion. Propaganda is often associated with political or ideological campaigns and may employ a range of techniques, such as emotional appeals, selective presentation of information, and demonization of opponents. Examples include Nazi propaganda, Stalinist propaganda, or the cult of personality in North Korea.
9. **Satire:** Satire is a form of humor that uses irony, sarcasm, and ridicule to expose or criticize human folly, vice, or stupidity. Satire is often used to comment on political or social issues. It may employ parody or caricature to exaggerate or distort the truth for comic effect. Examples include "The Daily Show" or satirical magazines such as "The Onion" in the USA.
10. **Poor Journalism:** Poor journalism refers to reporting that is inaccurate or biased or that lacks adequate research and verification. Poor journalism often stems from sensationalism, click baiting, and the use of unreliable sources. It may also involve misrepresentation or omission of facts, thereby distorting the public's understanding of events and issues. Example: In 2019, ABC News broadcast a report on the conflict between Turkey and the Kurds in Syria, showing footage of explosions and claiming they were from this conflict. It was later revealed that the footage originated from a shooting range in Kentucky. In 2018, the website BuzzFeed published an unverified dossier alleging that Russia possessed compromising information about President Trump, which was widely criticized as an inadequate source and a failure of journalistic due diligence.

Some studies have identified as many as 16 different types of dis-, mis-, and malinformation (Santos-D'Amorim & de Oliveira Miranda, 2021). These also include hate speech, name theft, and framing.

As we can see, fake news can in fact have a harmless side, that is, a satirical and entertaining side. This is not the case with disinformation. Disinformation is the toxic, malicious sibling in the family of fake news, misinformation, or malinformation. Disinformation is intended to deceive and manipulate people.

The disinformation toolkit includes, for example, cheaply AI-generated and operated websites that mimic professional and traditional media. Through these fake news sites, disinformers spread misleading content ("pink slime sites"), which is then picked up and disseminated by large language models via their chatbots or so-called sock puppet accounts, which pump emotionally charged "memes" into the public sphere via social media channels. Click farms manipulate the trending sections of social media platforms and their recommendation systems.

The term "fake news" is therefore far from sufficient to describe everything that is deliberately used to mislead people. Nor is "fake news" any longer an adequate umbrella term for the multitude of disinformation strategies.

Most effective disinformation content is not even 100% fabricated but contains a kernel of truth or a real reference to a current event. However, this real reference is taken out of context, reinterpreted, and weaponized by perpetrators who understand falsehoods containing an element of truth are more likely to be believed and spread. The term "fake news" cannot capture this new reality and all the new forms of disinformation.

As already mentioned, "fake news" has become a fighting term and is now part of the standard repertoire of populist politicians around the globe who seek to discredit and attack professional, critical journalism.

Such attacks have devastating effects on the public's media consumption, which in any case appears to be increasingly turning away from traditional media (Edelman Trust Barometer, 2025). Here, Donald Trump—and, following his lead, many other populist politicians worldwide—has played a major role by regularly attacking the media as "fake news." Both the targeted nature and the clear intent to cause harm in his "fake news" accusations against the media are—according to our terminology—nothing other than disinformation attacks on companies.

It is therefore absurd for the media to continue using the term "fake news" in this context—the very term that plays a central role in disinformation attacks on traditional media organizations. Words matter, and when scientists and journalists use the term "fake news" uncritically in their work, they lend legitimacy to a phrase that is both unhelpful and increasingly dangerous. They must call these attacks what they really are: disinformation attacks.

4.1 Objectives of Disinformation Campaigns

Disinformation attacks on companies may pursue various objectives, depending on the intentions and motives of the attacker.

Political Purposes Disinformation is disseminated for political purposes, for example, to discredit political or economic opponents, as the campaign team by Donald Trump against his opponent Hillary Clinton. Members of the campaign team spread the claim that she and her husband were running a child sex ring out of a pizzeria in Washington. Sometimes, the methods are more subtle and less bizarre. Populist politicians of the current generation have no qualms about conducting clear disinformation campaigns to gain political advantage. Attackers may disseminate false or misleading information about a company's political affiliations, donations, or activities to discredit the company or influence public perception of its products or services.

NGO Campaigns NGOs are masters at leveraging social media and have adopted many strategies from traditional political campaigns. It is entirely irrelevant whether the NGOs are considered "good" or "bad." In our experience, environmental or animal welfare organizations are no less adept at dirty tricks and disinformation than NGOs from the tobacco, arms, or chemical sectors. Attackers use social media, blogs, or other online platforms to spread rumors, fake reviews, or other forms of negative content (such as regarding supply chains or environmental impact) that can damage the reputation of a company or its products. NGOs are also, often without their knowledge, exploited by disinformation actors or even established specifically for the purpose of a disinformation campaign. I have recently written several articles and given lectures on how companies are targeted by professional disinformation actors via ESG guidelines, who ruthlessly exploit the symbiotic relationship between NGOs and journalists.

Economic Motives The initiators of disinformation campaigns in the economic sphere are driven by a variety of motives. One of the most insidious is the intent to inflict damage on the target company that translates into an advantage for the attacker, as is the case with covert short sellers or activist shareholders. The attackers primarily target the stakeholders and shareholders of a company. The targeted competitor may go under, be forced to withdraw a product from the market, replace its CEO, be prevented from entering a new market, and much more. We will return to this later. Disinformation attacks aim to cause lasting reputational damage to a company by spreading false or misleading information about its products, services, or practices. Such attacks can be used to gain a competitive edge over rivals by disseminating false or misleading information about their products, services, or practices. Attackers may use fake reviews, endorsements, or testimonials to make their own products or services appear more favorable compared to those of their competitors.

Strategic Objectives Disinformation attacks may form part of a broader strategic agenda aimed at destabilizing a particular industry or country. Attackers deploy disinformation to sow chaos and confusion and to undermine trust in institutions, thereby advancing their own political or ideological goals. One example is the attacks by Russia and China on Western vaccine manufacturers.

Commercial Interests False reports are created and disseminated to attract more attention, increase click rates, and thereby boost advertising revenue for the respective websites. An example of this is the fake news factories that became notorious in the small town of Veles, Macedonia (Ladurner, 2016).

Personal Motives There are quite a few employees who, after being dismissed, seek revenge against their former employers. Their desire for retribution is not limited to posting negative online reviews or contacting the media. We have witnessed cases where a single individual orchestrated a complex disinformation campaign against a company or investment fund. The motive was simple: revenge for perceived disrespect and dismissal.

Financial Gain Disinformation attacks may also be motivated by financial gain, such as through short selling of shares or market manipulation. Attackers spread false or misleading information about a company's financial performance or prospects to depress the share price or unsettle investors.

Competitive Advantage Disinformation attacks are used to gain a competitive advantage over rivals by spreading false or misleading information about their products, services, or practices. Attackers use fake reviews, endorsements, or testimonials to make their own products or services appear more favorable compared to those of their competitors.

Political Influence Attackers disseminate false or misleading information about a company's political affiliations, donations, or activities, or those of its management, to discredit the company or influence public perception of its products or services.

References

Althuis, J., & Haiden, L. (2018). *Fake news. A roadmap*. NATO Strategic Communications Centre of Excellence.

Edelman Trust Barometer. (2025). 2025 Global report—Trust and the crisis of grievance. https://www.edelman.com/sites/g/files/aatuss191/files/2025-01/2025%20Edelman%20Trust%20Barometer%20Global%20Report_01.23.25.pdf

Ladurner, U. (2016, December 15). City of Liars. Retrieved from: https://www.zeit.de/2016/52/fake-news-hersteller-unternehmen-mazedonien/komplettansicht?utm_referrer=https%3A%2F%2Fwww.google.com%2F

Roozenbeek, J., & van der Linden, S. (2021). *Inoculation theory and misinformation*. NATO Strategic Communications Centre for Excellence.

Santos-D'Amorim K, de Oliveira Miranda MKF (2021, March 26). Misinformation, disinformation, and malinformation: Clarifying the definitions and examples in disinfodemic times. *Encontros Bibli: Revista Eletrônica de Biblioteconomia e Ciência da* Informação. https://doi.org/10.5007/1518-2924.2021.e76900

Wardle, C., & Derakhshan, H. (2017, September 27). Information disorder—Toward an interdisciplinary framework for research and policymaking. Retrieved from: https://shorensteincenter.org/wp-content/uploads/2017/10/Informa- tion-Disorder-Toward-an-interdisciplinary-framework.pdf?x78124

Why Is Disinformation Effective? 5

All of us have certainly experienced this: you hear or read a piece of news or a story that is so novel, so unusual, so entertaining, or so infuriating that you feel an urgent need to share what you have just learned with others. In pre-Internet times, this meant making a phone call or telling an astonished group at dinner or at work, only to discover that the supposedly new story was nothing more than an old rumor. How embarrassing! This awkward situation raises a very interesting question: Why are we, as enlightened individuals, so vulnerable to misinformation? What is happening in our minds?

Today, we no longer need to make a phone call or wait until dinner or the lunch break to share an electrifying piece of news. A few clicks are enough for the message to spread further.

There are many studies addressing why we are so susceptible to rumors, why we believe certain things and not others, and why some information spreads virally. A useful approach to better understand this is to look into the "rumor mill," as there are significant overlaps between the mechanisms and dissemination of disinformation and the findings from research on the spread of rumors (Holzinger & Wolff, 2009).

There is always some element of truth in rumors, no matter how far-fetched they may be. They always contain a kernel of truth. A rumor becomes more powerful the more components it contains that can be linked to actual circumstances or the expectations of the recipient.

"In essence, the rumor is disruptive because it can turn out to be true," claims Jean-Noël Kapferer, Professor at the Paris School of Economics and then Chair of the "Foundation for the Study and Clarification of Rumors" (Kapferer, 1987). Kapferer considers the rumor to be the oldest medium in the world (the original title of his book is "Rumeurs. Le plus vieux média du monde"). According to Kapferer, rumors are based on "raw, confused facts," to which an explanation is then attached (Kapferer, 2013).

U. Wolff, *Disinformation Attacks On Businesses*, Management for Professionals, https://doi.org/10.1007/978-3-658-51407-5_5

But what makes rumors so irresistible to us? Why are we willing to believe certain things while fundamentally rejecting others that may in fact be true? Why are there still people who seriously believe the moon landing was a Hollywood fake, in Roswell/New Mexico—a UFO is said to have landed there, or US President John F. Kennedy was allegedly assassinated by the Mafia? On the one hand, there is the proximity to reality, which makes a rumor appear credible. An effective rumor must contain a kernel of truth. Only then does the rumor become "believable."

On the other hand, on the recipient's side, there must be a pronounced willingness to accept the rumor, allowing it to permeate and take effect.

> "People are excessively influenced by rumors, even when these contradict what they have seen with their own eyes," explains Ralf Sommerfeld from the German Max Planck Institute for Evolutionary Biology. He and his colleagues studied the emergence, dissemination, and impact of rumors in 126 test subjects. He arrived at a remarkable conclusion: "Even people who possess all the necessary and important information ultimately tend to trust rumors rather than objective facts" (Der Spiegel, 2007).

Sommerfeld also provides an explanation for this phenomenon:

> "Gossip and hearsay have a strong manipulative potential." People are culturally accustomed to making decisions based on orally transmitted information. In this context, gossip and rumors play an important role, especially in situations where people cannot observe everything themselves and must rely on indirect information.

As communicators who are primarily involved in legal disputes or crisis situations, we encounter this repeatedly: In a case of significant public interest, either the client or their lawyer refuses to make a statement—even a completely innocuous one—to present the client's perspective. This categorical refusal creates a knowledge and information vacuum for the media and media users, that is, the public, who—as I quote Sommerfeld here—"rely on indirect information." From physics lessons, we know that a vacuum does not actually want to remain a vacuum and will always strive to draw in air from its surroundings. This is precisely what happens with an information vacuum: the emptiness of the information space does not draw in air but rather rumors and misinformation to fill the void. Renée DiResta has succinctly described this cognitive mechanism in her excellent book "Invisible Rulers":

> If the facts are sparse, we rely on our imaginations to fill in the blanks, often drawing on community lore or popular tropes. We spread the rumor because we want to know the truth and want to participate in the community conversation—particularly when the facts involve an ambiguous or troubling incident with the potential to impact our lives (Renée DiResta, 2024).

Whenever supposed information is not made accessible to the public or is only passed on covertly, it is the hour of rumors, the hour of speculation, conjecture, conspiracy theories, and above all, of disinformers who ruthlessly exploit such an information vacuum to fill it with harmful content. Rumor researcher Jean-Noël Kapferer observes in this context:

> More than ever before, three fundamental rights are in conflict today: the general right of the public to information, but also the personal rights of the accused (the presumption of innocence in favor of the accused loses its value if he is accused in the media), and finally the right of the judiciary to conduct investigations impartially so that the truth can be uncovered. Two forces exert opposing pressures: the investigating judge knows everything but is not permitted to say anything because he must maintain investigative secrecy; journalists, on the other hand, are expected to say everything while knowing nothing. The media are the provisional winners. However, since they lack reliable information, they resort to rumors, this black market of ever-ready but also manipulable information (Kapferer, 1987).

Science has investigated what makes us so susceptible to misinformation. "First Draft"—a publication from the "Shorenstein Center for Media, Politics and Public Policy at Harvard's Kennedy School"—has since moved to the "Information Future Lab" at Brown University in the USA—offers an excellent overview, which I follow here (Shane, 2020) and whose individual points I will elaborate on later.

Cognitive Biases determine how we think, what we believe, which information we are willing to accept and select (e.g., those that appeal to us), and which we reject (those that do not correspond to our views). Cognitive biases help us to recognize patterns, whether real or merely perceived. They shape our judgments, our perceptions, and our decisions.

Cognitive biases are constantly operating in the background, that is, in our subconscious, and make use of so-called cognitive heuristics—shortcuts that allow us to make quick assessments of a matter or situation. This was very important for our ancestors, for example, when a saber-toothed tiger appeared at the entrance to the cave. The cavemen had no time to deliberate on what to do in such a situation. They had to act, following a predetermined pattern—self-made, handed down, and learned experiences.

Science has now identified over 230 different cognitive biases that shape our thinking and behavior. Anyone who still believes they are capable of clear thinking considering this immense influence through cognitive biases is evidently also subject to one of these cognitive biases (Wikipedia, 2024).

Outstanding scientists such as the American social psychologist Elliot Aronson, who has studied cognitive dissonance and stereotyping (as in his book "Mistakes Were Made—but Not by Me"), have demonstrated how people employ mechanisms to resolve contradictions for themselves when faced with conflicting beliefs. In this way, it is possible to believe in a flat Earth or to support a hypocritical politician.

Why am I writing this? Because disinformation specifically targets these cognitive biases in humans and affects us at a deep, intrinsic level. It triggers us and attempts to steer our thinking and actions in a particular direction. The virus of disinformation can latch onto any individual cognitive bias and damage our system.

What can we do? We must recognize that we are not masters in our own house. We need to analyze ourselves honestly and relentlessly to discover which cognitive biases we are subject to.

Wikipedia features an excellent interactive graphic ("The Cognitive Bias Codex") listing over 230 cognitive biases. Clicking on any of the listed biases leads to a dedicated explanatory page for each one. This is among the best resources I have found on the subject.

Let us consider some of the shortcomings of cognitively biased humans (and that includes all of us):

- We do not want to think and are, therefore, from an evolutionary perspective, **"mentally lazy."** We do not wish to engage with complicated matters. We want simple solutions and explanations. That is why our brain is so efficient—because we do not have to think intensively about every action. It is exhausting to consider whether the news I have just consumed is true or false. So, I prefer to take the easier route. The simpler something is to process, the more likely we are to believe it is true. We deceive ourselves and thus give ourselves the wonderful feeling that quick, simple judgments often feel right, even when they are not. There is also a particularly unpleasant aspect: when things become complicated, we have the option of not seeing or ignoring them. We may have read somewhere online that a piece of information has already been debunked, but we have already forgotten (or want to forget) that. In this way, we remain on the easy path (Pennycook, 2018).
- Because we find thinking strenuous and prefer shortcut cognitive processes, humans have developed so-called **heuristics.** *(A heuristic refers to methods that, with limited knowledge and incomplete information within a short timeframe, nevertheless lead to probable conclusions or practical solutions.)* This helps us to draw conclusions and make quick decisions—including decisions about whether something is right or wrong. We do not require complex, lengthy analyses; we have heuristics that assist us in processing information on the internet and sifting through news.

Evolution had a reason for equipping us with the ability to think heuristically. Imagine the situation of a Stone Age human returning to their cave after a hunt and encountering a saber-toothed tiger. The Stone Age human does not have much time to weigh up whether the saber-toothed tiger might not be so dangerous, perhaps because it is already full. Nor do they have time to consider whether the saber-toothed tiger currently eyeing them might belong to the more amiable members of its species. No, the Stone Age brain triggers a clear alarm, having stored the information that big cats with long teeth represent a clear danger to be avoided or eliminated. This insight provides the Stone Age human with an action plan within milliseconds, which must be executed to survive.

- One of these evolutionarily sophisticated heuristics is based on the **"heuristic of social proof."** If, for example, our academic acquaintance, Professor John Doe, shares a report, it appears to many to be much more likely that the report is true. After all, Professor John Doe is no fool. The problem, however, is that Professor John Doe, due to his own psychological makeup, can also fall for misinformation, professor or not. In the end, the real fool is the one who relied on their heuristic system and believed the professor. This has particularly significant consequences on social media, as Claire Wardle describes in "First Draft News": "On social media, the heuristics (the mental shortcuts we use to make sense of the world) are missing. Unlike in a newspaper, where you know which section you are in and see visual cues indicating whether you are in the opinion or cartoon section, this is not the case online" (Wardle, 2020). People are influenced by their social networks, and the opinions of people in one's social environment exert influence. If a person's social network shares or believes misinformation, it is more likely that the person will do the same.

- **The Echo Chamber Effect:** People tend to trust information that they share within their social networks, such as with friends and family members. This can lead to an "echo chamber" effect, where individuals are more likely to believe and share news that is circulated by their trusted social networks, even if it is false. Social media platforms are designed to amplify content that generates high levels of engagement, such as likes, shares, and comments. These platforms use algorithms that tend to show users only content that reflects their interests and beliefs. As a result, users may be exposed only to information that confirms their pre-existing beliefs and values, rather than being confronted with contradictory information. This makes life easier (see "mentally lazy" and "heuristics").
- **Cognitive Dissonance** is the negative experience encountered when confronted with information that contradicts one's own beliefs. This results in psychological stress. It can lead people to reject credible information to reduce the dissonance. The initial reaction is clearly negative and results in a defensive attitude. Moreover, contradictory information often provokes irritation, which may be directed at the information itself or at the person (or even the medium) presenting the new, challenging information. How do people respond when faced with conflicting information? In many cases, the strategy adopted by those challenged was to reaffirm their own opinion by revisiting familiar information, rather than seeking new evidence to resolve their uncomfortable cognitive discrepancies (Taddicken & Wolff, 2020). This brings us to the overarching concept of confirmation bias.
- **Confirmation Bias** refers to the tendency to believe information that confirms one's own beliefs and to reject information that contradicts them. Disinformation actors can exploit this tendency to reinforce existing beliefs (Nickerson, 1998). People tend to seek out information that confirms their pre-existing beliefs and values and to ignore information that contradicts them. This can make us more susceptible to misinformation that aligns with our existing views. For example, a person who strongly adheres to a particular political ideology may be more willing to believe and spread a fake news story that supports their viewpoint, even if the story is false. Even if someone is skeptical about a particular claim and researches it to determine its veracity, confirmation bias can lead them to unconsciously interpret their research in a way that fits their existing beliefs.
- **Emotional Appeal:** Misinformation plays on emotions such as fear, anger, or hope to provoke a strong emotional response that can override our critical thinking abilities. Images (both static and moving) play a crucial role here: a fake news story about a natural disaster that includes images, videos, and emotive

language can trigger a powerful emotional reaction in readers, prompting them to believe and share the story. This often results in people forwarding the message impulsively while in an emotionally charged state, without first verifying its accuracy or authenticity. Essentially, this insight can be summed up by the well-known phrase "A picture is worth a thousand words." The images captured by war photographers in Vietnam played a decisive role in mobilizing people to protest the war. The images from recent wars in the Middle East have also had a significant impact. Today, however, we face the problem that images and videos ("deepfakes") can be convincingly faked with minimal effort and disseminated to manipulate the emotions of the public.
- **Source Credibility:** People are more likely to believe information from sources they consider trustworthy, such as mainstream news channels or people they know. For this reason, some disinformation websites ("pink slime sites" and "doppelgängers") disguise themselves as reputable news organizations.

Disinformation actors exploit the credibility of a source to spread their disinformation under the banner of a major newspaper, TV, or radio station. A fake news story that appears to originate from a credible news source such as CNN or the BBC is more likely to be believed by readers, even if the story is false. Such Trojan horses have recently appeared in the marketplace of mis- and disinformation. They take advantage of the fact that people are more likely to trust news sources that are familiar to them and that align with their political views (Media Insight Project, 2017).

The American organization "NewsGuard", which assesses the trustworthiness and reliability of news websites, claims that around 10% of online news currently consumed by US readers originates from fake news sites (Tett, 2020). These figures are from 2020. More recent data from NewsGuard indicate that the problem in the USA has worsened since then. According to the current Reality Gap Index by NewsGuard, 49% of Americans now believe at least one of the major falsehoods currently circulating online (NewsGuard, 2025). This reveals a worrying trend that is certainly not limited to the USA.

The spread is further fueled by the sharp increase in the use of AI chatbots, which are now being used in place of Google searches. NewsGuard examined the role of AI chatbots in the dissemination of misinformation and disinformation. In its "AI Misinformation Monitor of Leading AI Chatbots March 2025," the organization presented a concerning development:

> The 11 leading chatbots collectively repeated false claims 30.9 percent of the time, offered a non-response 10.6 percent of the time, and a debunk 58.48 percent of the time. The 41.51 percent fail rate (percentage of responses containing false claims or offering a non-response) is broadly consistent with previous months' results, suggesting a plateau in progress across the industry (NewsGuardTech, 2025).

This means that chatbot queries are effectively infected with misinformation and deliberately placed disinformation, which then spreads through our everyday conversations, research, and even scientific work. A significant share of the blame lies with the chatbot providers themselves, who have so far failed to teach their AI to distinguish between false and fabricated information and who continue to use disinformative content from the pink-slime sites and lookalike platforms to train their large language models.

- **Illusory Truth Effect**: When we are repeatedly confronted with false information, it can start to seem more familiar and therefore more credible, even if we know it is false. The psychologist Charles Goetzinger demonstrated this in the 1960s at Oregon State University with an interesting experiment. His finding: We initially respond to an implausible message with annoyance and rejection. But the more often it is repeated, the more often we see or read it, and the more familiar it becomes, until eventually it appears true to us. A message that is read several times and thus seems more familiar requires less cognitive effort to evaluate. And because we are reluctant to think too hard, this feels good (see above: "mentally lazy"). Researchers have shown that it apparently does not matter whether a person is intelligent or less intelligent: repetition catches up with all of us (De Keersmaecker et al., 2020). Donald Trump made good use of this phenomenon after his election defeat: his claim that the election was rigged by his political opponents is now shared by around 35% of Americans (Poynter Institute Politifact, 2022). However, this number has decreased in recent months, as the message that there is no evidence of election fraud has also been repeated often enough.
- **Motivated Reasoning:** Even thinking for ourselves does not always bring us closer to the truth, especially when we use our reasoning to confirm what we already believe, rather than to uncover the truth through hard, demanding intellectual work. This is known in the literature as "motivated reasoning." Numerous studies in cognitive psychology have shown that a little logical thinking makes a significant contribution to forming accurate beliefs. For example, people who think more analytically (i.e., who use their analytical skills rather than relying solely on their 'gut feeling') are less superstitious, less likely to believe in conspiracy theories, and less susceptible to seemingly profound but meaningless statements (such as 'Wholeness soothes infinite phenomena'). These findings suggest that the main reason for the acceptance of disinformation may lie in cognitive laziness, especially in the context of social media. "A great deal of research in cognitive psychology has shown that a little bit of reasoning goes a long way toward forming accurate beliefs. For example, people who think more analytically (those who are more likely to exercise their analytic skills and not just trust their "gut" response) are less superstitious, less likely to believe in conspiracy theories and less receptive to seemingly profound but actually empty assertions (like "Wholeness quiets infinite phenomena"). This body of evidence suggests that the main factor explaining the acceptance of fake news could be cognitive laziness, especially in the context of social media, where news items are often skimmed or merely glanced at" (Pennycook & Rand, 2019). When we talk about "motivated reasoning," we must also consider the influence of highly personal cognitive biases on research. It was not only Michel Foucault who recognized that researchers' work is shaped by their personal, individual psycho-

logical makeup, as well as by their cultural background. Feminist scholars have rightly criticized the fact that research has for years been dominated by a "male" impetus (and still is), or that white researchers have steered research in a "white" direction, especially in medicine, or consider research conducted under National Socialism in Germany, which was clearly designed to confirm prejudices against Jews and other non-Aryan people.

We should not be so naïve as to boldly proclaim that we are aware of the power of cognitive biases and that, because of this awareness, we are therefore able to fend them off. What would help us more is to recognize that searching for the truth is exhausting, and we are therefore inclined to use less demanding strategies, such as heuristics and many other cognitive biases that have now been identified by science.

- Our **limited attention** builds on Pennycook's insight: in everyday life, we simply lack the time to verify the truthfulness of every piece of information, unless it is our job or our passion. The sheer volume of information we are exposed to each day, combined with the media battle for our attention, reduces our attention span and makes us more susceptible to misinformation. Motivated reasoning, combined with a limited attention span, leads us into a state of mental exhaustion if we constantly try to assess the truth or falsehood of the information that bombards us daily. The author Sean Illing has described this mental exhaustion and its consequences as follows:

  > The issue for many people isn't exactly a denial of truth as such. It's more a growing weariness over the process of finding the truth at all. And that weariness leads more and more people to abandon the idea that the truth is knowable (Illing, 2020).

- **Pluralistic ignorance** is the inability to understand what others think or believe. This can lead us to the mistaken assumption that we know what opinion is held by most of the society or a particular group. As a result, we may be convinced that the majority of society supports a certain social change when in fact it is only desired by a minority. "This phenomenon is amplified when these minority fringe groups are very loud and very aggressive in their approach and when their positions are reflected in widely distributed media. The researcher Stephan Lewandowsky refers to this as 'The Loud Fringe'" (Lewandowsky, 2011).
- **Lack of media literacy**: A person who is not familiar with the typical features of a news report, such as source references and fact checking, is more likely to accept a false report or a manipulated image/video as true. This is why calls for media studies to be taught as a school subject are growing louder, so that our children can learn from an early age to distinguish news and information from false reports or disinformation. Companies, too, should consider whether they ought to train their employees in media literacy.

5.1 Misinformation Travels Faster

A false report can be greatly amplified in the social sphere when it is spread by certain individuals or organizations (so-called superspreaders). These include, for example, Donald Trump or influencers such as Kim Kardashian. As already described above, so-called bots—tiny programs that drive disinformation by automatically liking posts en masse or posting preformulated comments—can also fuel the spread of disinformation. However, the following holds true: humans outperform machines. According to research, human superspreaders are far more effective, and there are reasons for this. While bots can significantly disseminate a message, they are nowhere near as effective as top influencers or superspreaders, who respond to comments and messages in their networks in a highly personal and emotional manner—just as humans do, not machines.

There are several studies on which types of (false) information spread most rapidly on social media. A sobering finding is that misinformation spreads faster and more widely than truthful information. Researchers found that falsehoods on Twitter are 70% more likely to be retweeted than the truth. In this study, false news reached about 1500 people roughly six times faster than the truth. The study also found that bots spread both true and false information to the same extent, concluding that it is individuals who disseminate false information more effectively (MIT Management Sloan School, 2018; Langin, 2018).

The data from this study support the "novelty hypothesis". False news is more novel than the truth, and people are more willing to share information that sounds new. By spreading seemingly exclusive news, disseminators also enhance their status and value within their community: they suggest that they have rapid and exclusive access to news sources that others do not. For this behavior, they are rewarded by the community with "likes" or other interactions on social media. It is, of course, even more effective if the novel news being spread also evokes strong emotions in readers: fear, disgust, envy, and even astonishment and joy. The impact of strong emotions on the spread of news is not a new insight: scandalous, sensational, or emotionally charged reports have always been the gold that lay in the street for traditional media. Traditional media have even created their own genre for this: tabloids and the yellow press.

Social networks are fueled by the sharing of emotional content. The architecture of these platforms is designed so that every time a user posts content and it receives a like, comment, or share, the brain releases a small surge of dopamine (also known as the "happiness hormone"). As social beings, we intuitively sense which types of posts best align with the prevailing attitudes of our social environment.

> And so, on this issue of information disorder, this performative aspect of how people use social networks is critical to understanding how mis- and disinformation spreads (Wardle & Derakhshan, 2017).

The high level of emotionalization generates many direct responses to disinformation. In particular, platforms such as Facebook, Instagram, TikTok, LinkedIn, and others offer various ways to respond directly, such as likes, comments, or sharing content. So far, the algorithms that determine which content is displayed in a user's feed are programmed to show the user the most interesting posts possible and to keep them on the platform for as long as possible (Netflix, 2020). The algorithm rates those posts as interesting that receive high levels of user interaction. This means that disinformation that provokes strong emotions is also presented particularly prominently by the platforms. In addition, emotionalization leads to a pronounced tendency to share disinformation.

These effects were scientifically investigated during the 2016 US election campaign. On the one hand, it was found that disinformation was shared significantly more often than other contents; on the other hand, it became clear that Facebook played an outstanding role in this. Personal reactions and the function of the algorithms reinforced each other in this context.

5.2 Why the Lie Is "Sexy"

As with a rumor, a falsehood or targeted disinformation is often driven by a kernel of truth or at least sheer plausibility. Fake news can be entirely fabricated—but they are particularly convincing when they are based on a true event or fact. It is only through malicious manipulation and altered proportions that such a fact becomes disinformation, creating a powerful but untruthful message.

In many cases, arbitrary figures are used, which, through exaggeration, create a completely different, distorted picture of reality. Proportions, conditions, or the temporal context are skewed. It is often only through excessive exaggeration that an ordinary fact becomes a message with the potential to excite, serving as the basis for fake news.

This supports the novelty hypothesis mentioned above. The kernel of truth in a fake news story provides an undeniable cognitive anchor for the recipient. The person targeted is immediately put on the defensive by such a factual core. If one wishes to counter disinformation with a nuanced rebuttal, it is first necessary to explain why the rebuttal is being made and why the disinformation is, in fact, disinformation. This explanation is therefore more extensive, complex, and less memorable than the fake news, which is reduced to a simple message. The rebuttal often fails due to our mental laziness and the effects of cognitive dissonance.

The psychologist Stephan Grünewald describes it as follows:

> Disinformation is dramaturgically brilliant; it is tailored to a specific goal. It is much simpler and clearer. That is to say, the lie is sexier.

And:

> The lie shapes our reality in such a way that we can clearly see what is up and down, and what is right and wrong (Grünewald, 2018).

The kernel of truth and the veneer of supposed credibility merely form the basis of disinformation. The most important factor for the intended reach and opinion-shaping success is the strong appeal to emotions. The key to its impact on recipients is the generation of intense feelings such as anger, fear, or sadness. The result is outrage and a high degree of activation among the targeted group.

5.3 Polarization Pays

Disinformation, therefore, usually deals with emotionally charged topics such as crime, sex, the refugee crisis, or powerlessness in the face of prevailing circumstances. Often, several of these aspects are combined. Highly complex issues are reduced to clear dichotomies along the lines of "good–evil," "perpetrator–victim," "locals–foreigners," "elites–the people." The aim is to achieve the greatest possible reduction in complexity.

In the economic sphere, such polarizations can also be exploited by disinformation actors: "companies–employees," "insurance corporations–policyholders," "corrupt banks–small savers," or "small shareholders–corporate management"—essentially, it can be boiled down to the age-old, power- and force-based polarity of "David–Goliath."

As we will see later, there are certain industrial sectors that are particularly susceptible to disinformation campaigns. These are primarily companies that are already confronted with a pre-existing mindset in the population. These predispositions provide a disinformation attacker with a fast track for the rapid dissemination of their disinformation. Among such companies, the pharmaceutical industry, banks, energy corporations, the arms industry, commercial elderly and healthcare providers, the food industry, the chemical industry, car manufacturers, and several others are included.

Disinformation is further amplified using images or "memes" that have a high potential to provoke strong reactions. These too often originate from other contexts or have been manipulated, distorted, or carry a mocking or even insulting tone. The visualization of the supposed facts is intended to make the disinformer's message even more striking. Even without additional text, this creates the lowest possible threshold for access, as images are simply more memorable and leave a stronger impression than mere, sparse text.

Ideally, disinformation must also fit into the historical, regional, and social context with which the recipient can identify and resonate emotionally and requires little cognitive effort. This is particularly effective when a topic is already fraught with great uncertainty, predispositions, prejudices, or stereotypes. Disinformation can then tap into the recipient's worst fears. What the recipient has always suspected now appears to be confirmed; prejudices and partially formed opinions are further reinforced, while the truthfulness of the disinformation is no longer questioned.

To lend credibility to these distorted truths, disinformation often refers to a reputable or supposedly reputable source. It is assumed that no one will bother to verify it. There are several variants of this.

Either the alleged primary source does not exist at all, or it does exist, but its actual statement has been completely falsified with fraudulent intent. The supposed credibility is further enhanced by citing sources that are generally associated with the opposing side.

Particularly popular is the reference to sources considered especially reputable, such as public service media or official sources from government and administration. The author of the disinformation can be confident that hardly anyone will read an official parliamentary document, delve into the depths of an investigative report, or engage with the official crime statistics.

The same purpose is served by referring to alleged experts or eyewitnesses. This was particularly noticeable during the heated debates about coronavirus measures, when even dubious dentists were thrust into the spotlight by disinformers as "virological experts." Of course, they are medical professionals and do exist, but their expertise regarding Covid viruses is, to say the least, questionable.

When it comes to real experts, the same approach can be taken as with other quotations: they are either invented or arbitrarily misrepresented. The likelihood of verification is minimal here as well, while the gain in supposed credibility is maximal. A dentist is credited with expertise simply because he is a doctor, even though his training is entirely different from that of a virologist.

This means that, in the initial stage of constructing disinformation, the author strives to create the appearance of the highest possible credibility for the basis of their statement. This credibility is, at least ostensibly, derived from others who are considered beyond reproach.

As the campaign progresses, the disinformation may be picked up externally by a media outlet like a reputable newspaper. This would be the ultimate accolade for the disinformers and their work. The original author now has another citable source at their disposal, which could even be verified (and thus, for example, be used in a Wikipedia entry). In fact, this is self-referentiality. The quotation of one's own statement is itself quoted again, this time reinforced by the remark: "… as even the XY newspaper reports." I will examine below how this disinformation tactic, for example, took hold among vaccine opponents, particularly in relation to the claim that vaccinations and autism are linked.

By filtering out unwanted and contrary information, echo chambers or filter bubbles are created, into which little or no information or opinions penetrate that do not correspond to the already established worldview or existing knowledge base. In this way, any relativization or reflection on one's own opinion and knowledge is avoided or even rendered impossible. This effect is all the stronger the more selectively the user curates their media consumption (Brodnig, 2017).

5.4 In the Grip of "Alternative Facts"

In this way, an alternative "truth" emerges that no longer allows for any exchange with the information and interpretations of an open societal discourse. Thus, not only does a closed set of opinions develop within the echo chamber but also a factual situation shaped by disinformation that completely diverges from that presented by established media. The term "alternative facts" describes this phenomenon, in which invented or manipulated facts are presented as equivalent to researched and verifiable facts.

In groups of like-minded individuals, there is an additional ideological reinforcement, leading to more radical positions. In the absence of opposing viewpoints, even initially more moderate views tend toward the extremes (Brodnig, 2017).

Producers of disinformation deliberately aim to intensify social conflicts and radicalize opinions. In some cases, these conflicts are only fueled by disinformation in the first place. Through the careful construction described above, these claims appear to be based on so-called "alternative" facts.

Most media outlets that disseminate disinformation were created specifically for this purpose. This gives rise to an information and opinion universe that is founded on distorted or false facts. Parts of this alternative media landscape also mix real and fabricated facts. By embedding disinformation within credible information, its plausibility is increased on one hand, while on the other, the risk of its being scrutinized is reduced. This also increases the likelihood that a reputable medium will pick up and publish the disinformation.

The high level of emotionalization triggers the mass dissemination of disinformation, both through personal sharing and through the algorithms of social media platforms. As a result, disinformation does not only appear in the technical environment of the original producer but also quickly surfaces in various contexts and on different platforms. These may include news aggregators as well as private online accounts. Thus, recipients encounter it repeatedly, and constant repetition makes it appear ever more credible. The more people support something, the more plausible it seems.

The now widespread use of social media facilitates this repetition. The most diverse formats and sources can be combined and disseminated almost at will, in the shortest possible time and with minimal effort. Disinformation can be spread via social media but also on blogs or as comments on other posts, as well as through interaction with the online presence of traditional media.

Producers of disinformation use both genuine accounts operated by real people and fake accounts or programmed social bots. As a result, and due to the mass dissemination by other users, disinformation is repeated across a wide range of channels and in a variety of formats. However, this phenomenon is by no means limited to the internet. It is also flanked by disinformative print publications or pseudoscientific literature, as well as by traditional media that pick up this false information, disseminate it on their channels, and thereby lend credibility to the dis- or misinformation. I have illustrated how this works above with the example of the Paris bedbug hysteria of 2023.

5.5 "Flood the Zone with Shit"

Targeted and strategic disinformation is not only about embedding a particular opinion, supposed fact, or judgment in the minds of recipients. Disinformation campaigns orchestrated by state actors are primarily intended to create confusion. The British magazine "The Economist" identifies two grandmasters of public confusion: Vladimir Putin and Donald Trump's former campaign strategist Steve Bannon, who crudely described this tactic as "Flood the Zone with Shit" (Spencer, 2021).

> The aim is to overload the public with so many different explanations for a poisoning, plane crash, or other untoward event that people begin to think the truth is unknowable. In that kind of oversaturated media climate, opposition parties wedded to old-fashioned notions of truth and evidence can find it hard to make themselves heard. Many people may simply put their trust in a powerful leader to tell them what's what instead. No wonder strongmen seem to have a love-hate relationship with the internet (Spencer, 2021).

It is also interesting to note the tactics China employs to drown out the voices of system critics on the internet: this is known as "Wumao"—the 50 Cent Party. The Chinese government uses this term to describe a group of people paid by the state to post pro-government messages online. The name "Wumao" refers to the 50 cents allegedly paid to each individual for every propaganda post. According to Harvard University, most Wumao are government officials and at one point are said to have posted 500 million messages on social media. If the loyal 50 Cent Party members discover a critical discussion about the Chinese government in an internet forum, or if a group of people is planning a demonstration against the authorities, the 50 Cent Party members swarm into the forum and post related topics, such as the organization of a grand local parade, spectacular fireworks, or other achievements of the Chinese party. The result is that attention previously focused on criticism of the party is effectively diverted and drowned out.

The US sociologist Damon Centola describes the Wumao tactic as follows:

> And the idea was if you have enough of these people talking to each other, it basically creates a critical mass, where the other people talking about legitimate protest issues or legitimate grievances feel like their conversation isn't relevant anymore; what's relevant is the sort of celebration of a local parade or a fireworks display. And so, it winds up changing the expectations of what we can and can't talk about on social media just by virtue of creating a critical mass of people who are doing something different than other people were doing. And it's been incredibly effective for derailing activists' efforts on Chinese social media (Centola, 2023).

The Wumao avoid any engagement with government critics. The aim is to change the subject or to bury it under a flood of enthusiastic messages. The Wumao are assisted by bots that inundate social media with posts at lightning speed.

5.6 Disinformation: Once in the Mind, Always in the Mind?

In a thought-provoking article, the scientist Stephan Lewandowsky, Professor of Cognitive Science at the University of Bristol, explores the question of whether and how disinformation, once embedded in memory, can ever be erased. He concludes, "Disinformation sticks. Once we know something, it is hard to delete it from our memory" (Lewandowsky, 2019). He reports on an experiment based on the deliberate disinformation spread by the US government that Iraq possessed weapons of mass destruction. This disinformation, which was later exposed as such, has remained entrenched in the minds of many Americans to this day. Lewandowsky and his colleague presented participants with certain war-related news items, some of which had subsequently been corrected, and asked them about their beliefs as well as their recollection of the original information and its correction. The researchers found that many participants who were certain that the information had been corrected still believed it to be true. They gave this phenomenon a name: the "I know it's false, but I believe it's true" behavior, identifying it as a key effect of disinformation. But why does the human memory find it so difficult to let go of information that has been identified as false? Lewandowsky sees one reason in the fact that people construct a "mental model" of a story as it unfolds:

> The primary factor is that people construct a 'mental model' of a story as it unfolds—for example, they may learn that a warehouse fire was caused by negligence. Once a model has been constructed, any correction that identifies an important component of the model as false may fail because removal of that component would create an unexplained and unfilled gap in the mental model. In consequence, people may know very well that a story has been corrected when asked directly, but they may nonetheless rely on the notion of negligence when asked to explain aspects of the fire.

So, what can be done? "Debunking" is of little help here. The clarification often promoted by the media has little effect in such cases. The gap created in people's mental models must therefore be meaningfully filled for those affected by disinformation, and this must be done with a "causal alternative."

> It follows that for a correction to be successful, it must be accompanied by a causal alternative. Telling people that negligence was not a factor in a warehouse fire is insufficient—but telling them in addition that arson was to blame instead will reduce or eliminate any future reliance on the negligence idea. People can update their mental model by replacing one causal component with another.

In the case of the experiment, the alleged weapons of mass destruction in Iraq must, therefore, be replaced by another reason for the start of the war, something that is emotionally as powerful as the weapons of mass destruction. Only then can the disinformation be successfully displaced. But this does not always work: if a causal alternative is not available or is simply too complicated, the piece of disinformation remains where it is. Moreover, if a new explanation is complicated, the disinformers are pleased, as they are guaranteed to offer a less complicated way to fill the mental gap.

At this point, we can clearly see how powerless traditional media are in their fight against disinformation and how they are forced to recognize day after day that their mission—their mandate to explain and inform—is often doomed to fail. For years, the media has been denounced as "fake news" by their critics, and apparently with great success: the media and journalists are confronted with a steadily increasing loss of trust among media consumers, a topic to which we will now turn.

References

Brodnig, I. (2017). *Lies on the Internet. How fake news, populists, and uncontrolled technology manipulate us*. Brandstätter Verlag.

Centola. (2023). Hidden Brain podcast: "The Snowball Effect" Transcript. Retrieved from: https://www.hiddenbrain.org/podcast/the-snowball-effect/

De Keersmaecker, J., Dunning, D., Pennycook, G., et al. (2020). Investigating the robustness of the illusory truth effect across individual differences in cognitive ability, need for cognitive closure, and cognitive style. *Personality and Social Psychology Bulletin, 46*(2), 204–215. https://doi.org/10.1177/0146167219853844

DiResta, R. (2024). *Invisible rulers*. Public Affairs / Hachette Book Group.

Exposure Labs. (2020). The social dilemma. Published 2020 on Netflix. Retrieved from https://www.thesocialdilemma.com

Grünewald, S. (2018). Deutschlandfunk (German Public Radio), Studio 9. Stephan Grünewald in conversation with Ute Welty ("Why lies are more appealing than the truth").

Holzinger, S., & Wolff, U. (2009). *In the name of the public. (Translation: "In the name of the public")*. Gabler Fachverlag.

Illing, S. (2020). Flood the zone with shit: How misinformation overwhelmed our democracy. vox.com. Retrieved from: https://www.vox.com/policy-and-politics/2020/1/16/20991816/impeachment-trial-trump-bannon-misinformation

Kapferer, J.-N. (1987). *Rumeurs. Le plus vieux média du monde*. Édition du Seuil.

Kapferer, J.-N. (2013). *Rumors: Uses, interpretations, and images*. Transaction Publishers.

Langin, K. (2018). Fake news spreads faster than true news on Twitter—Thanks to people, not bots. Retrieved from: https://www.science.org/content/article/fake-news-spreads-faster-true-news-twitter-thanks-people-not-bots

Lewandowsky, S. (2011). The loud fringe—Pluralistic ignorance and democracy. *Shaping Tomorrows World*. Retrieved from: https://www.shapingtomorrowsworld.org/lewandowsky-pluraligno.html

Lewandowsky, S. (2019). Disinformation and human cognition. *Security and Human Rights Monitor*. Retrieved from: https://www.shrmonitor.org/disinformation-and-human-cognition/

lub/afp. (2007). People are more likely to believe gossip than the truth. Retrieved from: https://www.spiegel.de/wissenschaft/mensch/verhaltensforschung-menschen-glauben-eher-klatsch-als-wahrheit-a-511796.html

Media Insight Project. (2017). 'Who shared it?': How Americans decide what news to trust on social media. Retrieved from: https://apnorc.org/projects/who-shared-it-how-americans-decide-what-news-to-trust-on-social-media/

MIT Management Sloan School. (2018). False news spreads faster than the truth. Retrieved from: https://mitsloan.mit.edu/ideas-made-to-matter/study-false-news-spreads-faster-truth

NewsGuard. (2025). Reality Gap Index. Retrieved from: https://www.newsguardtech.com/special-reports/july-2025-reality-gap-index/

Nickerson, R. (1998). Confirmation bias: A ubiquitous phenomenon in many guises. *Review of General Psychology, 2*, 175–220.

Pennycook, G. (2018). A perspective on the theoretical foundation of dual-process models. In W. De Neys (Ed.), *Dual process theory 2.0* (pp. 5–27). Routledge.

Pennycook, G., & Rand, D. (2019). Why do people fall for Fake News? *The New York Times.* Retrieved from: https://www.nytimes.com/2019/01/19/opinion/sunday/fake-news.html

Poynter Institute Politifact. (2022). Over 65% of the country believes that the 2020 election was fraudulent. That number was around 35% a year ago. Retrieved from: https://www.politifact.com/factchecks/2022/feb/02/viral-image/no-most-americans-dont-believe-2020-election-was-f/

Shane, T. (2020). The psychology of misinformation: Why we're vulnerable. *FirstDraft*. Retrieved from: https://firstdraftnews.org/articles/the-psychology-of-misinformation-why-were-vulnerable/

Spencer, J. (2021). Know what a 'propaganda-condom' is? Retrieved from: https://www.economist.com/1843/2021/03/15/know-what-a-propaganda-condom-is?

Taddicken, M., & Wolff, L. (2020). "Disinformation", science communication: Emotions and strategies of coping with dissonance online. *Media and Communication, 8*(1), 206–217.

Tett, G. (2020). The uncomfortable truth about fake news. *Financial Times Magazine*. Retrieved from: https://www.ft.com/content/01622cd8-90ad25e377c0ee1f

Wardle, C. (2020). Understanding information disorder. *First Draft*. Retrieved from: https://firstdraftnews.org/long-form-article/understanding-infor-mation-disorder/

Wardle, C., & Derakhshan, H. (2017) Information disorder—Toward an interdisciplinary framework for research and policymaking. Retrieved from: https://shorensteincenter.org/wp-content/uploads/2017/10/Informa-tion-Disorder-Toward-an-interdisciplinary-framework.pdf?x78124

Wikipedia. (2024). The cognitive bias codex. Retrieved from: https://upload.wikimedia.org/wikipedia/commons/6/65/Cognitive_bias_codex_en.svg

6 Crisis of Confidence in Traditional Media: An Accelerant of Disinformation

The gatekeeping function of traditional media has been called into question in recent years by the rise of social media and other online platforms. In the past, traditional media such as newspapers, television, and radio played a crucial role in shaping public opinion by deciding which stories to report and how to present them. They acted as "gatekeepers" by filtering out information they considered irrelevant, unreliable, or untrustworthy. In this way, traditional media provided their audiences with a trusted source of news.

Today, anyone with an Internet connection and a social media account can become a publisher and reach a wide audience with their message, regardless of the accuracy or reliability of these new publishers. Individuals and organizations who take issue with the role of traditional media or feel fundamentally treated unfairly by journalists are no longer dependent on traditional media houses with their newspapers, magazines, radio, and TV stations. Through social media channels, they inform the public and no longer must face the critical questions of journalists. US President Donald Trump set a precedent by primarily using Twitter, Facebook or his social media platform TruthSocial to shape policy. The multi-billionaire Elon Musk also grew tired of journalists' questions and simply abolished the press office of his companies. Instead, he tweeted and later even bought the social media platform Twitter, which he renamed "X."

The emergence of social media and the distribution opportunities provided by the Internet (blogs, e-books, podcasts) have led to a democratization of the media and the demise of many publishing institutions. Local newspapers, in particular, which relied on small-scale advertising (obituaries, personal ads, sales, wanted ads, product promotions), suffered severe losses as they lost the battle for revenue streams to Internet-based platforms and search engines. In the USA, there are now vast "news deserts"—regions where no newspaper is published at all.

Some large international publishing houses had the financial strength to face the new challenges. The German company Springer S.E., once Europe's largest media group, sold off all its newspapers except for the tabloid "Bild" and "Welt" and now

U. Wolff, *Disinformation Attacks On Businesses*, Management for Professionals,
https://doi.org/10.1007/978-3-658-51407-5_6

generates revenue from nonmedia ventures. Expansion into the US market and recent acquisitions of online-based US media such as "Politico," "Business Insider," and "Morning Brew" are expected to secure future profits. At Springer, the print-based media business is now only maintained in a palliative manner. Print circulation is declining, as is the confidence of editorial teams (Statista, 2023a, b).

Even the German media institution Gruner + Jahr ("Stern," "Geo"), once a publishing powerhouse, was forced to capitulate. Magazines were closed, sold, or drastically downsized. Gruner + Jahr was taken over by the private broadcaster RTL, which is not exactly known for quality journalism. The initial uproar in the press and politics ultimately gave way to pure resignation, especially among journalists. Thus, the sale of Gruner + Jahr to a tabloid-oriented private TV channel extended the long list of once-proud publishing houses in decline.

There are, however, newspapers that have successfully reinvented themselves and still maintain a loyal readership. Notable examples include "The New York Times" in the USA and the weekly "Die Zeit" in Germany, both of which continue to offer high-quality journalism.

In addition, since the late 2000s, publishers have been cutting costs as stringently as beggars on the roadside. The fees paid to freelance journalists have reached a level embarrassing threshold of shame. Photographers are seriously being asked by magazine interns whether they would like to have their images published in magazines free of charge. Business trips for research purposes are being cancelled; instead, research is conducted from the office, using—yes, indeed—of all things, the Internet. Research trips now take place predominantly in digital form.

Only a few publications still afford themselves the luxury of investigative teams and send reporters to crisis zones, admired and envied by those who must remain at their desks in newsrooms or home offices. Yet it is precisely these individuals—and many seem not fully aware of this—who, with every login to their user interface, enter the world's largest war zone: the Internet and social media, a space where any means is permitted to achieve dominance over opinion and interpretation. Here, between the Digi-Taliban, Insta-ISIS, and Twitter militias, wars are waged that repeatedly shake the world with their intensity.

In Myanmar, Facebook was used to incite people against each other, resulting in genocide against the Rohingya minority.

> There were massacres, mass rapes, and the burning of entire villages. Between 600,000 and one million people were displaced. Most fled to neighboring Bangladesh; others to Thailand. The United Nations describes these actions as ethnic cleansing with 'genocidal intent' (Kreye, 2021).

Meta, Facebook's parent company, admitted that its platform played a shameful role in the genocide of the Rohingya. In an internal document from August 2019, a Meta employee wrote:

> We have evidence from a variety of sources that hate speech, divisive political speech, and misinformation on Facebook … are affecting societies around the world. We also have compelling evidence that our core product mechanics, such as virality, recommendations,

and optimizing for engagement, are a significant part of why these types of speech flourish on the platform (Amnesty International, 2022).

Myanmar is and remains not a singular social-media-based massacre: time and again, for example, people in India come together via WhatsApp and beat to death alleged sex offenders. Wagner mercenaries use social media to broadcast executions of deserters and prisoners, just as ISIS terrorists used horrific execution videos on social media to recruit followers for their perverse ideology.

There is no question: traditional media still play an important role in shaping public opinion, but their sheen has faded, the self-confidence of many once great and celebrated newsrooms has suffered a severe blow, and their gatekeeper function, once the pride of an entire industry, is now in doubt. Anyone who meets with freelance or staff journalists today and asks about their well-being risks suddenly witnessing a veritable outpouring of tears.

It must also be clearly stated: the decline of traditional media began even before the rise of social media, especially at the local level. The Internet, and subsequently social media, accelerated the economic collapse. However, the real problem—the growing loss of trust in journalism—only truly gained momentum with the increasing polarization of society. I dare to doubt whether traditional media—in view of the rapid developments in information technology—would have been able to maintain their monopoly on the gatekeeper function at all. Many publishers recognized the advantages of digital transformation too late. With the advent of social media, the number of users of traditional media declined. The mass extinction of traditional media on the one hand and the rise of social media on the other have demonstrably led to the widespread dissemination of misinformation and disinformation, as well as to a fragmentation of the media landscape.

A key role here is played by the modern newsroom, where editorial teams assess online articles according to click rates, reading time, and the resulting conversion rates. These factors now determine the popularity of an article, rather than its social, political, cultural, or scientific relevance. The article with the most interactions is the winner of the day, no longer the one that truly contributes to social development or the elucidation of complex issues. SEO specialists optimize headlines and articles so that search engines prioritize them. This leads to exaggerated and sensationalist headlines that do not do justice to the content.

For every disinformer, this modern evaluation matrix of a digital newsroom is a godsend, because what ultimately increases the interaction rates of an article? It is emotionalization (including through images and videos), polarization, scandalization, sexualization, and brutalization—essentially the entire repertoire of a tabloid newspaper. Disinformers must skillfully tailor their disinformation to these evaluation criteria. If they succeed in getting their "news" published online by a medium and well received by the readership, the editor-in-chief applauds and calls out, "More of that!" And it is not only the editor-in-chief who applauds but also the finance departments of the newsroom operators, because the higher the number of clicks, the higher the advertising revenue.

The consequences when sensationalism and clickbait combine in newsrooms are illustrated by the case of a 13-year-old Russian-German girl from Berlin who, in 2016, claimed to have been raped by migrants living in Germany. The news cycle was in overdrive, as was the Russian propaganda machine. Every article on the subject guaranteed high click rates and interactions across various platforms. In this case, too, the topic was picked up and amplified by traditional media. For days, it was given prominent coverage in print, on TV, on the radio, and online. Even though the spokesperson for the Berlin public prosecutor's office made it clear to the media at the time: "We are investigating sexual abuse of a minor and currently have two suspects." The public prosecutor's office also stated that there were indications the sexual contact had been consensual. The office explicitly clarified: "Neither suspect was a refugee." Nevertheless, demonstrations took place across Germany, fueled by the Russian propaganda machine and supported by right-wing parties such as the AfD and NPD. The prosecutor's statement alone once again ensured lively debate on social media.

The prosecutor's statement was of no concern to the media and social media channels driven by the Russian side, as their aim was not to report accurately but to destabilize German society by providing right-wing parties with ammunition for their smear campaigns against Angela Merkel's government at the time. And they succeeded.

A victory for the disinformers and a defeat for critical journalism.

6.1 Changes in User Behavior

Social media has given rise to an entirely new category of media. This new medium, and its networking with other users, only comes into being through the actions of its users. Each individual user creates their own account, decides with whom they wish to communicate, and determines the media content that appears in their timeline.

The user becomes a "prosumer"—both producer and consumer. They can connect with other content creators without relying on intermediaries such as traditional media.

Almost all internet-based media services are now accessible anytime and anywhere via smartphone. Among younger age groups, smartphone penetration is now universal. But smartphones not only encourage passive media consumption but also active creation and curation of media content, as seen on Instagram, Facebook, Snapchat, and many other platforms.

Alongside these, traditional media such as television, radio, and newspapers continue to exist in their established forms. They too now make use of the opportunities offered by the internet and social media.

Anyone commuting by bus, underground, or train today will notice one thing above all: people with a smartphone in their hand. Readers of newspapers or books have become a rare sight in public spaces. Media is now consumed on the move. It is more convenient and faster.

Media usage has changed accordingly. The mix of consumed media now includes new sources of information. Studies show, however, that public service television and radio remain the most important sources of information for the majority of the population, as they have been for many years. Among younger consumers, however, other media are now at the forefront, such as social media, which now dominate media consumption. Linear television, by contrast, is increasingly consumed by a significantly older audience. Attempts by public broadcasters to counter this trend sometimes result in curious offerings aimed at attracting younger viewers. But they have long since moved on, watching Netflix and the like. This reflects a trend already experienced by the music industry: self-determined media consumption, at any time of day or night and in any place in the world, by people who no longer wish to have their choices dictated by rigid frameworks set by the media industry. The approximately 900 employees of the British broadcaster Sky (Comcast) felt the impact of this. They received their redundancy notices in autumn 2025, as the broadcaster reorganized to compete with the major US streaming providers (Financial Times, 2025) under a streaming-first strategy. It is the slow death of linear TV.

In Germany, the USA, and the UK, younger generations are turning away from traditional media and increasingly relying on digital sources of information. In Germany, under-30s use social media and search engines at above-average rates, while only 25% of 14- to 29-year-olds watch television in the evening, compared to 75% of those over 70 (Statista, 2022). In the USA, more than half of under-35s state that social media and video platforms are their main news source (Reuters Institute, 2025; Nieman Lab, 2025), 37% regularly follow influencers for news (Teen Vogue, 2024), and 41% of under-30s do not watch live television (Attest, 2025). At the same time, almost half of Generation Z prefer searching via social platforms over Google (eMarketer, 2024; New York Post, 2024). In the UK, similar patterns are evident: younger audiences are increasingly turning away from public broadcasters and newspapers, while social media has overtaken television as the primary news source (Reuters Institute/YouGov, 2023; The Guardian, 2025).

Linear radio programs, too, reach significantly older rather than younger listeners. Among under-30s, music or podcasts are listened to via streaming services. This age group also reads the most text from digital providers. While overall media consumption does not differ significantly between age groups, a clear trend toward digital and internet-based offerings has emerged among younger people. Mobile media use is also much more pronounced in this demographic than in the general population. The ability to access media anytime and anywhere is therefore becoming increasingly important.

It is also evident that, among content distributed via social media, newspapers and public service broadcasters continue to serve as preferred sources of information. This demonstrates that, in addition to maintaining their strong position through traditional distribution channels, established media have successfully recognized and utilized the potential of internet-based platforms. However, on social media, the next most important sources of information are individuals such as bloggers, celebrities, or other opinion leaders (influencers). There is thus considerable interest in unfiltered and uncommented information.

As early as 2018, the American Pew Research Center reported:

> Social media sites have surpassed print newspapers as a news source for Americans: One in five U.S. adults say they often get news via social media, slightly higher than the share who often do so from print newspapers (16%) for the first time since Pew Research Center began asking these questions. In 2017, the portion who got news via social media was about equal to the portion who got news from print newspapers (Shearer, 2018).

These figures have since shifted further in favor of social media as a news source. Social media is now considered the preferred news source for Americans. Nearly a quarter of Americans obtain their news via news websites or apps (23%). Among respondents, 18% reported reading their news on social media sites, 12% search for news online, and 5% prefer podcasts. This means that the proportion of Americans using social media as a news source has increased by 6% since 2023 (Pew Research Center, 2024).

6.2 The Great Loss of Trust

There is frequent discussion of the loss of trust in traditional media. Journalists and their readers, listeners, and viewers: they appear to be growing apart. The expectations of readers toward journalists are increasingly at odds with the expectations journalists have of themselves.

This is also reflected in another survey by the Pew Research Center, which found that US journalists' attitudes differ markedly from those of their audience regarding "bothsidesism"—that is, whether journalists should always strive to cover all sides of an issue equally. While just over half of the journalists surveyed (55%) believe that not every side always deserves equal coverage in the news, three-quarters (76%) of media consumers think that journalists should always endeavor to report on all sides equally (Forman-Katz & Jurkowitz, 2022). It is especially younger journalists—six out of ten between the ages of 18 and 29—who do not believe that all sides must be heard in news reporting.

At the beginning of 2023, an opinion piece appeared in The Washington Post that shook the foundations of American journalism. The title: "Newsrooms that move beyond 'objectivity' can build trust" (Downie Jr., 2023). The author was Leonard Downie Jr., the long-serving editor-in-chief of the Washington Post:

> But increasingly, reporters, editors, and media critics argue that the concept of journalistic objectivity is a distortion of reality. They point out that the standard was dictated over decades by male editors in predominantly White newsrooms and reinforced their own view of the world. They believe that pursuing objectivity can lead to false balance or misleading 'bothsidesism' in covering stories about race, the treatment of women, LGBTQ+ rights, income inequality, climate change, and many other subjects. And, in today's diversifying newsrooms, they feel it negates many of their own identities, life experiences, and cultural contexts, keeping them from pursuing truth in their work (Downie Jr., 2023).

The response from The Washington Post readers was remarkable, resulting in an astonishing 858 comments as of 28 August 2025.

Downie, who now teaches journalism in Arizona, writes that during his time at The Washington Post, he had objectivity imposed on him as a reporting standard by "male editors" and predominantly "white newsrooms." This, he argues, should now come to an end. Activism instead of clear, objective, and rigorous reporting?

René Pfister, former Washington correspondent for the German news magazine *Der Spiegel*, addressed the topic in a thought-provoking column entitled: "Activists in the media: How to destroy trust in journalism—a user manual." He writes:

> One might consider Downie's essay a product of 'woke' America. But the progressive journalism that Downie sees as the future of the industry has long since arrived in Germany (Pfister, 2023).

Pfister, who also published the highly recommended book *One Wrong Word: How a New Left-Wing Ideology from America Is Threatening Our Freedom of Speech* (German title: "Ein falsches Wort - Wie eine neue linke Ideologie aus Amerika unsere Meinungsfreiheit bedroht"), further:

> Now, many journalists have also adopted a pseudo-scientific vocabulary with which they attempt to impose their worldview. During the pandemic, those who gave a platform to critics of mask mandates or school closures were allegedly contributing to a 'false balance' and thus advancing the cause of conspiracy theorists. Those who point out problems with the integration of immigrants are, in the eyes of some colleagues, engaging in a 'shifting of discourse' to the right.

For any media outlet that continues down this path, there is a real danger that media consumers will no longer feel fully informed and will seek out alternative news sources, retreat into echo chambers, become susceptible to disinformation, and further contribute to the polarization of our society.

This alienation is being experienced by the media worldwide. This becomes evident in the debate about so-called "advocacy journalism" and the growing criticism of the overt bias of some journalists in public broadcasting, less so in the Anglo-Saxon world, but increasingly in German-speaking countries. The noble goal of objectivity is steadily fading away and is not being quietly abandoned but is being loudly and clearly buried by some journalists. Media users feel lectured to, rather than informed.

The loss of trust in the media is certainly another factor contributing to the dramatic decline in newspaper circulation. Newspapers are increasingly seen as dispensable.

A widely noted study by Gallup and Knight, which surveyed 20,000 adult Americans, shows that a clear majority express pessimism when asked whether the media are fulfilling their democratic mandate to provide factual and trustworthy information. Many Americans feel that the media's critical role in informing the public and their stance toward those in power is being undermined by increasing partisanship. Americans have not only lost faith in the ideal of objective media, but they also believe that news organizations are actively supporting party-political division (Knight Foundation, 2020).

It is precisely this alienation from traditional media that provides disinformers with a "window of opportunity." Attacks on traditional media have now become standard practice for demagogues, populists, and professional agents of confusion from the circles of conspiracy theorists. Unfortunately, traditional media repeatedly invite such attacks.

6.3 Growing Polarization Threatens Our Society

For 23 years, the global communications agency Edelman has published its "Trust Barometer." For this, 32,000 people in 28 countries are surveyed. While the 2022 Trust Report was titled "The Cycle of Mistrust," the survey results for the 2023 report focus on "Navigating a Polarized World" (Edelman Trust Report, 2023). The report identifies four forces driving the increasing polarization of the world:

1. Economic anxieties: Economic optimism is collapsing worldwide. In 24 out of 28 countries, the number of people who believe their families will be better off in 5 years is at an all-time low.
2. Institutional imbalance: Business is now the only institution regarded as both competent and ethical; government is seen as unethical and incompetent. Business is under pressure to fill the gap left by the state.
3. Mass-class divide: People in the top income quartile live in a different reality of trust compared to those in the lowest quartile, with differences exceeding 20 percentage points in Thailand, the USA, and Saudi Arabia.
4. The battle for truth: A shared media environment has given way to echo chambers, making it harder to solve problems collectively. The media are not trusted, with trust in social media being particularly low.

The report notes a rapid decline in trust in three institutional leaders: government officials, business leaders, and journalists. It is especially among lower income groups that distrust is growing. In contrast, higher income groups have more trust in institutional leaders.

This distrust leads to polarization. This is clearly in the interest of state agents from hostile nations but also of domestic actors such as populist politicians, who, through influence and disinformation campaigns, fuel distrust in our institutions and thus further intensify the polarization of our society.

Distrust of journalists, who are increasingly seen as lacking in competence—this is a sobering finding of the Trust Report. Christiane Schulz, CEO of Edelman Germany, is quoted in the report as follows:

> Globally, the main drivers of Polarization are above all a lack of trust in the respective government, a lack of shared identity, and systemic injustice. In addition, the so-called economic pessimism, social anxieties, and distrust in the media. The crux of the matter: the

> intensity of Polarization has an impact on trust. In countries where the population perceives their society as polarized, there is less trust in institutions, which in turn further intensifies Polarization—a vicious circle (Dillmann, 2023).

The Edelman Trust Report is just one of several studies that attest to a loss of trust in the media. Nevertheless, 59% of Americans consider journalists to be extremely or very important for the well-being of society. That is, after all, a majority (Pew Research Center, 2025).

What do people do who turn away from traditional media? They turn to new media. The actual gatekeepers of journalism are thus losing more and more access to these individuals and are now competing with bloggers, content creators, YouTube stars, and others.

6.4 Conclusion

The crisis of trust in traditional media is the result of a complex interplay of various factors.

1. Misinformation and disinformation: The increasing spread of misinformation and disinformation on the internet has undermined trust in traditional media. Critics argue that traditional media are either unable to report the truth or deliberately avoid certain topics to promote their own political agenda.
2. Polarization and fragmentation: National societies are experiencing growing polarization and fragmentation. As a result, many people now consume only media that reflect their own beliefs and opinions, often within the realm of social media or on YouTube channels.
3. Changes in the media landscape: In recent years, there have been massive changes in the media environment. The rise of social media, the proliferation of online news portals, and the increasing influence of opinion leaders and political influencers have contributed to the decline in the significance and relevance of traditional media, as reflected in the shift of politicians toward new media, especially during election campaigns. Traditional media are perceived as hostile or as "fake news."
4. Financial pressure: Traditional media are under considerable financial pressure as more people consume news online and advertising revenues decline. Media companies have cut staff and made compromises in quality to save costs. The quality of the media suffers as a result, with expensive and time-consuming on-site investigations being abandoned. This leads directly to the next point.
5. Errors and scandals: Errors and scandals in reporting undermine trust in the media and reinforce the position of critics, who then point the finger at the media and loudly proclaim "fake news". Mistakes in reporting occur repeatedly. This is normal. However, nowadays such errors are exploited to demonstrate how flawed and inadequate journalistic reporting is.

References

Amnesty International. (2022). Myanmar: Facebook's system promoted Violence against Rohingya; Meta owes reparations. Retrieved from: https://www.amnesty.org/en/latest/news/2022/09/myanmar-facebooks-systems-promoted-violence-against-rohingya-meta-owes-reparations-new-report/#:~:text=In%202014%2C%20the%20Myanmar%20authorities-,own%20policies%20on%20hate%20speech

Attest. (2025). US media consumption report. Retrieved from: https://www.askattest.com/blog/articles/2025-us-media-consumption-report

Dillmann, D. (2023). Edelman Trust Barometer 2023: Polarization tendencies in Germany. Retrieved from: https://pr-journal.de/lese-tipps/studies/30009-edelman-trust-barometer-2023-tendencies-towards-Polarization-in-germany.html#:~:text=The%20Edelman%20Trust%20Barometer%202023%2Cmedia%2C%20business%20and%20NGOs%20surveyed2023,media%2C%20business%20and%20NGOs%20surveyed

Downie, Jr. L. (2023). Newsrooms that move beyond 'objectivity' can build trust. Retrieved from: https://www.washingtonpost.com/opinions/2023/01/30/newsrooms-news-reporting-objectivity-diversity/

Edelman Trust Report. (2023). Navigating a polarized world. Retrieved from: https://www.edelman.de/sites/g/files/aatuss401/files/2023-04/2023%20Edelman%20Trust%20Barometer%20Report%20-%20GER_2.pdf

eMarketer. (2024). Search Behavior is being redefined thanks to generational shifts. Retrieved from: https://www.emarketer.com/content/search-behavior-being-redefined-thanks-generational-shifts

Financial Times. (2025). Sky to cut hundreds of jobs in UK as broadcaster shifts to streaming era. Retrieved from: https://www.ft.com/content/402f5cfb-c27a-4210-81c1-c2760c45ebaf

Forman-Katz, N., & Jurkowitz, M. (2022). U.S. journalists differ from the public in their views of 'bothsidesism' in journalism. Retrieved from: https://www.pewresearch.org/short-reads/2022/07/13/u-s-journalists-differ-from-the-public-in-their-views-of-bothsidesism-in-journalism/

Knight Foundation. (2020, August 4). American views 2020: Trust, media and democracy. Retrieved from: https://knightfoundation.org/reports/american-views-2020-trust-media-and-democracy/

Kreye, A. (2021, December 7). Why the Rohingya are suing Facebook. Retrieved from: https://www.sueddeutsche.de/politik/rohingya-facebook-meta-klage-1.5482494

New York Post. (2024). Gen Z ditches Google for social media search engines. Retrieved from: https://nypost.com/2024/09/12/tech/gen-z-ditches-google-for-this-next-most-popular-search-engine/

Nieman Lab. (2025). For the first time, social media overtakes TV as Americans' top news source. Retrieved from: https://www.niemanlab.org/2025/06/for-the-first-time-social-media-overtakes-tv-as-americans-top-news-source/

Pew Research Center. (2024). News platform fact sheet. Retrieved from: https://www.pewresearch.org/journalism/fact-sheet/news-platform-fact-sheet/

Pew Research Center. (2025). How Americans view journalists and their role in society. Retrieved from: https://www.pewresearch.org/journalism/2025/08/20/how-americans-view-journalists-and-their-role-in-society/

Pfister, R. (2023). Activists in the media: How to destroy trust in journalism: a user's guide. Retrieved from: 2026e9dbaa3c

Reuters Institute. (2025). Digital news report. Retrieved from: https://reutersinstitute.politics.ox.ac.uk/digital-news-report/2025

Reuters Institute/YouGov. (2023). How young people consume news and the implications for mainstream media. Retrieved from: https://reutersinstitute.politics.ox.ac.uk/our-research/how-young-people-consume-news-and-implications-mainstream-media

Shearer, E. (2018). Social media outpaces print newspapers in the U.S. as a news source. *Pew Research Center*. Retrieved from: https://www.pewresearch.org/short-reads/2018/12/10/social-media-outpaces-print-newspapers-in-the-u-s-as-a-news-source/

Statista. (2022). Report: Mediennutzung in Deutschland (Translation: Media usage in Germany). Retrieved from: https://de.statista.com/statistik/studie/id/3177/dokument/mediennutzung-statista-dossier/

Statista. (2023a, May 5). BDZV: Circulation of newspapers sold in Germany. Retrieved from https://de.statista.com/statistik/daten/studie/72084/umfrage/verkaufte-auflage-von-tageszeitungen-in-deutschland/

Statista. (2023b). Development of the circulation of daily newspapers sold in Germany in the second quarter of selected years from 1991 to 2022. Retrieved from: https://de.statista.com/statistik/daten/studie/72084/umfrage/verkaufte-auflage-von-tageszeitungen-in-deutschland/.

Teen Vogue. (2024). How young people get news from influencers. Retrieved from: https://www.teenvogue.com/story/news-influencers-young-people

The Guardian. (2025). Social media overtakes TV as main source of news. Retrieved from: https://www.theguardian.com/media/2025/jun/17/social-media-overtakes-tv-as-main-source-of-news-in-us-analysis-finds

7 Media Prankster Joey Skaggs: The Journalist Catcher

I first met Joey Skaggs in the mid-1990s in a sewer beneath Manhattan. We were part of a so-called culture jamming group (Wikipedia, 2023), which that evening wandered through Manhattan's sewer system all the way to the Bronx, where, in the dead of night, we emerged from a manhole dressed as monsters, to the terror of the local residents.

The journey through the sewers was long and at times arduous, and Joey and I had plenty of time to talk. I had only moved to New York a few years earlier and had never heard his name before. What I also did not know at the time was that Joey had already been fooling the media for 30 years and had gained a certain notoriety for it. I was fascinated by the professionalism, logistical effort, and strategic skill he employed to mislead even the most reputable TV stations, radio broadcasters, and print media, both in the USA and internationally.

That the media do, from time to time, prefer a good story before the dry facts, I already knew. I was once part of the media system myself. But that there are people who so rigorously exploit the weaknesses of the media and journalists to satirically expose the shortcomings of the media—I had never heard of that until I met Joey Skaggs one night in a sewer pipe beneath Manhattan.

7.1 Mainstream Media as Canvas

The film magazine "Highlike" wrote in connection with a documentary about Joey Skaggs: "'Media Prank' and 'Culture Jamming' were the most important anti-media countercultural tactics. Skaggs was the 'grandfather' of the so-called 'media hoax.' Long before he discussed 'fake news' or 'memes', he used lies and manipulation against the corporate media themselves, creating humorous, cynical, and ironic effects. Time and again, he made the mainstream media taste their own poison" (Viera Ferreira & Roberto, 2021).

U. Wolff, *Disinformation Attacks On Businesses*, Management for Professionals,
https://doi.org/10.1007/978-3-658-51407-5_7

Joey Skaggs began as an artist in Manhattan. He graduated from the "New York High School of Art & Design" and received a Bachelor of Fine Arts from the "School of Visual Arts," where he also taught media communication, including "Culture Jamming and Media Activism" (https://joeyskaggs.com/about/). Today, he gives lectures worldwide on various approaches to addressing social issues through art. "Like the Wizard of Oz, he reveals the man behind the curtain and vividly demonstrates the influence mass media have on society."

Back then, as an artist in Manhattan, he had poor experiences with the media. "I was fed up with the way they (the media) reported on me as an artist, so I started fabricating news. I wanted to make clear just how irresponsible the media are in their work." From then on, he, the artist, used the media as a medium, just as a painter uses canvas as a medium for art. "With these new techniques—using the media as they use their subjects—I made the media part of my arsenal." Joey Skaggs radically exploited the vulnerability and gullibility of the media, teaching many a journalist and media outlet some painful lessons.

He still does so today. After 50 years. And he has no intention of stopping.

Anyone who looks at Joey's oeuvre can hardly believe the absurd stories with which Joey Skaggs managed to make his way into the media (https://joeyskaggs.com/work/). Even more incredible, however, is the fact that the media, who are supposed to act as gatekeepers, published these absurd stories. For example, Joey Skaggs appeared as a priest traveling through the city with a mobile confessional ("Portofess"—a portmanteau of "Porta Potty" and "Confession"), which closely resembled a portable toilet. His reasoning: if the faithful no longer go to church, then the church will come to them. The photo of Joey Skaggs on a bicycle with the confessional on a trailer went around the world and even made it into the German media at the time (see Fig. 7.1).

Or his project "Metamorphosis, Cockroach Miracle Cure": Skaggs appeared as the scientist "Dr Josef Gregor" (named after the protagonist Gregor Samsa in Franz Kafka's novel "The Metamorphosis") at a press conference he had convened, claiming to have created a strain of super-cockroaches immune to poisons and radiation. From these insects, he said, he had extracted a hormone that he and his followers were taking. So far, they had cured all known ailments, such as colds, acne, anemia, and menstrual complaints. The renowned news agency UPI picked up the story, leading to its widespread dissemination in the USA (see Fig. 7.2).

The news show "Live at Five" heard about the eccentric insect researcher who claimed, after years of research and scientific investigation, to have discovered why cockroaches are so resilient and invited him onto the program. Joey Skaggs announced that his miracle cure could even make people immune to nuclear radiation. To illustrate this, he pulled out a petri dish containing two enormous live cockroaches in front of the cameras and a disgusted audience.

The notorious media prankster also played with media mechanics through a so-called Celebrities Sperm Bank, which claimed to store sperm from famous rock stars. His plot: there was to be an auction of celebrity sperm, but the bank was allegedly robbed at night, and the rock stars' sperm was stolen by blackmailers. Of course, none of this was true; the sperm bank was nothing more than the entrance to

Fig. 7.1 Portofess

a house in Manhattan owned by his friend. The women were waiting outside the door, shocked and horrified. They were actresses, just like the supposed lawyer who "represented" one of the two women, announced plans to sue the sperm bank, and, visibly agitated, answered questions from the print journalists and TV crews. Real, unsuspecting bystanders, drawn by the spectacle, soon gathered around the eccentric group in a Manhattan side street, along with police officers who, in their attempts to keep the agitated crowd under control, became unwitting participants in the performance.

7.2 The Shark Man: Artof the Prank

Joey Skaggs's cinematic coup "Pandora's Hope" was a kind of personal protest against genetic engineering. The geographical backdrop for this action was Hawaii, where Joey Skaggs lived. Once again, he planned this prank down to the smallest

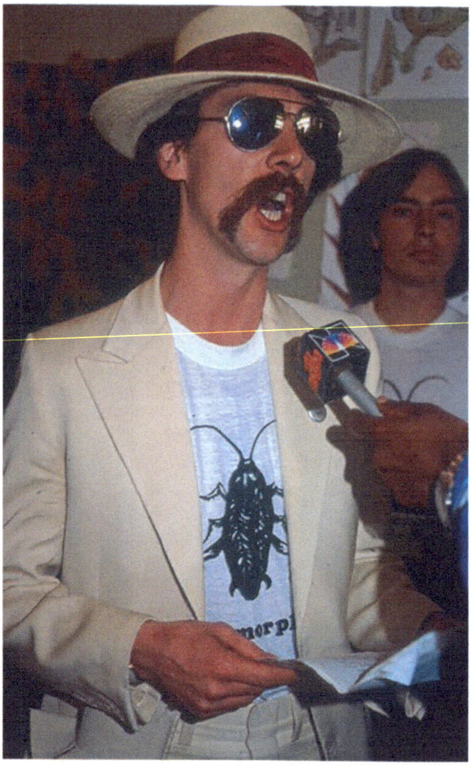

Fig. 7.2 Scientist "Gregor," alias media prankster Joey Skaggs, holds a press conference in which he presents the benefits of his cockroach-based medicines

detail. The aim was to create a fake documentary about the benefits of possible genetic modifications to the human body. At its core, it revolved around the invented story of a man who, after an accident, had his severe jaw injury treated with gene therapy using shark stem cells. His jaw healed, but his lost human teeth were replaced by regenerating shark teeth. For every tooth he lost, another would grow in its place. A dental technician friend crafted a remarkably realistic set of shark teeth for Joey Skaggs. A supposed reporter conducted highly professional interviews with alleged scientists and dentists, who, on camera, celebrated the Shark Man as a miracle and praised genetic engineering. The goal was to get the "documentary" shown at as many film festivals as possible. In fact, between 2013 and 2015, eight well-known film festivals in the USA accepted the film and screened it to astonished audiences. In this way, many people saw the story of the man with the shark's jaw.

The media reported on the Shark Man. Joey Skaggs did not even bother to disguise himself for his appearance as the Shark Man. The journalists failed to recognize the well-known media hoaxer. Joey Skaggs only revealed later, in another documentary that is still available today, that the supposed documentary was a fabrication. This documentary, about the artistic life of Joey Skaggs, the media prankster, is entitled "Art of the Prank" and was also shown at a film festival.

In this documentary, Joey Skaggs is described by Buck Wolf, News Director of HuffPost Trends at the "Huffington Post," as a "quality controller of the media."

Much like a programmer who uses special software to test the security and reliability of a program, Joey Skaggs relentlessly searches for loopholes and weaknesses in the media. The best illustration of how this works is Joey Skaggs's masterpiece, the "Cathouse for Dogs" from 1976: "With the dog brothel, we staged a theatrical performance for the press."

It all began with an advert in a New York newspaper, calling on owners of male dogs to bring their pets to a Manhattan apartment, where bitches in heat awaited them. For 50 US dollars, the dogs could freely indulge their animal instincts in front of their cocktail-sipping, photo-snapping owners. The advert included a phone number for those interested in registering at the "Cathouse for Dogs." Joey Skaggs recalls that the phone did not stop ringing that day. Naturally, the media jumped on the story. They came to report and to film. He told the journalists that the bitches were injected with substances to keep them in heat. What the journalists did not know was that all the dog owners were actors. Only the dogs were real, and so it happened that one of the dogs, in the presence of the cameras, gave in to his instincts and mounted a bitch, much to the delight of the journalists and especially the camera crews.

The New York TV station WABC (as well as many other media outlets at home and abroad) reported on the dog brothel under the title "It's a Dog's Life." The station even won a coveted "Emmy Award" for this report. As was inevitable, not everyone was pleased about the canine pleasure house. Joey Skaggs recalls:

> The reports about the dog brothel caused animal rights activists to run amok, and religious organizations went on the barricades.

All this culminated in a court summons that Joey Skaggs received from the Attorney General of the State of New York. He was accused of running an illegal brothel for dogs. Together with his lawyers, he responded to the summons. This hearing took place, of all days, on 1 April 1976. For his press-covered appearance, Joey wore a red T-shirt featuring a cartoon dog and the large letters "April Fool's Day." That let the cat out of the bag, and the dog brothel theater was exposed as a hoax. The media were appalled and embarrassed. They could not believe they had fallen for this prank.

Joey Skaggs had taken his game with the media to the extreme. He gave the journalists exactly what they wanted, and in return, they abandoned all caution. The story was simply too good. Suddenly, the media outlets that had reported on it themselves became the subject of coverage—ironically, by those who had chosen not to report on it. Joey Skaggs:

> I decided that I no longer wanted the media to report about me; instead, I would report to expose the media and their prejudices. The dog brothel was the culmination, the point at which I asked myself: "If they're willing to believe something like this, what other nonsense would they fall for?

When we later discussed his work (see my interview with Joey Skaggs), he told me:

> My father repaired cars. He didn't get upset when he saw wrecks, because for him, that meant work—an opportunity to support the family. He suppressed any compassion he might have felt for someone else's misfortune. It was an interesting lesson he had to learn at a young age. He said it jokingly, but there was some truth to it. Later, in my own work, I realized that I too had to set aside my empathy when I deceived journalists who fell for one of my performances. Not because I had any personal financial interest, but because I wanted to speak out against perceived injustices, and the best way to get them to report on my work was to report on what drives the media.

He therefore created a well-crafted, staged, media-friendly plot that journalists could not resist, only for them to discover, after the plot was revealed, that Joey Skaggs had used them as a mouthpiece for his own causes.

7.3 An Element of the Plausibility

One of the most important ingredients in Joey Skaggs's media pranks is his cast of invented characters: the scientist researching the resilience of cockroaches; the man who grew shark teeth after a stem cell transplant; the operator of a celebrity sperm bank, or the priest who drove his mobile confessional to visit his faithful flock. "A good media hoax needs a good story and, above all, images." These incredible stories, which Joey Skaggs has created over the past decades as an art activist, were not only the subject of reports in the US media. Media outlets around the world picked up his pranks and spread them unchecked. Buck Wolf, News Director of HuffPost Trends:

> Every story by Joey Skaggs begins with an unbelievable lie that people simply want to believe.

But this lie must be skillfully crafted to stick in people's minds. Joey Skaggs describes a key ingredient as follows:

> It's exactly that thin, fine line between what could be possible and the realm that is so exaggerated that no one really wants to believe it. What you definitely need is an element of the plausibility.

And there it is again: the element of the possible—something plausible that taps into existing prejudices or clichés:

> If you know how the media works, it's pretty easy to throw them the bait.

For Joey Skaggs, playing with the media has an educational dimension. He demonstrates how even high-quality media—behind which, as we sometimes forget, there are always people—can abandon their gatekeeping role and thus open the floodgates to disinformation, seduced and blinded by an attractively packaged story.

There is an old tongue-in-cheek piece of advice from the media world, often attributed to the American writer and journalist Mark Twain:

> Never let the facts get in the way of a good story.

7.4 Our Daily Media Scandal

It was precisely this dangerous weakness of journalists—to abandon all caution for the sake of a good story—that led me to include Joey Skaggs and his media pranks in this book on disinformation attacks and to let him speak for himself (see the following interview).

Scandals involving forgeries in the media are nothing new, nor are they a thing of the past. Fabricated stories are not just the domain of internet conspiracy theories; some of the most shocking examples have come from the newsrooms of renowned media organizations.

One major forgery scandal from Germany has become ingrained in the cultural memory: the "Hitler Diaries," published in 1983 by the once-renowned German magazine "STERN." In a frenzy, the gatekeepers of this respected magazine turned into squealing fanboys, pushing aside the last critical voices who pointed out that the diaries, purchased for millions, might be forgeries. The magazine paid for this with a massive and lasting loss of reputation from which it has never fully recovered.

In 2003, the *New York Times* found that one of its rising stars, Jayson Blair, had fabricated quotes, invented scenes, and even plagiarized the work of other reporters. The scandal reached such proportions that the newspaper published an exceptionally lengthy apology on its front page under the headline "Correcting the Record."

Two decades earlier, *The Washington Post* had to endure a similar reckoning when reporter Janet Cooke was awarded the Pulitzer Prize for a heart-wrenching article about an 8-year-old heroin addict in Washington, DC. The problem? The boy did not exist. When the truth came to light, the *Post* had to return the Pulitzer Prize and issue a full retraction.

And in the United Kingdom, *The Independent* faced a credibility crisis in 2011 when columnist Johann Hari was caught appropriating quotes from other sources and rewording them to fit his narrative. His downfall was chaotic and public: suspensions, corrections, and ultimately a forced apology. The episode sparked a broader debate in the UK about journalistic integrity and the trustworthiness of the press.

Every day, false stories or fabricated interviews find their way into the media and are consumed by millions of people. It would seem, then, that it is not all that difficult to smuggle forgeries past the gatekeepers of media organizations.

What we learn from the satirical and media-critical actions of Joey Skaggs, as well as from forgery scandals, is this: disinformation campaigns aimed at damaging a company must, to achieve their full effect, be strategically planned, contain powerful images, and feature a striking protagonist. They must evoke emotion, possess a certain plausibility, and ideally be linked to a current event. Apparently, not even the toughest gatekeepers in the media are safe from such disinformation campaigns.

"Someone will always break something": An interview with media prankster Joey Skaggs

Question: You have been pulling off media pranks and exposing the media for many decades. You say that you use the media as your artistic medium. What motivates you?

JOEY SKAGGS: I am a formally trained artist. I consider my work, my actions and performances, to be my art. For me, art means communicating. I choose the media as my medium because it is so immediate and has such a wide reach. I can comment and observe how things develop, document the phenomenon, critique it, and then move on to the next "canvas". My motivation is whatever angers and frustrates me: destructive and pervasive status quo thinking. This kind of thinking is the opposite of what matters to me. A major theme for me is what people want to believe about God and the meaning of life. The danger of organized religion is probably the most important issue for me. I prefer to accept that I do not know the answers to the big questions. As uncomfortable as that may be intellectually, I can live with it. All my other actions are about the abuse of power, exploitation, and a distorted value system that is egocentric and materialistic.

Question: You were once described as a "penetrator of the media." Do you see yourself in this role?

JOEY SKAGGS: It is a nice quote, but in my work I do not see the media as my only target. The news media are made up of people whose values are just like everyone else's. I do not do this to make friends. I do it to propose alternatives and to stimulate conversation and the exchange of ideas, in the deep hope of change for the better.

Question: The main characters in your pranks are sometimes so incredibly bizarre that one always wonders, why does anyone believe this? And yet you manage to get journalists to drop all caution and filters. What is happening there?

JOEY SKAGGS: If you make it suggestive, provocative, sexy, or ridiculous, if you make it enticing with a visual image or the promise that something will happen, it is only natural that someone in the media will fall for it. If I do a good enough job, write a good press release, and stage a good performance, the rubbish attracts the flies. I give so many obvious clues, such as my names like "Dr Dick Long" in the "Save the Geoduck" campaign; "Joe Bones" with the Fat Squad, "Josef Gregor" in "Metamorphosis," the cockroach miracle cure. Many journalists are so fixated on deadlines, attention, and "likes" that they are willing to set aside critical analysis in favor of wishful thinking. It is the poorly informed who misinform the uninformed.

Question: You have said that with your pranks you exploit the vulnerability of the media and the gullibility and prejudices of journalists. Has anything changed in this respect over the past decades?

JOEY SKAGGS: Technology has changed. The system for transmitting information is now the Internet. But unfortunately, prejudice and biased opinions still exist. We are still drawn to what we want to hear, think, and believe. And we do not want to be pushed out of our comfort zones. There is still war, racism, injustice, and environmental pollution. Some of the very same issues I was already addressing over 50 years ago. No, in my view, the evolution of human consciousness continues to be painfully slow. In some cases, I even see us regressing.

Question: You say that all your pranks are based on a certain plausibility and that the stories must move between plausibility and the "oh, spare me" zone. How do you manage to stay on that line?

JOEY SKAGGS: It's a fine line, a lesson in juggling. I have to improvise, when necessary, always keeping the desired outcome in focus. I assume I can handle whatever comes up. It's a challenge and fun to play these different characters. The media unwittingly become complicit in the hoax with me. When New York's WNBC TV news show "Live at Five" booked Dr Josef Gregor from "Metamorphosis"—the entomologist who had developed a super strain of cockroaches and made a vitamin pill from their hormones—they were already hooked before I even entered the studio, looking completely absurd. They ignored the obvious clues. The rest was easy. They were stuck because they had booked me for a live interview. All I had to do was play along and say exactly what I wanted to say: that we are destroying the planet, and that I did not want to become a survivalist or kill my fellow human beings over a can of beans. It was hard for me not to laugh, but that's my job.

Question: The media has changed. With 24-h news channels and online media, the news cycle has become faster. Is that good or bad for your business?

JOEY SKAGGS: There are so many ways to find a confirming source of information to suit any value system. People are now conditioned to share personal information indiscriminately. So, it's easier to reach an audience. If I want to say something against one view or another, I know where to look. Demographic data are easier to obtain. I think understanding your target audience is one of the keys to success. My short answer is: business is good, and as things stand, it always will be. I'm not afraid of being out of work. Like my father, the car mechanic, who was never afraid of unemployment. Someone will always break something.

Question: With the rise of social media and the abundance of misinformation, journalists should be more cautious and take their role as gatekeepers against misinformation more seriously. And yet you still manage to slip past the controls even today. How do you do it?

JOEY SKAGGS: The role of "gatekeeper" has become an impossible task with the proliferation of information sources on the Internet. Through social media, everyone now has a voice. I have never found it difficult to come up with concepts that can attract attention. Unfortunately, the same is true for people with malicious intent. The solution is that everyone must be their own gatekeeper and question everything. The world has become a much scarier place.

Question: Your pranks are exceptionally well planned. You use entire teams to pull off a prank. Is there a basic recipe for a good prank?

JOEY SKAGGS: There is no universal recipe for pulling off a good prank. But in a satirical recipe I wrote years ago for a Slovenian publication entitled "How to Catch and Cook a Journalist" (Joey Skaggs, 2003) I compiled a series of suggestions and techniques to help anyone fool the news media. It is still relevant today. It's a tongue-in-cheek article that pokes fun at the media's tendency to report on sensations and exaggerate facts. It contains a detailed guide on how to lay the bait, cast the hook, and then land a big fish. It also explains what to expect when you realize you've been caught.

Question: I imagine you are very interested in the discussions about fake news and disinformation campaigns. Apart from the fact that your pranks do not pursue malicious aims, where do you see yourself in the field of tension between fake news, disinformation, and misinformation?

JOEY SKAGGS: My work is my passion. I am a media junkie and follow what is happening in the world very closely. I am concerned about the direction we are heading with the possibility of creating fake news and deep fakes for malicious purposes. In an interview from 1987 for the book "Pranks, Vol 11", published by "Re/Search", I expressed concern about the future of technology and predicted that it would soon be possible to fabricate any story, making it impossible for us to distinguish what is real and what is fake. I quote myself: "With the ability to generate, assemble, and collage photos on the computer, eventually creating holograms, we will have a living Hitler in South America who is entirely fabricated … we will have a home video of JFK having sex with Marilyn Monroe, or whatever twisted story we want to invent. And due to technological advances, it will be virtually impossible to detect that it is a fake. We are technologically on the brink of a truly frightening media reality. If we do not sharpen our tools and our integrity now, we will face even greater problems." Well, we are there. It is now difficult to believe or trust anything we see in the public sphere. That is why it is important for all of us to question the sources of information to which we are exposed. Media literacy should be taught more extensively in schools. In my opinion, courses in common sense and ethics should also be compulsory.

Question: Behind the media are people who work professionally with the full range of our emotions. Which emotions do you try to evoke in journalists?

JOEY SKAGGS: I try to spark the curiosity of journalists. I want them to ask questions like, "What is the story about? Can I use it? Is it suitable for the publication or the network? Does it tell a complete story? Is there good visual material? Does it fit with what I want to tell my audience? Can I do it quickly? Is it a front-page story? Does it have significance? Will there be a follow-up story?" Basically, I try to sell my ideas to journalists, just like anyone else who has something to market. However, I have the advantage that, as in pataphysics, I design both the problem and the solution myself (*Author's note: Pataphysics is a whimsical philosophy developed by Alfred Jarry in Paris in the 1890s, which explores imaginary solutions to imaginary problems*). I approach my work with a similar mindset to Jarry and to P.T. Barnum, who famously said, "There's a sucker born every minute." If I simply presented myself as Joey Skaggs, an individual with something to say, no one would pay attention to me. But by creating characters such as a cockroach scientist with a miracle cure, the owner of a celebrity sperm bank, the proprietor of a dog brothel, a Native American surgeon at Hair Today, Ltd., or a whistleblower trying to stop BioPEEP, I can give myself a voice in the media and reach millions of people with shocking and outrageous concepts.

Question: In the film about you ("Art of the Prank"), London-based author and PR specialist Mark Borkowski says, "Sometimes the facts are boring. People are more interested in the story than in the facts. People don't want to know the truth. They want to play with the story." Is Borkowski referring more to media consumers or more to journalists?

JOEY SKAGGS: Mark Borkowski is probably referring to both media consumers and journalists. In my experience, journalists often shape a story to fit their own biases or those of their employer. Even though my pranks involve deception, it is not uncommon for journalists to report invented or distorted information that they have made up themselves. For example, in my dog meat soup prank, I posed as a Korean businessman who wanted to buy unwanted dogs from animal shelters for consumption. Some journalists reported that they had spoken to me on the phone, which was a complete fabrication. In reality, I never took a single call, but I did record every incoming message.

Question: I don't see you using social media in your recent PRANKS. Why is that?

JOEY SKAGGS: I have used the internet as a tool and a weapon since its early days, in combination with analogue media, advertising, PR techniques, and guerrilla performances. "Sexonix", "Final Curtain", and "April Fools' Day Parade" are just some of the performances that depended on it. I have used social media accounts when necessary. However, pranks on social media are too ubiquitous and obvious, and the challenge is too small for me. Most of it is not very creative.

Question: Which prank would you consider your greatest coup and your favorite prank so far?

JOEY SKAGGS: The next one, which I haven't done yet!

References

Ferreira, V., & Roberto, W. (2021). Highlike. Retrieved from: https://highlike.org/joey-skaggs/

Skaggs, J. (2003). The well-cooked journalist: A traditional Joey Skaggs recipe. Retrieved from: https://joeyskaggs.com/wp-content/uploads/2013/12/Recipe_ENG.pdf

Wikipedia. (2023). Culture jamming. Retrieved from: https://en.wikipedia.org/wiki/Culturejamming

Part II

Disinformation: From the Political Sphere into the Economic Sphere

8 Disinformation Attacks on Companies: "A Clear and Present Danger"

Disinformation attacks on companies are real; they exist, and they constitute a "clear and present danger." However, this fact has apparently not yet fully registered in the executive suites of many companies. They still locate the problem in the political sphere or regard it as an IT issue. As a result, it is delegated to IT departments rather than to communications departments.

As we have seen, the political sphere is indeed the breeding ground for disinformation. Disinformation has probably existed since humans first learned to speak, and, as we have observed, it was already being used long ago to prepare for wars and genocides.

Modern disinformation has been turbocharged by digitalization and has not only learned to walk but also to sprint. It has discovered a new domain: companies and the economy.

We all carry a smartphone in our pockets, and with it a potential tool for a disinformation attack. The tools for such digital attacks are available on every mobile phone and are therefore affordable for everyone. Even in its simplest, most basic form, such an attack can have devastating effects. Just think of the many negative reviews after restaurant visits, hotel bookings, medical appointments, or purchases on eBay and Amazon. Not every review is genuine, and not every negative review is motivated by honest intentions.

These review attacks are small but effective assaults on companies and provide ample material for legal disputes.

Consider this further: Why do so many people read the negative reviews first (which can ultimately influence their decisions)? Is it because they want to avoid unpleasant surprises? The answer is more complex, and there are indeed studies on this. According to these, customers who have had negative experiences with a service or product are apparently more likely to write a negative review (Marketing Charts, 2013). There is also another motivation at play when doomscrolling through negative reviews: consumers want to avoid being negatively surprised ("risk reduction"). That is why they read the negative reviews first, which, according to research,

U. Wolff, *Disinformation Attacks On Businesses*, Management for Professionals,
https://doi.org/10.1007/978-3-658-51407-5_8

are also trusted more than positive reviews, as the latter could be bought or manipulated. Then there are those who are simply curious or seek drama, conflict, and controversy and find a scathing critique far more interesting than a pleasant, positive review. As mentioned, the issue is somewhat more complex.

Here, too, our tendency toward cognitive laziness (see Chapter "Why Does Disinformation Work?") comes into play. Studies show that users are particularly influenced by extreme opinions. Why? Because such opinions are often simply constructed and therefore intellectually easier to digest.

Let us now consider scaling up such mini attacks on a service provider. It is then no longer just about individual reviews but about the very foundations of a company: its shareholders, banks, employees, customers, or suppliers. It concerns those who support the very existence of a company.

Communication in recent national revolutions, such as the Arab Spring or the women's revolutions in Iran, was largely based on smartphones. These are attacks on states, on political systems, entirely without the support of state TV or radio broadcasters or even print media. What applies in the political sphere also applies in the economic sphere and thus to companies.

> Digitalization makes such attack scenarios affordable. Consequently, the spread of disinformation in aggressive corporate competition is a logical consequence. (ASW Report, 2019)

Beyond our pockets and desktops, entirely different arsenals can be assembled, depending on the target and tactics of the attack. When large organizations or even states assume the role of attacker, money and manpower are hardly limiting factors—as we have seen in the disinformation attacks by China and Russia on vaccine manufacturers BioNTech, Pfizer, AstraZeneca, and Moderna.

8.1 Mercenaries of Disinformation

We have previously mentioned the "mercenaries of lies," who should more accurately be called "mercenaries of disinformation." Just as there are contract killers or hackers who carry out their dirty work for a fee, there is also "disinformation for hire," also known as "DaaS (Disinformation-as-a-Service)." Anyone determined to do so can commission a tailor-made attack and buy a disinformation campaign using the most advanced tools, and all that for not even a handful of dollars. These service providers are easy to find—namely, where all sorts of shady characters offer their services: on the Dark Web.

"DarkOwl," a security service provider based in Denver, Colorado, is certainly unique in its range of services. DarkOwl describes itself as a "leading provider of darknet data in the industry." The company continuously collects information from the Dark Web to identify potential risks for its clients at an early stage.

The specialists in Denver have observed a marked increase over the past 2 or 3 years in Ukrainian- and Russian-speaking Disinformation-as-a-Service providers on the Dark Web. There, "these providers advertise for clients in darknet forums focused on cybercrime. They use the tools of online brand building and mass marketing for malicious purposes, such as destroying a competitor's brand and reputation" (DarkOwl, 2024). To illustrate what is on offer in this field, I present you with an excerpt from the services offered by such a mercenary group:

> We offer anti-reputation services for a company or an individual. We can:
>
> - Create anti-reputation for a company, service, or individual
> - Create and publish negative content and optimize it for search engines
> - Write negative reviews and comments on social media
> - Create multiple negative narratives and experiences to legitimize the claims
> - Stage stories (theatre)

The following service package from another disinformation group is more complex and is offered as a bundle for sale. Here, the focus is not only on disinformation and reputational damage but also on disruption and sabotage:

> - We can disrupt the daily operations of a company
> - We spam the company by flooding its website and listed contact addresses with enquiries
> - We can continuously call the company from different phone lines and talk nonsense
> - We can harass the company every minute from different IP addresses via chatbots on the website and send delivery companies fake addresses.

There are providers who set up a blockchain-based botnet to conduct disinformation campaigns. That is already a higher league. However, the price they charge is relatively low: the cost is between 500 and 700 US dollars to destroy a competitor's reputation.

Another Russian provider (DarkOwl, 2022) offers

> "Targeted, customized messages via WhatsApp; large-scale information management on social media through credible social media accounts on OK.ru, Facebook, and Instagram; as well as the removal of content from search engines through targeted critical search engine optimization (SEO)." Others, meanwhile, work with a "network of controlled biorobots that can disseminate any desired information to the masses" (DarkOwl, 2022).

However clumsily these offers may be worded, they can be highly effective. Above all, there must be a market for this type of service.

The dangers of disinformation attacks on companies are also recognized by international intelligence and law enforcement agencies. In the USA, both the CIA and the FBI act as investigative and intelligence authorities in this area.

As I mentioned at the outset, when writing the first edition of this book, the basis for investigations and reports on disinformation attacks was still weak. That has since changed. Cases of companies targeted by such attacks are becoming increasingly well known.

The report "#Disinformation—Situation, Forecast and Defense" by the German Federal Association "Alliance for Security in Business" (ASW)—which we will cite repeatedly throughout this book and refer to as the "ASW Study"—is certainly the most comprehensive and in-depth investigation into disinformation attacks on companies that I have encountered to date (as of 2024). This is also because the companies organized within the ASW were willing to speak openly in interviews when asked about disinformation attacks, prevention, or containment. This is highly unusual, as German companies are generally very reticent when asked whether they have ever experienced an attack on their business. On one point, however, almost all companies surveyed were certain: in the near future, disinformation attacks on companies must be given significantly greater attention (ASW Federal Association, 2019).

In the near future? Why not already? Well, the ASW study reflects the situation as of 2017 and thus also the attitudes of companies at that time. Martin Grothe, managing director of Complexium GmbH, a company specializing in the detection of threats in the digital sphere, contributed to the study. He believes that awareness of disinformation attacks has since increased. The ASW study states:

> Disinformation is becoming one of the central threats of the 21st century for German companies.

If that is not a wake-up call for the business community! The former head of the Hamburg State Office of Criminal Investigation, the second largest criminal investigation office in Germany, remains skeptical. Frank-Martin Heise, who now advises companies on economic crime, says, "However, it seems to me that awareness of the dangers posed by disinformation attacks against companies and their governing bodies is still insufficiently developed. The fact that false information can be a dangerous weapon should be given much greater attention."

The business consultancy PwC has also recognized:

> Disinformation is now penetrating the corporate sector as well. Organized crime and sophisticated actors are adopting the techniques and methods of disinformation, using the same creation and dissemination mechanisms as those employed in politically motivated disinformation campaigns (PricewaterhouseCoopers, 2021).

8.2 Attackers Weaponize Social Media

The US company Graphica uses artificial intelligence to analyze activities and trends on social media. In a white paper, the analysts examined how attackers weaponize social media to target a company or brand.

> The speed and scale at which narratives emerge and evolve on social networks have made social media a domain ripe for disinformation and conspiracy theories, despite constant efforts by social media platforms to evolve content moderation policies. But it's not just QAnon, Russia, and presidential elections. Weaponized cybersocial threats and viral events impact businesses at their bottom line. Such online movements can lead to boycotts that reduce market share, while negative sentiment reduces share prices, and the list goes on. The intentional manipulation and amplification of information or a negative viral moment of a brand can leave an organization's key stakeholders—from customers and investors to employees and shareholders—lacking trust (Graphica, 2021).

The threat to companies has long since been recognized by intelligence services, not only in the USA but also in Germany. Germany has its own intelligence service to protect its constitution. Groups whose political aims threaten or attack the German constitution are registered and monitored by the Federal Office for the Protection of the Constitution. Since 2023, the constitutional protection authorities have been distributing an "Information Sheet on Economic Security—Protection against Disinformation" (Federal Office for the Protection of the Constitution, 2023). However, anyone reading the informative flyer will quickly notice that the Office for the Protection of the Constitution adopts a political perspective. For example, the flyer states:

> Foreign states also use disinformation to pursue their economic policy interests. In the increasingly fierce battle for dominance of opinion, these states also deploy their intelligence services alongside overt means.

There are now plenty of cases of disinformation attacks on companies, both high-profile and less well-known. The perpetrators are motivated by a wide range of factors: criminal, vengeful, greedy, political, entrepreneurial, and more.

We can now look back on a whole series of cases in which companies have been attacked through deliberately disseminated and media-placed allegations, through strategic lawsuits or criminal complaints, through tips to the media or forged "expert reports" that were deliberately spread in the media, leaked information, and much more. The range is broad and diverse. Here are some examples:

- US media received a forged memo from the US Department of Defense claiming that the planned takeover of a technology company by a semiconductor giant raised national security concerns. The share prices of both companies subsequently fell.
- In 2024, a defense company was confronted with media reports questioning the quality and reliability of its armored personnel carriers supplied to Ukraine. Behind this was a rival company, which orchestrated the reports together with a major daily newspaper and did not shy away from using fake images from the Russian intelligence service FSB.
- "Corporate raiders" orchestrated an illegitimate capital increase at a successful crypto start-up in Switzerland, thereby depriving the young German founding team of its majority stake in the company. The corporate raiders were targeting the investments previously raised by the founders, amounting to around USD 100 million. To justify their unscrupulous actions, they fed a renowned business newspaper false information about the founders. The investors were outraged by the allegedly fraudulent behavior of the founders. The company collapsed. This was followed by a cascade of legal disputes between the defrauded founding team, the corporate raiders, the investors, and the company's insolvency administrator.
- In 2012, "Papa John's Pizza" fell victim to a disinformation campaign on social media. False rumors were spread claiming that the company's CEO, John Schnatter, had made derogatory remarks about President Obama and donated money to the "Ku Klux Klan." Although there was no evidence to support these claims, the rumors quickly circulated on social media and led to a boycott of the company. As a result, Papa John's suffered a significant decline in sales and was forced to issue a public apology.

- "Starbucks" was targeted by a disinformation campaign alleging that the company had removed Christmas symbols from its holiday cups to be more politically correct. The rumors triggered a social media storm against Starbucks, with many customers claiming the company was waging a "war on Christmas." Although the rumors were untrue, they negatively affected the company's reputation. During the war between Israel and Hamas, Starbucks was attacked for selling coffee cups featuring a watermelon design (the colors of the watermelon represent those of the Palestinian flag). Disinformation agents spread the rumor that Starbucks was attempting to win back the pro-Palestinian movement in the USA, which had previously boycotted the company. The result of this disinformation attack was outrage against Starbucks within the Jewish community, leading to yet another boycott.
- "Unilever," a British Dutch multinational consumer goods manufacturer, became the target of a disinformation campaign in India in 2018. Rumors were circulated that Unilever's products contained harmful chemicals and that the company was using India as a testing ground for these products. Although there was no evidence to support these claims, the rumors led to a social media campaign against Unilever and a decline in the company's sales in India.

The list of cases that have occurred internationally could be extended much further. Moreover, there is a high number of unreported cases, as many victims do not report attacks on their companies at all, and unlike cyberattacks, disinformation attacks are not yet legally defined or categorized.

8.3 Corporate Raiders in Conflict Zones

A new form of disinformation attack on companies appears to be spreading in Ukraine: forced corporate takeovers during times of war and crisis. Since the outbreak of war, the current Ukrainian government under Volodymyr Zelensky has been trying to keep its powerful and corrupt oligarch clique in check to curb widespread corruption in Ukraine. The program is called "restructuring"—which sounds positive, but for some "clean" companies, it poses a real threat. The online portal politico.eu (Dettmer, 2023) reported on Julia Kiryanova, CEO of "Smart Holdings," one of the country's largest investment firms, focusing on metals, gas, agriculture, real estate, and shipbuilding, which is increasingly having to defend itself against hostile takeovers. The attackers' aim is to acquire Smart Holdings at the lowest possible price. Among the attackers, Julia Kiryanova suspects "high-ranking government officials." She says it is dangerous to resist, "(…) because if there is no law, anyone can be persecuted for no reason."

> Kiryanova believes Russia's war on Ukraine is being used by powerful and politically connected players in Ukraine to enrich themselves by extorting, plundering, and weakening commercial rivals—as well as an opportunity to redistribute corporate assets, partly in a bid to strip the old elite of wealth to shape a new one. And it's all being done with scant regard to the rule of law (Dettmer, 2023).

The weapons used by corporate raiders in such hostile takeovers are the classic tools of disinformation. Suddenly, Smart Holdings and other Ukrainian companies find themselves facing allegations of criminal activity, or they suddenly appear on the Ukrainian sanctions list of the "Security Service of Ukraine" (SBU). The justifications for this are questionable and range from alleged business ties to Russian companies to tax irregularities. Alarm bells are now ringing in Kyiv, not least because the fight against corruption is a prerequisite for EU accession. Shortly before the Ukrainian SBU raid, Smart Holding received a takeover offer amounting to just a third of the company's value. A similar fate befell "Parimatch", a major betting provider in Ukraine.

We will discuss in detail later how a national judicial system can be used to carry out disinformation attacks on companies. Strategically placed criminal charges or flimsy civil lawsuits against management and companies, accompanied by orchestrated media coverage, are part of the standard arsenal of attackers.

When discussing disinformation attacks, I consider it essential to clearly distinguish between the terms "fake news," misinformation, and disinformation (see Chap. 4). If we conflate these terms, the statistics regarding the actual number of disinformation attacks remain questionable. The term "fake news" still frequently appears in recent literature, when in fact what is meant are disinformation attacks.

We must also be careful not to assume that every negative media report about a company marks the beginning of a disinformation campaign. Whether it is a case of misinformation or actual disinformation must be examined very carefully before deploying extensive countermeasures.

On several occasions, we have been able to reassure agitated or anxious clients after discovering that the false information about a company originated from the convenience or negligence of journalists. Such misinformation does not pursue any objective but is simply attributable to the sloppiness or ignorance of the journalist.

However, in our daily practice, we also regularly encounter media reports based on deliberately leaked or even falsified information. In these cases, the malice and intent to cause harm do not lie with the journalist disseminating the damaging information but rather with the informant, who has used the media and journalists as instruments for their attack.

8.4 Journalists as Tools of Disinformation Agents

Even if a journalist insists that they did not intentionally disseminate false, misleading, or otherwise impermissible information, both they and their media outlet remain liable. The question then arises as to whether due diligence obligations were breached. This is where things become interesting, as the journalist can only extricate themselves from this predicament by naming the source who provided the false information. But what reputable investigative journalist would betray their source to save themselves? In any case, I have never witnessed this in a legal dispute.

Malice can be attributed to a media outlet when its editorial team first formulates a thesis regarding a company's situation, then conducts research along the lines of this thesis, deliberately disregarding all exculpatory arguments that arise during the investigation in order not to jeopardize the pre-established thesis and to deliberately portray the company in a negative light. This is known as thesis-driven journalism and is the opposite of open-ended research. The Swiss journalist and publicist Kurt W. Zimmermann describes thesis-driven journalism as the "reversal of research and conclusion"—the opposite of what any serious journalist should practice.

> In the normal case, a journalist gathers information and forms an opinion from it. In thesis-driven journalism, they first formulate an opinion and then only collect information that supports this opinion. The other facts are concealed (Zimmermann, 2010).

A similar pattern can be observed with deliberately drafted and submitted criminal complaints or civil lawsuits against managers, which are based on scant information and are not primarily intended for the prosecutor but rather to attract journalists to the case and cast managers and companies in a negative light. This is a tool often used by investor lawyers seeking to acquire clients in this way and who regard the media as useful idiots.

Another form of attack—which we will discuss further in this book—is assaults originating from the depths of the internet. Data leaks repeatedly find their way into the media. The "Panama Papers," "Pandora Papers," "Lux-Leaks," and "FinCEN Files" have become particularly well known. These involve vast amounts of data on companies and individuals who have used complex corporate structures to exploit the world's tax havens. To be clear: the investigations and reports by journalists on these data leaks do not constitute disinformation attacks but are rather the result of thorough and diligent research. These famous data leaks, which every journalist covets, are clearly investigative in nature and in some cases have indeed led to criminal consequences for the individuals, corrupt politicians, and companies named in the leaks.

However, and this is something we see time and again, the fact that certain individuals or companies appear in these data leaks is repeatedly exploited by interested parties for targeted disinformation attacks aimed at damaging a company's reputation. For much of the public, it seems irrelevant whether person or company XY may have opened a bank account or company in Panama for entirely simple, legitimate business reasons. If the information that company XY holds a Panama account is placed in the "right" context, the originator of this information plays on the anticipated assumption of the audience that this must be because company XY has something to hide. Banks, tax authorities, and shareholders then become highly alert. Whether Panama, the Cayman Islands, the Channel Islands, or the British Virgin Islands (BVI)—all these locations have a certain notoriety for journalists and financial authorities, which disinformation agents skillfully exploit, regardless of the fact that such accounts may make perfect sense for the operation of a business, especially if, for example, the company actually conducts real business in Central America. The most recent and spectacular data dump consisted of the Epstein Files, which the U.S. Department of Justice released during the Trump II administration following intense public pressure. Journalists around the world pounced on the published Epstein Files, searching for well-known individuals from their jurisdictions who appeared in the sex offender's collected documents. However, the media published the names of prominent people who were connected to Epstein only in a business capacity and had absolutely nothing to do with his abuse of underage girls. That did not deter some journalists from writing that Mr. XY was named in the Epstein Files. While that may be factually correct, it by no means proves that Mr. XY is also an abuser. The mere mention in connection with the Epstein Files amounted to a media-driven character assassination of innocent people.

8.5 Disinformation Attacks by Activists

Disinformation attacks are increasingly being launched by activist investors, who use annual general meetings as a platform to stage their interventions and attempt to put pressure on company management. Activist investors may target individual C-level executives or supervisory board members, for example, to push for the breakup of companies, block planned takeovers, demand the sale of the company, stall unpopular product developments, or fill supervisory positions with their own allies. Alternatively, activist investors may pursue a political agenda, seeking to bring the targeted corporation into line with their views. This was experienced by several American companies during the second Trump administration, which took action against corporate DEI (Diversity, Equity, Inclusion) policies. Iconic American companies such as Harley-Davidson, Apple, Levi Strauss, Disney, and Goldman Sachs have all felt the power of activist investors, finding themselves caught in the crossfire of anti-woke and anti-DEI campaigns.

Activist investors have a wide range of communication tools at their disposal to achieve their objectives, including the dissemination of disinformation or deliberate falsehoods. For instance, during "Pride Month" 2023, the American department store chain Target was attacked with the claim that it was selling children's swimsuits designed to conceal a child's gender identity. As a result, Target employees were threatened by anti-LGBTQ+ groups. In some southern states, Target removed its Pride Month products from sale or relegated them to the back of its stores. This, in turn, outraged LGBTQ+ activists, who also began to protest. Target thus found itself under attack on all fronts, all due to a piece of disinformation spread by activists: the children's swimsuits allegedly designed to "standardize" children's gender did not exist. They were only available for adults (Associated Press, 2023).

The chemical and agribusiness group Bayer experiences this at almost every annual general meeting at its headquarters in Germany, when protesting farmers, genuine or alleged victims of chemical exposure, Monsanto victims, environmental activists, and others gather outside the venue, demonstrate, distribute leaflets, and give interviews to the media. Energy, defense, oil, and pharmaceutical companies; meat and automotive manufacturers; mining companies; and others face the same scenario year after year. These demonstrations by interest groups and NGOs are intended not only to prompt a change of course by the management of the affected company but also to inform the public via the media about the allegations—justified or not—leveled against the company. Sometimes, simple or even fact-free polemics are not enough, and gross disinformation is also employed.

In the USA, for example, "Eli Lilly", the manufacturer of contraceptive pills, was put under pressure by highly vocal and aggressive anti-abortion activists. Google's parent company, "Alphabet," and "American Express" were attacked by vocal interest groups for speaking out against the criminalization of abortion.

Representatives of the LGBTQ+ community attack companies, as do environmental groups and gun lobbyists; thus, the fragmentation of our society is also reflected in the annual general meetings of major corporations. Unfortunately, not all activists or NGOs are scrupulous with facts and truth; they often bend them to fit their agenda or spread false information via social media to broaden their activist base.

Such disinformation attacks by NGOs or certain lobby groups often result in damaging or even value-destroying false claims. I have written articles and given lectures on disinformation attacks that exploit the close, symbiotic relationship between NGOs and journalists. An example of such a disinformation attack via an NGO can be found in a later chapter of this book (Wolff, 2024).

No matter how much companies try to remain as apolitical as possible, they are pushed in one direction or another by activist campaigns. A good example is the somewhat older PR battle between Greenpeace and the oil company Shell over a decommissioned, massive, floating oil storage facility called "Brent Spar". Shell wanted to sink the tank in the North Sea, as prior scientific studies had shown that sinking the "Brent Spar" would not cause significant environmental problems (Wikipedia, 2023). Towing the platform ashore for dismantling would have been more expensive and less environmentally sound. The environmental organization Greenpeace seized the moment to stage a high-profile protest, occupying the floating tank and launching a campaign aimed squarely at stirring emotions and outrage. Once again, journalists acted as uncritical fanboys of the environmental organization and did not even attempt to question Greenpeace's claims.

Greenpeace claimed that there were still 5500 tons of oil in tanks that would contaminate the sea. Shell, on the other hand, claimed that it was only 100 tons, an amount the sea could absorb, and argued that it would be less environmentally sound to tow the tank ashore for dismantling.

Shell attempted to counter Greenpeace's campaign in the media, but the press had already made up its mind regarding credibility. Greenpeace was granted a credibility bonus by editorial teams, and the oil company's resistance collapsed in the face of massive public outrage and media coverage. The 147-m-high oil tank was towed ashore and ultimately dismantled there.

Later, on 5 September 1995, Greenpeace was forced to admit, somewhat sheepishly, that its estimate of the amount of toxic oil residues in the tank had been grossly inaccurate: the cited figure of 5500 tons was far too high. An inspection report by the Norwegian ship classification society DNV estimated the oil residues at 75 to a maximum of 100 tons, i.e., about 1.37–1.8% of the amount previously stated and widely publicized.

Considering these facts, Greenpeace had no choice but to apologize to Shell and the public for the misleading figures, issuing a notably self-critical press release: "Surveys on the credibility of various organizations and institutions repeatedly show the great trust placed in non-governmental organizations (NGOs). Greenpeace regularly ranks among the top. This credibility bonus also benefited the organization during the 1995 Brent Spar campaign, which led to the oil company Shell abandoning its plan to sink the decommissioned oil loading platform in the Northeast Atlantic. Instead of the previously stated 130 tons of oil sludge, 5,500 tons were suspected to be in the tanks of the Brent Spar. The error affects not only credibility in this individual case but also provides a compelling reason to examine campaign communications as a whole for the risks they pose to Greenpeace's credibility" (Steffens, 2005).

Another case involved a pig farming company that became the focus of animal welfare activists. It was a very large intensive farming operation, which was a thorn in the side of both residents and small farms in the area. The activists managed to secretly film shocking footage inside pigsties, which they then passed on to a German television current affairs program shortly before Christmas. This animal welfare organization also appeared to enjoy a credibility bonus in the editorial offices of the program. After the broadcast, the pig farming company was sanctioned by the authorities for the allegedly appalling conditions, and its operating licenses were revoked. The damage to the company was enormous. However, upon closer examination of the footage, it became clear that the secretly filmed material did not actually show our client's pig farm. It apparently depicted interiors of another company.

Nevertheless, the animal welfare organization achieved its goal. The Dutch company had to close and, due to the reputational damage it had suffered, could not expect to reopen a new breeding operation in Germany any time soon. However, the animal welfare organization also achieved another, unwanted outcome: several thousand pigs had to be culled following the closure of the business. A cruel collateral damage caused by animal rights activists, based on disinformation driven by self-interest.

Both the "Brent Spar" case and the pig farming case occurred at a time when social media either did not yet exist (Brent Spar) or was still in its infancy, meaning activists were not yet able to recruit large numbers of supporters via social media channels in a short period of time. With today's tools and communication channels, both cases would likely have spread even more rapidly. Today, there would be no need for the support of traditional media to disseminate highly emotional images such as the occupation of the Brent Spar platform or the dying piglets in the pig farm. Activists and NGOs can now attract attention much more quickly via online platforms and attack companies—guilty or not—with emotional images, videos, and stories.

8.6 State-Sponsored Disinformation Attacks on Vaccine Manufacturers

At the height of the coronavirus pandemic and in the midst of the race to develop vaccines, a perfect opportunity arose for state-sponsored disinformation agents to expand their field of activity: they moved from the political sphere into the economic sphere. As a result, the business sector now also faced a disinformation problem.

The Western manufacturers of Covid-19 vaccines—Moderna, BioNTech/Pfizer, and AstraZeneca—not only competed to produce the most effective vaccine but also faced powerful competition from authoritarian states, with Sputnik from Russia and Sinopharm/Sinovac from China.

Russia and China quickly recognized the propaganda potential of vaccines: they could use them to demonstrate their scientific progress and superiority to the world.

> Vaccine diplomacy is a natural extension of these efforts. The ability to develop and distribute an effective vaccine is, like mask diplomacy before it, an effective tool for autocrats to blunt domestic and international criticism and to showcase the competency and generosity of their respective governments. But with more than a half-dozen vaccines in early or limited use, vaccine narratives are more than an exercise in self-promotion; they are a tool to open enormous diplomatic and economic opportunities for vaccine-producing countries. The stakes are therefore high, as efforts to win the hearts, minds, and deltoids of global populations—particularly those in developing countries—are as much about market dominance as they are about soft power (Schafer et al., 2021).

The use of vaccines as part of a diplomatic soft power strategy worked as follows: Russia and China sought to present themselves as friends and helpers to other, "friendly" nations by supplying them with their domestically developed vaccines. The populations of these countries were then expected to feel indebted to Russia or China and to turn away from their common enemy, the West.

This approach also seemed to suit certain populist leaders who had a bone to pick with Western nations, namely Europe and the USA: Brazilian President Jair Bolsonaro accepted vaccine supplies from China, as did the populist-led Philippines. Russia supplied, among others, Argentina, Hungary, Mexico, Serbia, and the United Arab Emirates, celebrating each recipient in its anti-Western propaganda. The only problem was that the vaccines from Russia and China were not as effective as those from Moderna or BioNTech. To distract from their own shortcomings and avoid a propaganda disaster, Russia and China devised a plan: not only should the advantages of their own vaccines be highlighted, but Western vaccines and their manufacturers also needed to be discredited. Here, Russia and China could draw on their extensive experience in political disinformation.

Soon, the disinformation machinery was running at full speed. The world was warned about severe side effects and the low efficacy of Western vaccines. It was also claimed that they were only effective for certain age groups. Conspiracy theorists and vaccine opponents, especially from alternative, anthroposophical, and spiritual circles, amplified the disinformation orchestrated by Russia and China with their own outlandish theories across all channels, aiming to discourage people from getting vaccinated. Russia and China also received support from two other states, which, although they had no vaccines of their own to offer, shared a strong aversion to the West: Iran and North Korea.

The "Alliance for Securing Democracy" (ASD) is a bipartisan initiative based at the German Marshall Fund. It conducted a thorough investigation of the information war surrounding vaccines and arrived at some remarkable findings. The ASD researchers analyzed more than 35,000 vaccine-related online messages disseminated by Russian, Chinese, and Iranian politicians, government officials, and state media since the announcement by Pfizer/BioNTech that they had developed a vaccine. During the study period, the ASD also collected and evaluated more than 455,757 tweets from Russian, Chinese, and Iranian officials and state media representatives.

The sheer volume of disinformation unleashed had consequences. Western vaccine manufacturers had to defend themselves against the most absurd claims regarding side effects. Negative mentions included tweets and articles referring to alleged deaths or other adverse reactions to the vaccine. In addition, the attackers criticized the manufacturers for supposedly excessive vaccine prices, failure to meet delivery requirements, or other related issues. The reputation of the vaccines and their manufacturers was damaged. Alarm bells rang at companies that had invested vast sums in developing their products. Disinformation had thus reached the economy and industry.

The disinformation campaign also led to a lasting erosion of public trust in the vaccination campaign and undermined confidence in government leadership. This was very much to the liking of the Russian autocrat Putin, whose goal was to manipulate the narratives surrounding Covid vaccines. Here, too, the disinformers were willing to accept cynical collateral damage: While their disinformation campaigns apparently took hold, people refused to get the necessary vaccinations and parents refused to vaccinate their children, with the bitter consequence that deadly outbreaks of measles epidemics occurred, for example in Texas, or cases of diphtheria in Germany, resulting in children dying or being permanently disabled.

In their introduction to the study, the authors write:

> "That vaccines have become the latest flashpoint in the coronavirus-era battle of narratives is hardly surprising. Since the outbreak of the virus forced much of the world into lockdown last March, Russia, China, and Iran have used a combination of public diplomacy, propaganda, and overt and covert disinformation campaigns to portray their respective responses to the pandemic as superior to those of the West," write the ASD researchers in their report with the striking title, "Influence-enza: How Russia, China, and Iran Have Shaped and Manipulated Coronavirus Vaccine Narratives" (Schafer et al., 2021).

Here are some highlights from the report on how Russia, China, and Iran advanced their vaccine narratives:

- Reports of safety concerns related to the administration of certain Western-manufactured vaccines were often presented in a sensationalist manner, while important contextual information was downplayed or omitted entirely.
- Russian coverage of Oxford-AstraZeneca underwent a marked shift after the announcement of a deal in December to test a combination of the Oxford-AstraZeneca and Sputnik V vaccines. Following the announcement, there was an increase in positive reporting and a decrease in negative coverage of AstraZeneca in Russian diplomatic and state media.
- Of the three countries studied, Russia was the most likely to suggest links between the Pfizer vaccine and subsequent deaths among vaccine recipients. Of the 209 tweets from Russian, Chinese, and Iranian accounts mentioning Pfizer and the words "die," "dead," or "death" in the same tweet, 111 (53%) originated from Russian state media.

- Iranian coverage of Pfizer and Moderna took a markedly more negative turn after Ayatollah Khamenei decided on 8 January 2021 to ban the import of all vaccines produced in the USA and the United Kingdom. Despite the ban, Iran continues with plans to import AstraZeneca, a contradiction that state media justified by claiming that the Oxford-AstraZeneca vaccine is Swedish rather than British. In this context, coverage of AstraZeneca was consistently positive, suggesting that Iranian reporting is driven as much by necessity as by geopolitics.

It is worthwhile to take a closer look at the detailed report by ASD/GMF. It reveals in a striking manner how Russia, China, and Iran, through their disinformation campaigns, can destabilize a country like Germany politically.

References

Associated Press. (2023). Target's Pride collection features 'tuck-friendly' swimsuits for adults, not kids. Retrieved from: https://apnews.com/article/fact-check-target-swimsuits-transgender-pride-collection-892500330955

DarkOwl. (2022). The digital economy of disinformation on the Darknet: Controlling the narrative. Retrieved from: https://www.darkowl.com/blog-content/the-digital-economy-of-disinformation-on-the-darknet-controlling-the-narrative/

Dettmer, J. (2023). Sanctions cause rising business fears in Ukraine. Retrieved from: https://www.politico.eu/article/ukraine-war-corruption-companies-sanctions-cause-rising-business-fears/

#Disinformation—Situation, Forecast, and Defense. (2019). Retrieved from: https://asw-bundesverband.de/wp-content/uploads/studie_desinformation_web_v3.pdf

Federal Office for the Protection of the Constitution. (2023). Information sheets on economic protection: Protection against disinformation. Retrieved from: https://www.verfassungsschutz.de/SharedDocs/publikationen/DE/wirtschafts-wissenschaftsschutz/2023-04-14-infoblatt-desinformation.pdf?blob=publicationFile&v=2

Graphica. (2021). Weaponized social media—The new brand reputation challenge. Retrieved from: https://graphika.com/whitepapers/weaponized-social-media-the-new-brand-reputation-challenge

Marketing Charts. (2013). Bad customer service interactions more likely to be shared than good ones. Retrieved from: https://www.marketingcharts.com/digital-28628

PricewaterhouseCoopers PwC. (2021). Disinformation attacks have arrived in the corporate sector. Are you ready? Retrieved from: https://www.pwc.com/us/en/tech-effect/cybersecurity/corporate-sector-disinformation.html

Schafer, F., & Kohlenberg, S., & Alliance for Securing Democracy (2021). Influence-enza: How Russia, China, and Iran have shaped and manipulated coronavirus vaccine narratives. Retrieved from: https://securingdemocracy.gmfus.org/russia-china-iran-covid-vaccine-disinformation/

Steffens, B. (2005). Credibility—The most important asset of an NGO. *Greenpeace Press Release*. Retrieved from: https://web.archive.org/web/20131101192357/http://www.greenpeace.de/themen/oel/brent_spar/artikel/glaubwuerdigkeit_das_wichtigste-kapital_einer_ngo/

Wikipedia. (2023). Brent Spar. Wikipedia Apr 2023, 05:30 UTC. https://de.wikipedia.org/w/index.php?title=Brent_Spar&oldid=233255313. Status: 24 May 2023, 04:56 UTC.

Wolff, U. (2024). AI-supported disinformation attacks on corporate ESG policies via NGOs and activists. In *AI in media, communication and marketing*. Springer VS.

Zimmermann, K. W. (2010, January 13). Controversy surrounding the monster. Retrieved from: http://www.weltwoche.ch/ausgaben/2010-02/artikel-2010-02-medien-eklat-um-das-monster.html

The Perpetrators and Their Motives 9

During the research for this book, I spoke with many experts about the perpetrators and their motives. I pored over crime statistics and discussed them with investigators. The central question was always: What types of perpetrators are these? What do they want? Do the attackers think like cybercriminals, extortionists, and fraudsters, or do they pursue entirely different motives?

It became apparent that disinformation attacks do not yet exist as a criminal offense in the crime statistics of many countries. If a company reports a disinformation attack to the police, the investigating officers file it under another category, such as "cyberattack" or perhaps "defamation."

It is due to the ignorance and lack of information among companies that disinformation actors are lumped together with cybercriminals. In my lectures and discussions with company executives, I therefore make a clear distinction between cybercriminals and professional disinformation actors, and I like to use the following analogy:

Cybercriminals break into companies' IT systems. Once inside, two scenarios typically follow: 1. The cybercriminals lock down the system with special software so that the company no longer has access to its IT system. The company is thus completely paralyzed on many levels. Production comes to a standstill, salaries can no longer be paid, and employees lose access to databases, addresses, or accounts. Only when the company complies with the cybercriminals' demand and makes a substantial payment (in crypto) does it regain access to its IT system. Or, following a cyberattack, scenario 2: Here, cybercriminals, or so-called hacktivists (a portmanteau of "hackers" and "activists"), infiltrate a company's IT system. But instead of blocking the system, the attackers sift through the stored data, downloading, for example, ongoing product developments or business plans, as well as sensitive management emails, financial data, patent applications, or documents relating to ongoing litigation. They then use this stolen data either to blackmail the targeted company or sell it to competitors, or, in the case of an attack by hacktivists, pass the captured

U. Wolff, *Disinformation Attacks On Businesses*, Management for Professionals,
https://doi.org/10.1007/978-3-658-51407-5_9

data on to the media. Journalists welcome such leaks, which often form the basis for extensive negative reporting.

The difference between cybercriminals and **disinformation criminals** lies in their approach. Disinformation criminals do **not** break into companies' IT systems; instead, they infiltrate the minds of stakeholders and shareholders with their disseminated disinformation, aiming to "reprogram" their brains and hearts. In this way, disinformation attackers erode trust in the company, political and science institutions, media or the legal structure of a nation. They prompt customers to turn away from the company, banks to withdraw credit (see the case of Hazim Nada), and unsettle employees, suppliers, regulators, and politicians. The goal is to inflict maximum reputational damage on the company and paralyze its operations. A ransom note? A demand for money? Not at all! As a rule, disinformation attackers are not interested in money but in the harm they can inflict on the company. And this brings us to the motives of disinformation attackers: these are diverse and varied. But why do they do it if they are not after money? Why do they develop complex and elaborate campaigns to attack the company?

Frank-Martin Heise is an experienced former criminal investigator who headed Germany's second-largest state criminal police office, namely Hamburg. He oversaw 2500 employees before deciding to move into the private sector. Today, he is a successful business consultant who, with his company Intafors, supports national and international companies or individuals and investigates a wide range of issues.

I asked him about the motives of those behind disinformation attacks. "The motives are highly diverse," he explained to me. "Essentially, they can be grouped into three categories: First, there is the pursuit of power, that is, the desire for influence and prestige within a region or an industry. If, from the attacker's perspective, the chosen target company cannot be defeated in the market by legal means, other, less legal and more covert methods are employed."

Frank-Martin Heise here alludes to one of the most common motives in the field of disinformation: competition and rivals. He regards "information"—and disinformation—as a weapon used by attackers who exploit our information society and, above all, social media in their assaults.

In the corporate sector, this is often linked to a second motive, namely financial gain. However, unlike cybercriminals, disinformation actors do not demand money directly; instead, they profit indirectly from the attack: "The attacker's aim is simply to inflict economic damage on the opponent, whether to limit the market power of the target or to force the target to focus its personnel and financial resources on resolving the problem, thereby depriving them of resources for market expansion or a product launch."

A third possible motive, according to the former criminal investigator and business consultant, can be found on a personal level. "Out of revenge, envy, or because, in the perpetrator's subjective perception, there is still an old score to settle. That is when the attack is launched."

The motives of state-sponsored actors, who possess extensive human and financial resources—such as Russia or China—are quite different. We will return to this topic in more detail later.

While we can describe the perpetrators and their motives in the context of cyberattacks relatively well, we still lack a solid and robust data basis regarding disinformation attacks. Furthermore, companies are not particularly forthcoming when it comes to admitting that they have fallen victim to a disinformation attack. The reasons for this are not entirely clear to me, especially since the targeted companies will eventually have to address and remedy such attacks. And that can only be achieved through communication.

It is understandable that companies are now more willing to report cyberattacks, as these involve criminal acts such as data theft or extortion. The media also regularly report on such incidents. This was not always the case.

The first cyberattacks were dismissed by company managers as minor "IT problems," the work of hacking computer kids. This view has since changed radically, once managers realized that these are organized gangs or, as in the case of North Korea, even state-sanctioned cybercriminals who funnel billions into their impoverished state's coffers. UN experts estimate that North Korea extorted around 3 billion US dollars between 2017 and 2022 (Reuters, 2024). According to estimates, companies worldwide will spend a total of 245 billion US dollars in 2024 to protect their IT systems from cyberattacks (Grand View Research, 2024). The situation has therefore changed completely: companies now take cyberattacks seriously as a threat. A similar development is likely to occur with the threat scenario of disinformation attacks.

Current crime statistics provide little insight into the initiators of disinformation attacks. At most, the so-called "insider" type could be incorporated into our perpetrator-motive schema. However, even here, the motives only partially overlap with those of cybercriminals.

The following list of perpetrator types also reveals, in most cases, their respective motives. I have identified the following perpetrator types, based partly on my own experience and partly on research into known cases.

Here is my list:

1. State-sponsored actors
2. Former (disgruntled) employees or customers
3. Competitors
4. Investors, corporate raiders, short sellers
5. Hacktivists
6. NGOs/activists
7. Extortionists (rare)
8. Investor protection lawyers
9. Beneficiaries

This list does not claim to be exhaustive. New perpetrator types may emerge in the future, or there may be "hybrids" that belong to more than one category. For example, we were involved in a case in which a company was attacked, which was engaged in major patent disputes with two large international corporations. The company had a good chance of winning the patent litigation and walking away with a substantial sum of money. The legal adversaries, however, were determined to prevent this outcome and launched a disinformation campaign. The result: banks cut credit lines, employees resigned, and the company found itself in financial distress. The media reported on the situation, further exacerbating the company's difficulties, which now lacked the funds to continue the patent litigation. The patent claims were withdrawn. The motives of the perpetrators can often be inferred from their background.

Financial Gain
Through disinformation attacks, perpetrators seek financial profit, for example, by manipulating share prices or increasing demand for a product. Example: short sellers.

Competitive Advantage
Disinformation attacks are intended to damage a competitor's reputation, disrupt their business operations, or poach their customers or staff. Disinformation is used to prevent market entry through false information or to discredit rivals in a bidding process.

Political or Ideological Objectives
Disinformation attacks are used to advance a political or ideological agenda by spreading false information about a company or an industry. This ranges from state actors to hacktivists, activists, or NGOs. I have already mentioned the examples of Greenpeace and animal rights activists.

Revenge
Targeted disinformation attacks are sometimes used by disgruntled (former) employees to take revenge on a company or its representatives by spreading false information about them. The same applies to dissatisfied customers.

Sabotage
Disinformation attacks are used to sabotage a company or an industry by spreading false information that leads to damage or disruption. In cases of sabotage via disinformation, a mix of motives may be present, such as revenge, a desire for destruction, or activism.

Terrorism
Disinformation attacks as a form of terrorism occur when false information is deliberately spread to create fear or panic. This could involve, for example, a supposed leak at a chemical plant or an alleged cluster of radiation-induced cancers near a power station.

Disruptive Innovation
Disinformation attacks are used by newly established companies to disrupt established industries or business models by spreading false information that undermines trust in traditional companies.

Influence Operations
State or state-affiliated actors use disinformation attacks as part of broader influence operations, spreading false information to sway public opinion or undermine trust in democratic institutions. Russia and China have demonstrated how this works, for example, when they targeted Western vaccine manufacturers with their disinformation campaigns.

Malicious Intent
There are also perpetrators who derive satisfaction from malicious acts and launch disinformation attacks simply to cause harm or create chaos, without pursuing any higher motive or objective.

Let us now examine in more detail what drives the perpetrator groups mentioned above:

9.1 State or State-Affiliated Actors

Governments or government-supported entities conduct disinformation attacks on companies for geopolitical reasons. I have already mentioned several cases but would like to revisit the attacks by China and Russia on Western vaccine manufacturers BioNTech/Pfizer, Moderna, and AstraZeneca during the COVID-19 pandemic as an illustration. In this well-documented case, the aim was not only to promote Russia's and China's own vaccines but, especially in Russia's case, to destabilize Western societies by inciting people and turning them against their governments.

The state actors spread disinformation about the composition, efficacy, and especially the side effects of the vaccines. They questioned the motives of the vaccine manufacturers, built up influencers and activist groups, and disseminated disinformation on a large scale. This was followed by demonstrations and attacks on vaccination centers and doctors administering vaccines. People, angered by the severe restrictions during the pandemic and confused by disinformation, refused vaccination for themselves and their children. They forged vaccination certificates or emigrated—lured by further disinformers and profiteers—to Paraguay, Mexico, or Bulgaria, where they hoped for a life free from vaccines and masks. The damage was borne by an even more polarized society, which now had to deal with a large number of vaccine skeptics, as well as by the vaccine manufacturers, whose reputations were damaged and whose product safety is now in doubt, with certainly measurable economic consequences in the future as well.

Significant—and not only material—damage can be inflicted on a national economy, for example, when systemically important companies become the target of state-sponsored disinformation agents, or when one state competes with another over the sale of armaments to a third country. Another case that falls under the category of "disinformation attack by state actors" is the distressing and previously mentioned story of the entrepreneur Hazim Nada, whose transport company became collateral damage in the conflict between the United Arab Emirates and Qatar. In this instance, the state actors, namely the UAE, paid a service provider in Switzerland to create and disseminate the disinformation. Apparently with success, Hazim Nada's transport company collapsed because banks were no longer willing to grant essential loans.

However, not all attacks by state actors are driven by geopolitical motives. Russia is currently destabilizing numerous African governments through disinformation campaigns and, in return, supporting politicians or military figures favorable to its interests—both in Mali and Sudan. In the Central African Republic, for example, Russian Wagner mercenaries are profiting from the country's gold mines after a Russian disinformation campaign paved the way for their entry (New York Times, 2022a). In other cases, the aim is to defend economic interests and damage the reputation of internationally competing companies (for example, the arms industry). Another objective is the enforcement of one's own economic interests (for example, the export of goods).

Another example of a state-directed disinformation attack, which I have also previously mentioned, was the bedbug hysteria in Paris in the summer of 2023. State-affiliated Russian disinformation agents came across a post by a woman who found a bedbug in her bed at a Paris hotel, photographed it, and shared it via social media. The woman's post went viral, fueled by countless bots. Traditional media picked up on the topic and began broadcasting images and videos of pest controllers fumigating cinemas and underground trains in an attempt to combat the alleged bedbug infestation. These reports and images soon reached other countries, resulting in thousands of tourists cancelling their planned trips to Paris, as well as their hotel and restaurant reservations, thereby delivering a severe blow to the Parisian tourism sector, costing many millions.

It was only later revealed who was really behind the campaign: the Russians, who were not permitted to participate under their own flag at the 2024 Olympic Games the following summer.

9.2 Former Employees or Customers

Disgruntled former employees, dissatisfied customers, or individuals harboring personal vendettas against a company may seek to settle a score with the company or its management. Their motive: revenge, anger, frustration, and above all, a desire to harm the company. In connection with such former or frustrated employees, the term "insider" is often used.

Time and again, we have encountered former employees who sought revenge on their employer by approaching the media and recounting sometimes outrageous stories. On several occasions, one of our clients, a company in the elderly care sector, was targeted by former or disgruntled employees. With stories that were sometimes entirely fabricated, they approached a television broadcaster, which then began to conduct covert investigations in the care homes, sometimes using questionable methods. The reputational damage to the company was enormous. The fact that almost all legal proceedings against the broadcaster were won was only a small consolation.

In the context of disinformation attacks on companies, I am not referring to the insider who steals company data and passes it on to the media or competitors. This is only tangentially related to a disinformation attack, unless the data is further processed as part of a harmful disinformation campaign. However, if the disgruntled employee uses selected and decontextualized correspondence from the executive board to damage the company or associate it with toxic individuals or political actors, then we are dealing with a disinformation attack that can have serious consequences for the company.

Disgruntled customers, on the other hand, generally do not have access to information in the way an insider might, but this group of perpetrators can nevertheless launch an effective disinformation campaign via social media, for example, through reviews of products or services on various channels or in multiple online forums. The situation becomes critical for service providers or vendors when negative reviews accumulate conspicuously. Companies such as eBay, Amazon, or hotel booking platforms attempt to nip such targeted campaigns in the bud by only allowing reviews from individuals who can prove they have made a purchase or booking.

9.3 Competitors

Competing companies or their associates may employ disinformation tactics to gain a competitive advantage. They spread false information about a competitor's products, services, or business practices to damage their reputation and lure away customers.

We encountered such a case during the acquisition of an attractive but financially distressed company. Four parties were interested in the takeover. While it was expected that each would present itself in the best possible light to achieve its objective, what was less obvious to us was that competitors would use targeted disinformation campaigns to eliminate certain parties from the race.

One of the bidding companies, which had a very good chance of being awarded the contract, was based in Eastern Europe. One of the competitors leaked false information to the media, claiming that the head of the rival company was connected to organized crime. As supposed evidence, a scant piece of information from the company's home country was cited, stating that the public prosecutor's office was interested in the company director and his connections to the underworld. In doing so, the competitor deliberately played on existing prejudices and stereotypes that virtually every entrepreneur in Eastern Europe is corrupt and has ties to organized crime. This targeted disinformation took hold in the media, and indeed, the company was subsequently eliminated from the bidding process at an early stage.

A similar approach was taken by a major German car manufacturer, which exploited prejudices and xenophobic resentments during a fierce dispute with a supplier whose origins lay in Bosnia. Company representatives repeatedly emphasized this fact to journalists, referring to the reputable owner family, which had lived in Germany for many decades and produced for the automotive group, as a "clan." This xenophobic portrayal and unrestrained prejudgment of the opponent gained traction in the media (NTV, 2017). The myth of the "Bosnian clan" spread and damaged the supplier's reputation.

A case similar to that of the Eastern European bidder involved an American semiconductor manufacturer seeking to merge with another tech company. However, a competitor was strongly opposed to the deal. The transaction was sabotaged by the dissemination of disinformation claiming that the US government intended to review the deal again, allegedly because it posed a national security threat. The basis for this disinformation was a forged document purportedly issued by the Department of Defense. The share prices of both companies plummeted.

9.4 Investors, Corporate Raiders, and Short Sellers

Corporate raiders fight with tough tactics and do not shy away from targeted disinformation campaigns. When a hostile takeover of a company is planned, the attackers often attempt to drive down the purchase price in this way and to improve the terms of the takeover in their favor—and to the detriment of the company.

I have already mentioned the example of a Swiss crypto company whose majority shareholders were attacked by corporate raiders using false information that was deliberately spread through the media. They accused the founders of fraud and unlawful withdrawal of funds. The international investors, who had invested around 100 million in the company, were incited against the founding team. Newspaper articles based on disinformation were used in social media and in the investors' Telegram groups as evidence that the founding team was indeed committing fraud. After all, reputable media outlets had reported on the case. The campaign was fueled by the corporate raiders, who deliberately and at a rapid pace leaked damaging and false information to the drivers of the campaign, which then found its way into the investors' social media channels. With the involvement of investor protection lawyers, who sensed a "quick buck" from potential clients—that is, the allegedly defrauded investors—the campaign intensified on social media.

This story is not an isolated case. The American investor Carl Icahn, for example, gained dubious fame on Wall Street for his ruthless corporate raids and the associated disinformation campaigns. The irony of history: Icahn's own company is now threatened by a hostile takeover, after the notorious short seller "Hindenburg Research," led by Nathan Anderson targeted "Icahn Enterprises". It is Icahn himself who now claims the following about Nathan Anderson of Hindenburg:

> Mr. Anderson's modus operandi is to launch disinformation campaigns to distort companies' images, damage their reputations and bleed the hard-earned savings of individual

> investors," Mr. Icahn wrote. "But, unlike many of its victims, we will not stand by idly (New York Times, 2023).

There is, however, one major difference between Icahn and Hindenburg: Icahn's heyday was in the 1980s, when there was neither the internet nor social media. Hindenburg, by contrast, now exploits precisely these media relentlessly to achieve its objectives.

Short sellers, on the other hand, are a special breed in the field of disinformation. Their activities are aimed at driving down a company's share price, as they bet on falling stock prices and can make substantial profits in the process. A share price can be very easily manipulated in this direction through an effective disinformation campaign. Major short sellers such as Hindenburg Research or Muddy Waters, for example, have their own departments that scrutinize the companies they target in detail. Their findings are summarized in a report, which they publish and disseminate as their personal assessment of a company's situation. Legally, it is difficult to act against this, as it is an interpretation of the available, researched, and often valid company data. The media, often alerted before the reports are published, are interested in these assessments and turn them into a story. This media campaign is part of the short sellers' strategy. Once the media becomes involved, share prices fall. For example, when the short seller Muddy Waters attacked the German advertising marketer "Ströer", the share price collapsed: MDax company by 30%. Share buybacks by the family were able to prevent worse (Manager Magazin, 2016).

Hindenburg Research attracted global attention when the hedge fund targeted the business conglomerate of the world's third-richest man, Indian billionaire Gautam Adani, in early 2023 (Hindenburg Research, 2023). With the striking headline "Adani Group: How The World's 3rd Richest Man Is Pulling the Largest Con in Corporate History," Hindenburg promoted its latest investigation on the hedge fund's website. The media followed suit, and Adani's companies lost an unimaginable US$150 billion in a very short time (The Economic Times of India, 2023a, b). How much money the short sellers at Hindenburg Research made from this is not known to me.

9.5 Hacktivist Groups

Hacktivism is a portmanteau of "hacker" and "activism." Hacktivist collectives such as "Anonymous" are often involved in online activism and may conduct disinformation attacks against companies to promote a particular cause or ideology. Their motives range from advocating for political change and exposing injustices to disrupting the operations of companies they consider unethical. While hackers pursue personal interests, hacktivists pursue social and political objectives (Hampson, 2012). Hacktivists attempt to obtain confidential information from companies, which is then published in a way that attracts maximum media attention.

Typical targets for such hacktivists include defense contractors, oil companies, banks, tax or law firms, and the chemical industry. In recent years, data leaks from offshore service providers have attracted considerable attention, such as the Panama Papers, as well as leaks from other providers. In the case of the Pandora Papers, data from 14 offshore service providers were passed to the media to expose tax havens and tax avoiders, including politicians and former heads of state. While this does not in itself constitute a disinformation attack, companies or individuals named in these leaks were publicly stigmatized by interested parties and generally suspected of either evading taxes or wanting to keep something secret.

9.6 NGOs and Activists

I have already pointed out that NGOs are not always scrupulous with facts when it comes to achieving their objectives. NGOs and activists are highly skilled in the use of social media and are trained campaigners. For those interested in delving deeper, I recommend searching the Amazon books page with the keywords "NGO" and "campaign." From a communications perspective, NGOs are a very, very serious adversary for any company under attack.

NGOs enjoy a certain advantage with the media and, undoubtedly, with a large part of the public, as they are seen as "good" organizations always fighting on the right side—especially when opposing large corporations. The ASW Report #Disinformation describes it as follows:

> Hard facts quickly become secondary. Activist groups and NGOs also have an interest in presenting issues in a way that suits their agenda. They are not objective and often pursue their own economic interests. To generate donations, dramatized figures or images are more effective than the sometimes rather sober truth (ASW, 2019).

Despite their often careless and interest-driven handling of facts, NGOs find it easy to gain access to the media. NGOs are adept at creating scandals and appealing to emotions and know how to generate headlines—also because they are simply regarded as "the good guys." Journalists are often untroubled when scientifically unsound or grossly exaggerated claims are made, such as the NGO classics "Every three minutes a child …," "Every day xx women die from yy worldwide," or "Every month xx insect species become extinct." The evidence for such claims is often thin or sometimes even nonexistent, but outrage is guaranteed. Anyone who asks NGOs to see the studies on which these claims are based is likely to be told, "These are expert estimates" or "We derive this from our daily work on the ground." The authors of the ASW Report rightly refer to this as "factual arbitrariness" among NGOs and activists.

Easy targets for NGOs and activists are companies with critical supply chains, particularly those extending into developing countries. In these regions, it has become very difficult for most journalists to undertake expensive and time-consuming trips to research the facts. They rely on the one-sided claims of NGOs.

"In this context, every large, well-known corporation offers more friction and guarantees greater attention than a smaller supplier or customer who may be responsible for an incident. This leads to stories that may be very close to the truth but ultimately miss the core of the matter—to the detriment of blameless companies. For higher circulation or more donations, corporations are portrayed as suppliers to Islamic State or as responsible for environmental pollution or accidents in which their products may have been involved, but where responsibility lies with someone else," write the authors of the ASW study.

I have described in detail in an essay how easy it can be for disinformers to attack a company using "evidence" generated by artificial intelligence and disseminated via NGOs. The main aim of such a disinformation attack is to ruthlessly exploit the trust that journalists place in an NGO, having previously presented them with convincingly authentic AI-generated deepfakes, which the journalists then bring into their newsrooms. At the same time, the attack also seeks to take advantage of the budgetary and time constraints faced by editorial teams (Wolff, 2024).

Let me be clear: I consider the work of most NGOs to be of inestimable value. Without them, the world would be a worse place. However, NGOs do themselves no favors if they stretch the truth too far and drift into the realm of mis- and disinformation. Greenpeace, for example, has had to learn this lesson the hard way. It costs trust, it costs credibility, and it costs members and donations.

9.7 Extortionists

Some perpetrators use disinformation as a means of extortion. They threaten to circulate damaging or false information or reviews unless some form of protection money is paid. The motive here is financial gain, exploiting the fear of reputational damage or legal consequences.

Especially during the era of the gray capital market, when a multitude of unregulated funds and companies entered the market between 2000 and 2015, fund managers were subjected to disinformation campaigns. During this period, a veritable ecosystem of "media" emerged, allegedly dedicated to investor protection. Ultimately, the negative articles served to extort companies and funds, which could only secure the removal of these articles by paying a substantial "consultancy fee."

9.8 Investor Protection Lawyers/Litigators

Investor protection lawyers and other representatives of class actions act aggressively and vociferously, not only when soliciting clients but also in their public attacks on defendants. They fight with hard tactics and exaggerated statements, often playing fast and loose with the facts. They see it as their mission to portray their opponents as absolute villains, not only in court. The media—both traditional and social—serve as a megaphone to amplify their claims. The louder they shout, the greater the chance that as many potential clients as possible will hear them.

To launch their disinformation campaigns, investor protection lawyers and litigators resort to a popular tactic: they file criminal complaints against the management of the targeted company, thereby bolstering their civil lawsuits with a criminal investigation (provided the public prosecutor pursues the case). Nothing excites journalists more than a public prosecutor turning their attention to a targeted company and possibly even conducting a raid. We have also seen cases where investor lawyers have claimed that a fund manager was on the run or had bought a Ferrari for every day of the week. These false claims were intended to mobilize both prosecutors and potential clients. Investor protection lawyers have now also recognized the potential of internet campaigns and social media, which they use to spread their disinformation and attract clients.

9.9 Beneficiaries

The beneficiaries of the massive disinformation campaign surrounding the coronavirus pandemic were not only to be found in Moscow or Beijing. Many small, private actors created their own distribution channels on YouTube, in blogs, on their own websites or social media channels, or through publishers that spread the most outlandish conspiracy theories. They profited—and continue to profit handsomely—from this targeted disinformation. Populist, mostly right-wing parties and organizations also capitalized on this, welcoming an influx of new, confused sympathizers, while Moscow and China moved a step closer to their goal: the destabilization of Western society.

Whether through so-called pink-slime online media, fake media, or online presence via YouTube channels, professional disinformers have been able to make—and continue to make—substantial sums of money by stirring up emotions with their posts, spreading outrageous falsehoods or AI-generated images, and thereby generating user reactions. Anyone who takes the trouble to look at these online media and channels will notice that they actually display advertising—advertising that also appears in more reputable media, advertising from respectable, large companies that, in fact, have a reputation to lose. How is this possible? The secret lies in so-called programmatic advertising and the associated ad fraud, that is, fraud involving programmatic advertising.

Imagine you are reading an engaging article about interior design. In the sidebar, advertising suddenly appears for exactly the seating set you viewed on Amazon yesterday. Coincidence? Not at all! This is the result of programmatic advertising, essentially the "eBay for advertising" space—only much, much faster.

How does it work? Let us assume you visit your favorite news site. At that very moment, something fascinating happens within seconds: a system analyzes your profile— "Ah, a design enthusiast from New York interested in high-quality furniture!" Simultaneously, a miniature auction takes place in the background. Various advertisers—in this case, furniture manufacturers—bid for this valuable advertising slot. The highest bid wins, and, instantly, the relevant advert appears on your screen.

The advantages are obvious: companies no longer waste money advertising women's perfume to male users or dog food to cat lovers. They reach precisely those people who are genuinely interested in their products. Website operators, in turn, earn good money because their advertising space is utilized optimally.

Fraudsters, organized crime, terrorist groups, and even the North Korean dictatorship have discovered this system as a source of revenue. They set up fake websites and use computer-controlled "visitors" to simulate real users. It is as if someone opened a newsstand stocked only with counterfeit newspapers to collect advertising revenue. Or they pretend to be a reputable news site, sell the advertising space at a high price—and the advert ends up on a dubious website.

According to estimates by Juniper Research (2024) in its AdTech study, ad fraud caused a global economic loss of around 100 billion dollars in 2024. The World Federation of Advertisers (WFA) warns in its latest analysis (WFA, 2025) "Compendium of Ad Fraud Knowledge for Media Investors" of the increasing sophistication of these criminal activities, especially in so-called "mobile ads." The WFA forecasts that ad fraud will cause damages of 50 billion US dollars in 2025.

Organized criminal groups have developed sophisticated methods for this purpose. According to investigations by the Digital Citizens Alliance, they often operate entire networks of seemingly legitimate websites—from news portals to entertainment sites. The annual Bad Bot Report by Imperva, 2024 demonstrates how these groups generate artificial traffic using technically complex systems:

> Almost 50% of internet traffic comes from non-human sources. Bad bots now comprise nearly one-third of all traffic. Bad bots have become more advanced and evasive and now mimic human Behavior in such a way that it makes them difficult to detect and prevent (Imperva, 2024).

The trick, as documented by the Interactive Advertising Bureau (IAB), is this: the advert is delivered and billed but never actually seen by real people. Instead, botnets—networks of hacked computers—simulate website visits. The cybersecurity company HUMAN (formerly White Ops) has demonstrated how these artificial "visitors" are even equipped with fake user profiles, making them appear particularly valuable to advertisers.

The proceeds are then channeled through complex international corporate structures, as revealed by the FBI initiative "Operation eBook" in 2022. The criminals use companies in various countries to obscure the origin of the funds. The profits can then be used to finance further illegal activities.

The Trustworthy Accountability Group (TAG, 2024) regularly publishes reports on the links between ad fraud and organized crime. The problem is particularly difficult to combat because the technical systems are highly complex and fraudsters are constantly refining their methods.

The reports mentioned above make it clear: the scale of ad fraud is considerable. It is estimated that billions are lost every year through such fraudulent schemes. The problem is particularly difficult to combat because the technical systems are highly complex and fraudsters are constantly refining their methods.

Why do I mention this here? Because it shows you that targeted disinformation can, in fact, also generate money, including through disinformation attacks on companies, as we can see in the case of anti-vaccination activists, who have created their own highly lucrative disinformation ecosystem.

The case of InfoWars demonstrates how extreme disinformation and conspiracy theories can be used to amass great wealth. InfoWars, the media company run by American Alex Jones, has established itself as a fascinating example of the fusion of conspiracy theories, disinformation, and commerce. Jones, considered one of the most commercially successful conspiracy theorists, developed a business model that is both sophisticated and insidious. At the core of this model are his weekday radio show and the InfoWars online portal, which he uses as platforms to disseminate controversial content. Particularly noteworthy is the distribution of his revenue: more than two-thirds of the company's turnover is not generated through traditional media activities but through the sale of a wide range of products. The product range extends from dietary supplements and bulletproof vests to potency pills and supposed "protective products" against alleged government conspiracies. Jones dedicates about a quarter of his airtime to promoting these products. Alex Jones and InfoWars exemplify the skillful marketing of fears, conspiracy theories, and disinformation, which over the years earned Jones millions of dollars.

The story of InfoWars came to an end when Alex Jones and InfoWars were forced to file for bankruptcy in April 2022 (New York Times, 2024). This step was taken in response to several costly defamation lawsuits related to his statements about the Sandy Hook school massacre. Jones had spread information through his channels claiming that the massacre had never occurred. As a result, he was taken to court by the parents of the murdered children and ordered to pay hundreds of millions of dollars in damages (New York Times, 2022b).

References

ASW Federal Association. (2019). *#Disinformation—Situation, forecast, defense, status*. ASW Federal Association.

Grand View Research. (2024). Cyber Security Market (2025–2030). Retrieved from: https://www.grandviewresearch.com/industry-analysis/cyber-security-market

Hampson, N. C. N. (2012). Hacktivism: A new breed of protest in a network world. *Boston College International and Comparative Law Review, 35*, 511–542. Retrieved from: lawdigitalcommon.s.bc.iclr/vol35/iss2/6.

Hindenburg Research. (2023, January 24). Adani Group: How the world's 3rd richest man is pulling the largest con in corporate history. Retrieved from: https://hindenburgresearch.com/adani/

Imperva. (2024). The 2024 Imperva Threat Research report. Retrieved from: https://www.imperva.com/resources/resource-library/reports/2024-bad-bot-report/

Juniper Research. (2024). AdTech Market. Retrieved from: https://www.juniperresearch.com/research/iot-emerging-technology/advertising/adtech-market-report/

New York Times. (2022a). Putin wants fealty, and he's found it in Africa. Retrieved from: https://www.nytimes.com/2022/12/24/world/africa/central-african-republic-russia-wagner.html

New York Times. (2022b). Alex Jones files for bankruptcy. Retrieved from: https://www.nytimes.com/2022/12/02/us/politics/alex-jones-bankruptcy.html

New York Times. (2023). Carl Icahn's firm faces federal inquiry. Retrieved from: https://www.nytimes.com/2023/05/10/business/carl-icahn-hindenburg-research-inquiry.html

New York Times. (2024) From Pizzagate to the 2020 election: Forcing liars to pay or apologize. Retrieved from: https://www.nytimes.com/2024/03/31/us/politics/defamation-lawsuits-michael-gottlieb.html

NTV. (2017, May 10). The Hastor clan attacks Volkswagen. Retrieved from: https://www.ntv.de/wirtschaft/Der-Hastor-Clan-greift-Volkswagen-an-article19832358.html

Reuters. (2024). UN experts investigate 58 cyberattacks worth $3 bln by North Korea. Retrievedfrom:https://www.reuters.com/technology/cybersecurity/un-experts-investigate-58-cyberattacks-worth-3-bln-by-north-korea-2024-02-08/?utm_source=chatgpt.com

Tag Today (2024). Tag US fraud benchmark October 2024. Retrieved from: https://www.tagtoday.net/insights/usfraud2024

The Economic Times of India. (2023a, March 23). After the Adani storm, Hindenburg Research is preparing another report on a 'big one'. Retrieved from: https://economictimes.indiatimes.com/news/company/corporate-trends/after-adani-storm-hindenburg-is-coming-up-with-another-report-on-a-big-one/articleshow/98930451.cms

The Economic Times of India. (2023b). Adani family's partners used 'opaque' funds to invest in its stocks: OCCRP. Retrieved from: https://economictimes.indiatimes.com/news/company/corporate-trends/adani-familys-partners-used-opaque-funds-to-invest-in-its-stocks-occrp/article-show/103225731.cms?from=mdr

Wolff. (2024). Chapter 28, AI-driven disinformation attacks on corporate ESG policies via NGOs and activists. In C. Vaih-Baur et al. (Eds.), *AI in media, communication and marketing*. Springer Nature. 2025.

World Federation of Advertisers. (2025). WFA warns that ad fraud will reach $50bn a year by 2025. Retrieved from: https://www.thedrum.com/news/2016/06/06/wfa-warns-ad-fraud-will-hit-50bn-year-2025

10 Vulnerable Corporate Areas

A company offers a wide range of potential targets for disinformation campaigns. The number of potential vulnerabilities increases with the size, global reach, and complexity of the company. Both the core of the company and its peripheries—such as international suppliers, supply chains, and subsidiaries—can become the focus of attackers. A strict regulatory framework, such as compliance guidelines or ESG (Environmental, Social, Governance) criteria, can also invite disinformation actors to attack, as the more complex and far-reaching the rules, the greater the likelihood that they will be breached, whether intentionally or unintentionally. In my view, it is precisely the morally and ethically charged ESG standards that provide a perfect attack plan for disinformation actors. Compliance with ESG standards is a prerequisite for banks and investors to do business with a company. If a disinformation actor attacks a company for allegedly violating its ESG standards, the company's banks and insurers become alert and react very sensitively.

Whether it is child labor, animal testing, discrimination, or sexual harassment in the workplace, corruption, lack of management oversight, or business relationships with questionable clients—every day the media report on alleged mistakes and misconduct by companies. It is not uncommon for minor missteps to be sensationalized, exaggerated, and thus propelled into the realm of a full-blown scandal. Just look at the business reporting of traditional and online media, all of which are now connected to social media networks. Such news spreads like wildfire and is almost impossible to contain, especially since studies have shown that bad news spreads much faster than positive news. Anyone dealing with disinformation attacks on companies will quickly develop a keen sense, when reading business publications, for whether there might be someone behind a negative story who stands to benefit from it.

A disinformation attack shapes the image of a company, influencing the actions and trust of investors, banks, customers, authorities, and potential employees. Companies are sensitive constructs whose existence depends on many different factors. Banks, customers, and investors consume media, both traditional and social.

U. Wolff, *Disinformation Attacks On Businesses*, Management for Professionals,
https://doi.org/10.1007/978-3-658-51407-5_10

They may have set up Google Alerts and follow news about a business partner. Or they may be informed by another business partner, friend, or acquaintance that the media are reporting on a company with which they are associated. Or they may receive an anonymous email drawing their attention to a negative aspect of a company with which they are connected. All of this makes companies easy prey for professional disinformation agents.

Banks are highly sensitive considering stricter laws on money laundering and terrorist financing. A good example of this is the case of Hazim Nada and his company LORD, described at the outset. When a company becomes embroiled in a high-profile, high-stakes legal dispute, alarm bells ring for banks, suppliers, customers, employees, trade unions, or shareholders. This is especially true in the case of criminal investigations against a company's management, as we saw in the Volkswagen diesel scandal. Even if the public prosecutor's office merely suspects a criminal offence, the company's reputation suffers as soon as the media report on it.

10.1 Attack via Suspicion-Based Reporting

Disinformation agents benefit from a special provision: journalists enjoy certain freedoms in their reporting and are not always required to present evidence that would stand up in court when making claims, even if those claims later turn out to be false. This is the notorious "suspicion reporting." Georg Mascolo, one of Germany's most renowned investigative reporters and former editor-in-chief of the news magazine DER SPIEGEL, calls suspicion reporting "probably the greatest privilege journalists possess, and at the same time the greatest responsibility they must handle" (Banse, 2018). If journalists adhere to the strict requirements of suspicion reporting, no media lawyer can touch them. However, as mentioned, the rules are strict, and since not everyone abides by them, media lawyers in Germany are kept very busy. In the United Kingdom, there is a regulation like German suspicion reporting: the British "Public Interest Defense." British journalists are also permitted to report on unproven allegations. However, the public interest in the report must outweigh other considerations; the story must be thoroughly researched and written; and it must be balanced. In the USA, by contrast, journalists are subject to fewer rules: their work is protected by the First Amendment, that is, by freedom of the press and freedom of expression. Should a company or individual seek legal redress against unfavorable reporting, they face significant hurdles.

This spectrum of possibilities for suspicion reporting, framed by German law, is used by journalists AND exploited by attackers. An informed attacker knows how far journalists are allowed to go and prepares their "pitch" accordingly: they must provide a substantiated and fact-based suspicion. These "facts" must be verifiable. The suspicion must have high news value, and the attacker must demonstrate a strong public interest. With these ingredients, which are easily obtained with little effort, they can mix their toxic cocktail, which the targeted media outlet then serves to the public, calling into question or even destroying the reputation of a company, its managers, or its products and services.

10.2 Attacks at a Critical Moment

A well-planned disinformation attack is also based on skillful timing: if a company is facing major changes that are already attracting media attention—such as annual general meetings, corporate takeovers, mass redundancies, new market entries, or product launches—this is the attackers' moment. During my many years as a crisis communications specialist, I observed that even the seasons can serve as a kind of schedule for disinformation attacks: ideally, for example, a candle manufacturer is targeted during the darker months, that is, in autumn and winter, and especially before Christmas. Ice cream producers are targeted in summer, and livestock farms and meat processing companies are targeted before Easter, Christmas, and in the USA also before Thanksgiving. For NGOs and animal welfare organizations, November is particularly suitable, as this is a time when people are especially inclined to donate.

Companies become particularly vulnerable when they are facing major changes, financial challenges, or significant events. These may include restructurings, acquisitions or divestments, staff redundancies, crises and disasters (whether man-made or natural), or even annual general meetings. At such times, management resources are focused on these events and cannot be fully mobilized in the event of a disinformation attack. The situation is similar to that of a weakened body succumbing to an infectious disease: there are simply not enough defenses available. Examples of such vulnerable situations will be discussed in the following chapters.

"Timing! Timing! Timing!" is the credo of communications strategists, much like the "Location! Location! Location!" mantra of estate agents. The right timing, combined with a product launch, was essential for what is probably the best-known disinformation campaign against companies and their products: the attacks by Russia and China on Western vaccine manufacturers during the coronavirus pandemic. The planned launch of the vaccines provided all the ingredients for a successful campaign: people were fearful of Covid infection and its consequences. The strict measures imposed by governments caused uncertainty and incomprehension. Many Western governments had alienated parts of their own populations, who felt patronized. Pharmaceutical companies developed novel vaccines in record time, with governments drastically reducing the usual testing and approval procedures.

Russia and China recognized the opportunity and the psychological fragility of society at that time. With their armies of disinformation and internet trolls, they poured fuel on the fire by deliberately spreading false information about the efficacy and alleged side effects of the new vaccines. Russian and Chinese disinformation agents showered the population—already in a state of emergency—with lies, half-truths, and conspiracy theories, a population willing to believe *anything*—even the most absurd nonsense, such as claims that "those at the top" were planning to dominate the common people using the new vaccines, which supposedly contained nanochips. Among those identified as masterminds of this alleged plan for world domination were, of course, George Soros and Bill Gates.

Disasters of all kinds—whether natural disasters such as floods, earthquakes, wildfires, and hurricanes, or man-made catastrophes such as dam failures, explosions at chemical plants, or nuclear power plant accidents—are becoming an increasingly popular playground for disinformation agents. This has serious consequences: rescue and aid organizations are increasingly confronted with a flood of disinformation, as was recently the case during the devastating floods in Valencia, Spain. Another example was the disinformation campaign launched by Donald Trump, then during an election campaign, in a hurricane-stricken part of North Carolina, USA. He claimed that the US Federal Emergency Management Agency (FEMA) was distributing aid and financial support only to migrants and Democrats while neglecting Republican victims. Such disinformation campaigns in the context of disasters force aid organizations to divert desperately needed resources to counter disinformation.

To target a company, attackers focus on specific corporate areas that are particularly susceptible to disinformation attacks. The choice of which area to attack depends on the perpetrators, their motives, objectives, and strategy.

For example, if the perpetrator's aim is to recruit highly sought-after talent from a limited pool of potential candidates, they may attempt to damage the competitor's reputation as an employer. If the goal is to prevent a competitor from entering a market that the attacker considers their home territory, they may seek to unsettle banks, investors, and policymakers by spreading false or fabricated information about links to organized crime.

As we will see, the vulnerable areas within a company cannot be clearly separated. For instance, if a disinformation attack targets production processes, product quality, or services, this also affects the customer and supply chain sectors.

Let us now take a closer look at the corporate areas that might be of particular interest for a disinformation attack.

Another example of a well-timed disinformation attack is the assault on the French aircraft manufacturer Dassault. In May 2025, military clashes broke out between India and Pakistan. Both nations engaged not only on the ground but also in the air. India deployed French and Russian fighter jets, while Pakistan used Chinese aircraft. China closely observed the aerial combat. The stark outcome for the Indian Air Force: three of their aircraft were lost. The Pakistanis claimed to have shot down as many as five planes. China seized the opportunity to celebrate the superiority of its aircraft, mocking the French in the process. China deployed military attachés from its embassies worldwide to convince other countries that their aircraft were superior and did not hesitate to spread disinformation, particularly targeting Dassault's flagship, the Rafale jet. China and France are competitors in the global arms market, vying for jet sales. The French, especially Dassault, for whom the Rafale is a key product, fought back with all available means against China's disinformation campaign to protect the reputation of their fighter jet. According to the French, the Chinese employed the full arsenal of disinformation tools. The US news agency AP quoted the French as follows:

> They say the campaign included viral posts on social media, manipulated imagery showing supposed Rafale debris, AI-generated content and video-game depictions to simulate supposed combat. More than 1,000 social media accounts newly created as the India-Pakistan

clashes erupted also spread a narrative of Chinese technological superiority, according to French researchers who specialize in online disinformation (Associated Press, 2025).

10.3 Attack Surface: Production Processes

We are all familiar with cases in which companies have been accused of outsourcing the production of their products to distant countries, where they are assembled or sewn by children. The sportswear manufacturer NIKE is a prominent example, having been targeted by NGOs and aid organizations. The same applies to manufacturers of cheap fast-fashion clothing, who produce their garments in countries such as Bangladesh (Ross et al., 2012).

Many campaigns by NGOs and aid organizations are—as I have already made clear—not classic disinformation campaigns in which false information is deliberately spread with malicious intent. They are legitimate, and their criticism and work are necessary. In many cases, these actions have also led to positive changes and greater awareness of the origins of products. The companies targeted had to face the criticism and changed their behavior. Nevertheless, I count this type of activist attack among the forms of disinformation, partly because they are deliberately imprecise with the facts and their work has a propagandistic character. They exaggerate, scandalize, and use unsubstantiated statistics and figures. The question remains: do the NGOs want to harm the companies? Well, they certainly want to hit them hard and damage their reputation. Harm is therefore at least accepted as a consequence.

In a fire at a textile factory in Bangladesh, more than 100 people died (Burke & Hammadii, 2012), who had to work there in extremely cramped conditions. Previously, 280 textile workers died in a factory fire in Karachi, Pakistan. The media response to these terrible disasters was considerable, and it became clear under what degrading and dangerous conditions people must work there. This agitated emotional state of the media and the public opens the door to disinformation, through which a perpetrator group can inflict further damage on the company at the beginning of the supply chain.

Human rights groups and NGOs run very powerful campaigns, and they often do so with good reason. They take on the role of watchdogs, alerting the public when something goes seriously wrong. Do you remember the campaign by the human rights group "Global Witness" against blood diamonds from countries such as Sierra Leone, the trade of which financed the bloody conflicts of various African war factions? One of the world's largest diamond producers, "De Beers," was affected and, under public pressure, now claims to offer only diamonds from conflict-free zones (Cowell, 2000). However, criticism of the working conditions of the miners who extract diamonds for De Beers remains.

The same applies, for example, to Coltan, which is indispensable to produce mobile phones and whose extraction in Congo is destroying rainforests and the habitat of gorillas or the shocking activist actions by Greenpeace against the food company "Nestlé" over the use of palm oil in products such as the KitKat chocolate bar. Greenpeace produced a shock advert in which an office worker opens a KitKat bar wrapper and instead of chocolate finds a severed orangutan finger inside (Greenpeace, 2010). This was not the first time Nestlé had been in the public spotlight. In my view, this is entirely legitimate. However, during such hyper-emotionalization, there is always the risk that information gives way to disinformation or that opportunists use a reputation-damaging NGO campaign to pursue their own goals with further harmful disinformation.

10.4 Attack Surfaces: Product Quality, Reputation, and Services

The production processes of larger companies are usually very complex, and global supply chains are vulnerable to disruption, as the coronavirus crisis has recently demonstrated. The food sector is hypersensitive in this regard. Rumors and strategically placed disinformation can destabilize entire product ranges.

Whenever I want to illustrate disinformation attacks in lectures, I like to present the case of a fictitious baby food manufacturer. The example is suitable for several reasons: baby food is a sensitive issue. Babies are delicate and vulnerable, and young parents are very concerned about their child's wellbeing. Parents' danger sensors are highly attuned and extremely receptive to (dis)information, for example, about the contamination of a particular baby food product. Once strategically placed in the relevant online parenting forums, reinforced by forum participants with false identities (fake accounts, sock puppets) or bots, the baby food manufacturer can watch as sales of its "Garden Vegetables 6th Month" product plummet. If there are also journalists among the users of these parenting forums, the likelihood increases that the damaging information will spread beyond the "parent bubble" into the wider public. If the disinformers then also post in one of the discussion forums that the baby food manufacturer is doing everything possible to suppress information about the product contamination, it becomes extremely difficult, delayed, or almost impossible for the company to defend itself.

A real case involved a large fast-food chain, where tensions had already been simmering. It began with a dispute between the fast-food chain and its franchisees, which drew media attention to the company. Interested parties exploited this unwanted attention. Suddenly, reports appeared on social media that had nothing to do with the original dispute between the company and its franchisees. Now, the focus shifted to the quality of the food on offer, its preparation, and above all, hygiene. An avalanche of unappetizing images and comments poured over the company from social media. It is important to note that this occurred at a time when bots did not yet exist. However, the fast-food company's clientele is young and highly active on social media. Apparently, someone wanted to take revenge on the company, which was not exactly known for paying its employees well. Someone? In fact, it was quite a few people who still had a score to settle with the fast-food chain—former employees, but also customers. The management came under severe pressure.

What happened in the communication spaces of social media did not go unnoticed by the traditional media. A TV crew planted an undercover employee who secretly filmed footage. It was clear that the TV team did not intend to report objectively but rather sought out the most shocking and disgusting scenes, editing the footage accordingly. Once broadcast and scandalized, the issue escalated and customers began to avoid the burger chain. Social and traditional media celebrated a devilish alliance at the expense of the fast-food chain. The burger chain's headquarters was forced to make amends, promised improvements, apologized live on the TV channel that had aired the exposé, and immediately booked TV advertising on the same channel. One could get the impression that the burger chain had paid a kind of protection money.

Or consider the attack on Paris's tourism sector in the summer of 2023. It all began when a young social media user checked into a Parisian hotel and discovered a bedbug in her bed. This is, of course, unpleasant and unappetizing, but in times of rising temperatures and global tourism, it is no longer unusual.

The young woman took a picture of the bedbug and uploaded it to her social media channel. Russian disinformation agents noticed this post and did what they have developed considerable expertise in: with the full disinformative power of a state actor, they inflated the issue into a bedbug epidemic. Images of bedbugs circulated on social media—bedbugs in trains, cinemas, restaurants, and hotels.

The news pressure from social media reached the traditional media, which then showed images of French pest controllers fumigating trains and cinema halls to get rid of the little pests. The story was picked up worldwide, across all channels.

The Parisian tourism sector experienced a devastating season: travelers cancelled their trips to Paris. Hotels and restaurants were in despair, as was the French government. The tourism sector suffered millions in losses. Paris had to contend with a massive image problem, and all this just 1 year before the start of the 2024 Olympic Games in Paris, which were expected to attract millions of visitors.

It was not long before the French intelligence services identified who was behind the bedbug attack: Russia, which was not permitted to participate in the 2024 Olympic Games and instead resorted to sabotage through disinformation. One piece of Russian disinformation was particularly telling: Ukrainian refugees were alleged to have brought the bedbugs to Paris. The news channel "France24" reported:

> Russian propaganda is linking the current bedbug outbreak in Paris to Ukrainian refugees. To "prove" this false narrative, pro-Russian accounts on social media are sharing fake French media reports from Le Figaro, Libération, and Contrepoints, falsely claiming that "parasite experts believe the bedbug infestation in Paris is linked to the influx of Ukrainian refugees into the capital" (France24, 2023).

The man behind the curtain became visible, as did his motives. The traditional media, which had previously actively contributed to the panic, calmed down.

The impact of the disinformation attack on the Parisian tourism sector was enormous and remains evident: people are still searching on Google to find out whether travel to Paris is safe.

But why did Russia do this? Well, France is a strong supporter and partner of Ukraine. In addition, Paris was to host the Olympic Summer Games the following year, in which the Russians were not allowed to participate—at least not under the Russian flag (Reuters, 2024).

10.5 Attack Surfaces: Workforce, Recruitment, and Social Issues

The relationship between employer and employee has become more complex. What was once tolerated is now, rightly, punishable. In recent years, a wave of "#MeToo" cases has swept through companies—cases of sexual assault, mostly targeting female employees. Discrimination of any kind is fortunately no longer tolerated and can result in severe sanctions against companies and the individuals responsible within them. A toxic work environment, where employees do not feel valued or respected, and constant time pressures, employee overload combined with mediocre pay, are particularly off-putting to younger applicants who have different expectations of their working lives. On professional networks, job boards, or review platforms, one can read how former employees view the company they have left. Anyone looking for a job and considering applying will first check the internet and social media. Potential applicants can already learn a great deal here. The decision to apply to a company is often made only after a careful review of such review platforms.

On certain platforms, employers can be rated in detail by former employees. Companies receive between 1 and 5 stars. In times of demanding personnel, it is therefore in a company's best interest to achieve a good rating and as many stars as possible on such platforms.

On the other hand, there are companies with a strong interest in ensuring that a competing company receives as many poor ratings as possible, especially if both are fishing in the same applicant pool. It is hardly surprising that unfair means are sometimes employed. Review platforms do attempt to filter out fake reviews by verifying the employment relationship, yet it is still relatively easy to create fake profiles and sock puppets that can then post scathing reviews.

In other cases, it is not even necessary to exploit a review platform to clog up a competitor's recruitment pipeline. Work councils, trade unions, or even individual employees can achieve this by passing relevant information to the media. A logistics company like Amazon regularly experiences this at its logistics centers, when trade unions demonstrate against Amazon as an employer and publicly criticize working conditions in the media.

The German study "#Disinformation" highlighted another interesting facet of attacks on the HR sector: for example, there are "employees, opinion leaders, prominent key and management personnel, as well as office holders and owners" who "leave traces in the digital space through their actions or by being referenced by third parties" (ASW Bundesverband, 2019). This means that these individuals can be identified on business networks such as "LinkedIn" or appear at events that are reflected in the digital space. The information available about these individuals is sufficient for so-called "social engineering"—that is, the digital impersonation of a senior company employee, enabling the fake persona to access valuable company information.

Important information also regularly leaves the protected environment of the company during job interviews or through internship placements. This is especially the case when a company is specifically seeking staff for a new project or location and discloses this during the interview. It is unfortunate if applicants are not actually interested in the job, but rather in information about the new location, which is to be sabotaged through a disinformation campaign.

We have already encountered several cases in which interns employed by a company turned out to be undercover journalists or spies. Time and again, I am surprised at how carelessly and without any background checks companies hire people who then gain access to sensitive data. Companies that are constantly short-staffed, such as hospitals, care homes, or ground service providers at airports, are particularly prone to forgoing thorough background checks on applicants.

10.6 Attack Surfaces: Corporate Governance and Finance

Let us now turn to incidents such as market manipulation, insider trading, corruption, bribery, compliance violations, or potential over-indebtedness.

In large companies, executive management and supervisory boards face numerous decisions daily. Senior management is expected to keep track of everything happening within the company. However, it is impossible for management to read the minds of their colleagues. Especially regarding a company's financial situation, there is considerable scope for interpreting the figures. These differing perspectives can be exploited for targeted disinformation campaigns aimed at banks and investors.

The same applies to shareholder meetings, where shareholders can exercise their right to ask questions and speak, using the opportunity to spread targeted disinformation in front of an audience (and the press).

Anonymous reports to public prosecutors and tax authorities are a well-established means of putting corporate management under pressure, particularly when the media are informed that such an anonymous report has been filed with the investigative authorities. The same applies to reports to banking or foundation supervisory authorities. Whether the relevant authorities pursue such a report is usually of secondary importance in this type of attack. What matters more to the attacker is that the media pick up on the report and cover the story. Such a report about compliance violations, irregularities in the financial sector, tax evasion, corruption, or excessive debt unsettles banks, employees, customers, suppliers, and more. Such an attack creates unrest, fuels rumors, and makes the company vulnerable.

10.7 Attack Surfaces: Suppliers and Subcontractors

Suppliers, subcontractors, and third-party services are the Achilles' heel of a company. Today, companies must demonstrate that they have oversight of their supply chain. The individual links in a supply chain present a significant attack surface for disinformation. Alleged customers complain about the customer service of service providers. Manipulated subcontractors publicly communicate payment irregularities, thereby implying financial difficulties within the company. Attackers deliberately target a supplier of the intended company, claiming that it is allegedly collaborating with criminal gangs or spying on the company on behalf of a foreign state. Airports must expect that ground service providers will be targeted, with claims that, for financial reasons, they are no longer conducting adequate background checks on their staff, thus jeopardizing passenger safety.

The (alleged) misconduct of a supplier also reflects on the contracting company, especially when the supplier's name is unknown, but the contracting company is globally recognized. This is precisely what happened to Apple and its Indian supplier "Foxlink," which manufactures charging cables for iPhones. The factory in southern India caught fire, and part of the building collapsed. No lives were lost in the blaze, but the news agency Reuters quoted an Indian "government official" who claimed that fire alarm systems and extinguishers at the facility had not functioned. It was not Apple's first problem in India, which is increasingly being favored over China for Apple's production. This incident likely attracted considerable attention not only from human rights groups and activists. For China, too, Apple's problems in India are valuable information (Reuters, 2023). The reverse scenario is also possible: Over the years, a major German automotive group acquired a dubious reputation for its harsh treatment of suppliers. There was talk of extortion, forced insolvencies, or managing directors of supplier companies being driven to suicide. When a highly publicized legal dispute with a supplier arose, it provided an opportunity for attackers, particularly from the competitive environment. The already borderline and at times inhumane conduct of the automotive group toward its suppliers was supplemented with further information and "evidence" and made public. The reputation of the automotive group as a business partner suffered as a result.

References

Associated Press. (2025). French intelligence: China used embassies to undermine sales of France's flagship Rafale fighter jet. Retrieved from: https://apnews.com/article/france-china-pakistan-india-defense-rafale-64eec86b6e89718d6a49d8fdedf565f4

ASW Bundesverband. (2019). *#Disinformation—Situation, forecast, defense, status July 2019*. ASW Bundesverband.

Banse, P. (2018). Are they allowed to do that? Retrieved from: https://www.deutschlandfunk.de/verdachtsberichterstattung-duerfen-die-das-100.html

Burke, J., & Hammadii, S. (2012). Bangladesh textile factory fire leaves more than 100 dead. *The Guardian*. Retrieved from: https://www.theguardian.com/world/2012/nov/25/bangladesh-textile-factory-fire

Cowell, A. (2000). Controversy over diamonds made into virtue by De Beers. Retrieved from: https://www.nytimes.com/2000/08/22/business/controversy-over-diamonds-made-into-virtue-by-de-beers.html

France24. (2023). Russian propaganda falsely blames Ukrainian refugees for Paris bedbug outbreak. Retrieved from: https://www.france24.com/en/tv-shows/truth-or-fake/20231005-bedbugs-invade-russian-propaganda

Greenpeace. (2010). Nestlé, no palm oil from rainforest destruction! Retrieved from: https://www.youtube.com/watch?v=IzF3UGOIVDc

Reuters. (2023). Apple supplier unlikely to resume full India operations for two months after massive fire. Retrieved from: https://edition.cnn.com/2023/02/28/tech/apple-supplier-foxlink-fire-issues/index.html

Reuters. (2024). Russian 'disinformation' hyped Paris bedbug scare, French minister says. Retrieved from: https://www.reuters.com/world/europe/russian-disinformation-hyped-paris-bedbug-scare-french-minister-says-2024-03-01/

Ross, B., Mosk, M., & Galli, C. (2012). Workers die at factories used by Tommy Hilfiger. Retrieved from: https://abcnews.go.com/Blotter/workers-die-factories-tommy-hilfiger/story?id=15966305

Tools and Tactics: Mechanisms of Attacks 11

Due to the easy availability of highly sophisticated tools and their remarkably low prices, companies under attack are fighting an unequal battle against their adversaries. The effort and cost required for a company to detect an attack, initiate countermeasures, repel the attack, and then deal with the aftermath are vastly greater than those faced by the attacker. This asymmetry is further exacerbated using AI-supported technologies and the ever-increasing degree of automation in disinformation attacks, which make such attacks faster, more efficient, and more cost-effective.

Anyone planning a disinformation attack on a company today has access to a whole range of technologies that are easy to obtain and surprisingly inexpensive. A disinformation attack can now be launched from any smartphone, without any programming knowledge. Today's AI-generated deepfakes are of such high quality that most people can barely distinguish them from reality.

At the outset of such an attack, it is not the message that matters, but rather the identity—more precisely, the false identity. Attackers want to remain anonymous and avoid being caught by the police or judicial authorities.

An effective disinformation attack requires careful preparation and time, during which the attackers either create a new identity or simply appropriate or steal someone else's. Experts refer to such fake identities as "sock puppets." State actors have set up thousands of fake accounts on social media platforms, populating them with innocuous content to create the impression that they are "active." These are sleeper accounts. In the event of an attack, the perpetrators activate these accounts, which then disseminate disinformation en masse, as China did in connection with the French Rafale fighter jets that fell from the sky during the recent Pakistan–India conflict (see Chapter "Attack Surfaces").

During the research for this book, I contacted DarkOwl in Denver, Colorado, a specialist company that scans the shadowy darknet and closely monitors what is being offered there. Among other things, stolen credit card data and company passwords are sold here, as well as criminal services. Recently, according to DarkOwl analysts, there has been increased activity in disinformation services on the darknet:

U. Wolff, *Disinformation Attacks On Businesses*, Management for Professionals,
https://doi.org/10.1007/978-3-658-51407-5_11

> DarkOwl analysts have observed a now well-established digital economy in the darknet around the trade of social media accounts and its influencers—accounts sold in bulk that could be easily leveraged for a disinformation or misinformation campaign by a foreign government or agency with malicious intention," the analysts write. "Social media continues to be a powerful tool for conducting disinformation campaigns, especially since access to large quantities of pre-verified, fake social media accounts continue to be readily available for purchase on the darknet (DarkOwl, 2023).

I have already mentioned that Russian and Ukrainian groups are increasingly offering "disinformation-as-a-service" on the darknet, acting as digital contract reputation assassins. But what are their weapons? What are the tools and tactics they employ? To find out, I spoke with Mark Turnage, CEO of DarkOwl.

About Reputation Assassins and Deals on the Darknet—Interview with DarkOwl CEO Mark Turnage

Mark Turnage is the co-founder and CEO of DarkOwl in Denver, Colorado. He graduated from the University of Colorado, the University of Oxford, and Yale Law School. His company, DarkOwl, provides a darknet threat intelligence platform that enables companies and organizations to understand and mitigate their digital risks. DarkOwl allows organizations to monitor in real time the theft, breach, or other compromise of their protected data on the darknet, so they can take action to limit the damage before the information is misused. According to DarkOwl, the platform is "believed to be the largest non-governmental database of darknet content available to commercial users."

Question: Mark, your analysts scan the darknet for potential threats on behalf of large companies. In doing so, one particular group has attracted their attention.

Mark Turnage: About 2 or 3 years ago, Ukrainian- and Russian-speaking operatives emerged offering disinformation-as-a-service. They offer disinformation attacks, that is, to damage the reputation of individuals, politicians, or companies for a fee. We are talking here about contract killers for reputations.

Question: What do you think of these offers?

Mark Turnage: I should say at the outset that we have not been in contact with these providers. So, I cannot comment on the quality of their services. What I can say is that what they offer is technically sound. However, with these individuals, you can never be sure whether they are genuine providers or simply fraudsters. Nevertheless, we have some reasons to believe that they are not scammers. Russians are highly skilled in disinformation, and it appears that many of these actors are Russian. Some used to work for, or are still working for, the state and its propaganda or intelligence agencies. They are looking to earn some extra money by freelancing.

Question: Are companies prepared for such offers and disinformation attacks?

Mark Turnage: No, they are not, and that is alarming to me because you can cause enormous disruption in a large company with disinformation attacks like these. Just imagine if professional disinformation operatives targeted major oil companies and refineries, for example.

Question: After all, there are already disinformation attacks on companies.

Mark Turnage: Yes, and that is why companies should be aware of the risks that can arise for them from the disinformation sector.

Question: From your observations of the darknet, can you tell whether the number of disinformation attacks is increasing?

Mark Turnage: I cannot say that directly, but we have recently observed increased discussions and activity on this topic. Three years ago, we heard nothing about it. The number of disinformation-as-a-service offerings is growing. What has been happening in the political sphere is now moving into the business and corporate sector. The tools and tactics are the same. So, the thesis of your book is absolutely correct. It is going to happen. Most definitely.

Question: The difference is that large, complex, global enterprises offer more diverse and sensitive areas of attack…

Mark Turnage: That is correct. That is what makes the whole situation so complex in terms of detection and defense. By definition, a large enterprise offers a broader range of disinformation vectors.

Question: We can already see the first disinformation attacks that show us how the attackers are moving from the political sphere to the corporate sector, such as the attacks on Western vaccine manufacturers by Russia and China…

Mark Turnage: …or they also cross over into the realm of organizations, such as sports and anti-doping bodies. Russian hackers attacked the Anti-Doping Association's computers in 2016 after Russian athletes were banned from competing due to doping. From the data they obtained, they discovered that non-Russian athletes also had substances in their bodies, but these were not covered by the doping regulations or were approved by medical professionals. The Russians disseminated this information and claimed that many non-Russian athletes had also been doping. This was clear disinformation. Just imagine—they used it to target innocent young people… not companies or governments, but young athletes.

Question: Where can you find such hitmen to attack a company's or a person's reputation?

Mark Turnage: On the darknet. However, we have not yet looked at social media for such offers. However, offering these services on social media would make sense, as they could reach a wider audience.

Question: Yes, but then these providers would have to appear publicly.

Mark Turnage: You can conceal your true identity on social media.

Question: Have you been able to identify any specializations among providers?

Mark Turnage: There is one provider that offers WhatsApp campaigns. Another deletes unwanted content from the Internet but, at the same time, offers to post harmful content online. Another provider claims to use a "blockchain-based botnet" to conduct persistent disinformation campaigns—another advertises URL hijacking. With everything on offer, we must remember one thing: criminals are opportunists. They follow the money.

Question: How can a company prepare for an attack?

Mark Turnage: An experienced disinformation specialist will not start from scratch and reinvent everything when launching an attack. He will first search until he finds something small but true on which to base a disinformation campaign. Then he will add falsehoods and inflate this into a large-scale campaign. Let me be clear: the Russians are extremely skilled at this.

Question: Give us an example.

Mark Turnage: For example, imagine a situation where an accident or disaster occurs in a company; most CEOs tend to downplay it. The seriously injured become the slightly injured. The number of fatalities is minimized. The consequences of a disaster are mitigated or covered up. This is dangerous. Because when a company is caught whitewashing a difficult situation, it plays into the hands of the disinformers. Journalists, too. It awakens their hunting instinct. Unlike journalists, however, disinformers have a malicious interest in prolonging this concealment of the truth and raising questions such as, "What else is the company hiding from us? Can the company be trusted? Who controls the company? Is the company being protected by politicians or the government?" This distrust creates an opportunity for the disinformers to spread falsehoods "on top of the truth."

Question: What can a company do in response to an attack?

Mark Turnage: It must publicly lay out the unvarnished facts. This takes much of the momentum away from the attackers. It is painful in the short term, but in the long run the truth will prevail.

11.1 The Tools

Sock Puppets and Fake Identities

Let us return to ***sock puppets*** and ***fake identities***, which attackers use on social media to steer and manipulate discourse, and to hijack the prevailing narrative within a defined digital space.

Sock puppets are fake online accounts that present themselves as independent and authentic individuals, representing a particular agenda or viewpoint. These accounts are often used to deceive and manipulate discussions by participating in conversations, spreading disinformation, and creating the illusion of broad support or consensus.

Effective sock puppets, which are taken seriously by the community and not recognized as such, require a digital backstory that the attacker must first establish. The sock puppet should demonstrably already have friends and be linked to other users through its own comments. If an attacker controls an entire army of such fake identities or sock puppets, they can interact with each other and cross-link their content. In this way, these sock puppets quickly build up a solid history.

These fake identities can also be equipped with false credentials to achieve greater authority. They may pose as journalists, think tank representatives, doctors, or other experts to lend more weight and credibility to their views.

Bots

A ***bot*** (the word is short for "robot") is a programmed account that performs automated actions on social media platforms. A bot can automatically post, like, share, or comment on content. This is faster and more precise than a human. A bot does not sleep and does not need breaks. Bots are now estimated to account for more than half of all global web traffic, with some sources suggesting as much as 75%.

There are good and useful bots but also malicious and harmful ones. Useful bots are employed by search engines or by companies as AI-powered ***chatbots,*** which provide information and advice to customers.

Malicious actors use bots to amplify their harmful disinformation. They artificially inflate the activity of an account, making it appear more active and attractive. Bots can also be used to attack or harass individuals, or to manipulate online discussions.

Fake News Websites

Fake news websites are designed to closely resemble real, reputable media outlets in both name and design. In this way, they deceive primarily those with less media experience. In fact, fake news websites feature content presented in a news format but intended for manipulation and disinformation. Media laypersons often do not realize that they have landed on a fake news website. This also includes the rapidly growing number of fake news websites that mimic the appearance of genuine online media, such as TV news channels or well-known daily or tabloid newspapers. These online news sites, which masquerade as reputable newspapers, are known as "pink-slime sites". Pink-slime sites are pseudo-news portals that, instead of real journalism, mainly distribute automated and AI-generated articles with a hidden agenda. The name derives from a pink meat paste used in the production of sausages and chicken nuggets. These portals deliberately spread biased or false information and make it harder to distinguish between real and fake news. Artificial intelligence plays a key role: it generates texts, optimizes headlines, and controls distribution via social media—all under the guise of local reporting. The operators therefore no longer need to do much, except ensure that their disinformation does not stand out too obviously.

Trolls

Behind the ***troll*** on the internet are not bots but real people whose task is to... in forums and social media that promote a particular viewpoint, to launch aggressive attacks and incite the forum community through provocation. The aim is to stir up emotions within the community (New York Times, 2008). Trolling causes discussions to be derailed or participants to turn away in frustration. The community is disrupted. One of the most notorious troll factories is in St. Petersburg, Russia, established by the now-deceased head of the Russian Wagner mercenaries, Yevgeny Prigozhin. North Korea also operates its own troll factory, which participated in attacks on Western vaccine manufacturers. These trolls can spread massive amounts of malicious information about a company, its products, or its employees via a corporate social media account.

URL Hijacking

URL hijacking refers, in simple terms, to a situation in which someone redirects a web address (URL) to another website without the owner's permission. It is akin to changing a road sign so that people are sent to a different destination than intended. For example, if you enter a URL in your web browser, you are redirected to the disinformer's website. In URL hijacking, a malicious individual or group manipulates the URL so that it points to a different website or webpage.

This can occur in various ways. For instance, attackers may gain unauthorized access to the domain registration account and alter the settings to redirect the URL. They may also create a fake website with a similar URL to lure users into visiting it. One method is to change the spelling of the domain name, for example, by replacing the "I" (as in "India") with a lowercase "l" (as in "Lima"). Deliberately created typos, or transposed letters, are also commonly used in domains, especially for high-traffic domain names, such as the adult site "Pornhub", which a hijacker might register as "Ponhub" or "Pronhub". (Our domain check revealed that these domain names have indeed already been registered with various domain extensions.) Careless users with quick fingers can easily end up on the attacker's website via such redirections.

What is the goal of URL hijacking? Some seek financial gain by redirecting visitors to fraudulent websites, thereby increasing traffic. Others attempt to obtain the personal data of unsuspecting users or to install malware on their computers. In the context of disinformation attacks, those who mistype URLs are directed to fake news sites. Company websites can also be hijacked in this way. While not particularly original, it is extremely annoying. Occasional checks with a domain provider can help to limit such hijackings.

Ranking Manipulation and Search Engine Optimization (SEO)

Some disinformation attacks also employ techniques to manipulate search engine rankings. In these cases, websites or content are deliberately optimized with misleading or deceptive information to appear higher in search engine result pages (SERPs). As a result, false or misleading information becomes more visible and accessible to users searching for related topics. This can be achieved through various techniques, such as keyword stuffing, creating fake websites or content, using deceptive link strategies, or exploiting vulnerabilities in search engine algorithms.

For example, a malicious actor may wish to spread disinformation about one or more products to influence public opinion. In ranking manipulation, attackers create multiple websites that are optimized for search engines with specific keywords related to the targeted product. These websites or pages may contain misleading information, fabricated studies, or fake testimonials that support their claims about the product's safety.

To manipulate search engine rankings, attackers overload the website content with keywords ***("keyword stuffing"),*** even if these make no sense or are grammatically incorrect. These websites are interlinked to form a network, thereby increasing their credibility in search engine algorithms.

When people search for information about the targeted product, these disinformation websites then appear higher in the search results, making it more likely that users will encounter and believe the false information.

There is also a more modern approach: as classic Google searches are increasingly being replaced by chatbot searches, we are seeing a growing number of providers offering chatbot optimization training. The chatbots are trained fully automatically using a large number of questions, answers, and (supposed) sources, so they ultimately deliver the desired query result. This search optimization of chatbots is nothing new in itself, as Russian disinformation factories have been using the technology for a long time. However, they take a detour via the aforementioned pink slime sites, which the chatbots read and incorporate into their knowledge base.

Fake Reviews

Disinformers create false and deceptive customer reviews to manipulate public perception of a product, service, or company. This can significantly influence the purchasing decisions of potential customers. Attackers create and disseminate fake reviews across various platforms, including e-commerce websites, review aggregators, social media, and online forums. According to a study by Cavazos, **global**

losses due to manipulated and fake online reviews are estimated at 152 billion USD.

Let us take as an example a cosmetics company that produces a particular facial cream and offers a unique and attractive product on the market, putting its competitors under pressure. In response, a rival spreads fake reviews from individuals posing as customers. These fake reviews contain claims of alleged side effects, an unpleasant smell, or the cream's texture. Above all, the reviews cast doubt on the advertised effects of the cream. If there are several similar fake reviews or endorsements of the negative comments, the manufacturer of the cream faces a serious problem.

The reverse is also possible: positive fake reviews can make a product appear especially recommendable and trustworthy, thereby attempting to attract more customers.

A remarkable example of how fake reviews can be weaponized against an opponent was seen at the end of December 2024 on the German Amazon website. The case concerned the memoirs of former German Chancellor Angela Merkel, who had become a veritable hate figure among anti-vaxxers, East Germans, and right-wing groups. On the very first day of the book's release, hundreds of negative one-star reviews (with five stars being the maximum) appeared on Amazon. It is hard to believe that those who "reviewed" the book had read its 700 pages within 24 h. Some reviewers even openly admitted that they had NOT read the book. Notably, the same comments and strikingly similar wording about Angela Merkel and her chancellorship appeared repeatedly among the reviewers. This strongly suggests a coordinated campaign intended to undermine the book's sales, likely based on specially programmed bots. Despite these conspicuous patterns in the first weeks after publication, Amazon apparently did not intervene (Amazon, 2025).

Memes

A ***meme*** or several ***memes*** in disinformation campaigns are small, creative pieces of content featuring humorous or memorable images, videos, short phrases, or wordplay. In many cases, memes are also used to mock the comments of other forum users.

The emotionally charged and often visual nature of memes allows them to spread rapidly online, with the aim of disseminating false or misleading information and manipulating public opinion. In disinformation campaigns, memes contain false information, distorted facts, or propaganda. These memes are distributed on social media platforms, where they can quickly go viral and reach a large audience. They are remarkably effective, partly because they appeal to people's visual perception and are therefore more likely to be remembered.

The intention behind using memes in disinformation campaigns is to make false information more appealing and to spread it, thereby increasing its visibility and impact. Memes often appeal to people's emotions and can spread rapidly, making them a powerful tool for shaping public opinion.

Deepfakes

Deepfakes are computer-generated videos or images that convincingly replace the face or appearance of a person in an existing video or image with that of another individual. With deepfakes, entire actions by synthetic persons can be created with near-photorealistic accuracy. Combined with AI-generated voices that are almost indistinguishable from those of the targeted individuals, these AI personas appear convincingly real, making it difficult for viewers to distinguish them from real people. This can have devastating consequences. Deepfakes are created for various purposes, such as generating fake news, spreading misinformation, or producing entertaining content. The term "deepfake" is a combination of "deep learning," referring to the AI techniques used, and "fake," indicating the fabricated nature of the content. Deepfakes can create the impression that someone has said or done something they never actually did, leading to misinformation and manipulation.

Business consultants at PwC USA now regard deepfakes as the "nuclear option among disinformation techniques":

> Deepfake technology, considered the nuclear option of disinformation techniques given its sophistication and remarkable effectiveness, is now easier than ever to produce and distribute online. There were 7,964 deepfake videos online at the beginning of 2019. The number was 14,678 nine months later. Deepfakes, usually presented in video format and sometimes in audio, are synthetic media built with the help of deep learning. The technology is designed to trick viewers or listeners into believing a fake event or an untrue message, and it's sophisticated enough that few viewers can distinguish deepfakes from genuine images (PwC, 2021).

Deepfakes can be used to create digital personas that appear convincingly real. One example was provided by the Chinese Communist Party's propaganda machine with "Wolf News", a news channel featuring an anchorwoman ("Anna") and a male anchor ("Jason") who read and commented on the news. The two presenters discussed gun violence in the USA and the shameful inability of politicians to contain it. At first glance, everything appeared genuine, except for a few details: the lip movements were not synchronized with the spoken words, and the faces had a somewhat unreal, video game-like appearance. Most notably, the subtitles were riddled with grammatical and spelling errors. "Even though this newly discovered pro-China disinformation campaign may seem somewhat crude, it marks the beginning of a new chapter in the information war," writes the New York Times (2023). Yet what we witnessed in 2023 pales in comparison to what we are seeing today.

This is illustrated by the case of the internationally operating British engineering firm Arup, headquartered in Hong Kong. During a video conference with several company executives, an employee in the finance department was instructed to transfer around 25 million US dollars to another account. The amount itself was not unusual, but the video conference was highly irregular: apart from the unfortunate employee who made the transfer, no other participant in the call was real. The faces appeared authentic (the employee knew the real individuals), and the voices sounded just like those of the actual people. The attackers had clearly done their homework.

They had extracted video and audio material from the executives' public appearances and processed it using AI (World Economic Forum, 2025). A representative of a major international software corporation explained to me how cautious companies have now become to provide attackers with as little exploitable material as possible. Employees are asked to keep their voicemail greetings to under 3 s, as otherwise there is a risk that the recording could be misused for voice synthesis.

The impact of deepfakes in disinformation attacks is fundamental for targeted companies. Just imagine a video emerging in public in which the head of a building authority is seen in a back room receiving a brown envelope from a property tycoon. The faces match, and the facial expressions and voices are authentic. These are precisely the kinds of cases PwC refers to as the "nuclear option." Audiovisual content is many times more effective, convincing, and altogether more powerful than text-based content and is therefore ideally suited for disinformation campaigns aimed at damaging the reputation and credibility of individuals by depicting them in compromising situations.

11.2 The Tactics

Coordinated Campaigns

Disinformation campaigns often involve coordinated efforts across multiple platforms and accounts. Malicious actors strategically align their messages and actions, thereby creating the impression of a consensus that has been orchestrated by them.

With a sock puppet army, an interesting and sophisticated disinformation tactic can be deployed, known as ***"Consensus Crack Development."*** Here, many fake social media accounts controlled by the attacker engage in mutual interaction. It begins with a user making a seemingly legitimate claim, which, however, is based on rather weak but real foundations. As soon as this claim is posted, a discourse begins with the other sock puppets controlled by the attacker. While some sock puppets support the attacker's claim, others attempt to refute it. The tone of the discourse can be manipulated by the attacker—the master of the sock puppet army. This continues until the sock puppets reach a consensus, which is precisely the one intended by the attacker.

Astroturfing

When fake accounts are used en masse to spread identical or similar content, creating the impression of a growing grassroots movement, this is referred to as ***"astroturfing."*** "Astroturf" is a synonym for artificial turf, i.e., synthetic grass without roots, and thus the exact opposite of a grassroots movement. The aim of astroturfing is to oppose a prevailing opinion or to generate a dominant narrative.

A similar approach is ***flooding***. Here, identical content is disseminated en masse against an unwelcome social media account, so that the existing narrative shifts and all opposing opinions are drowned out. ***"Flood the Zone with Shit":*** Steve Bannon, former head of Breitbart News and former chief strategist to Donald Trump, is the originator of flooding and explained it in February 2018 in a conversation with author Michael Lewis as follows:

> The Democrats don't matter. The real opposition is the media. And the way to deal with them is to flood the zone with shit (Bloomberg, 2018).

With this tactic, he interferes with the machinery of reputable media, whose task it is to separate fact from fiction so that users have the necessary information for informed political decisions. Sean Illing of vox.com warns:

> If you short-circuit this process by flooding the ecosystem with misinformation and undermining the media's ability to overburdening mediation can disrupt the democratic process (Vox, 2020).

Networks

Attackers build cross-platform networks of bots and sock puppets to amplify their messages. These ***networks*** collaborate to boost content, manipulate current topics, and control coverage of a particular subject or event.

Disinformation actors can also extend their networks to ***alternative social media platforms*** and exploit them for their own purposes. These are platforms that offer less user protection, less stringent content moderation policies, and fewer controls for detecting and removing inauthentic content and accounts than other social media platforms. Such platforms may include, for example, sites for cinema films, medical forums, car forums, and many others.

Exploiting Information Gaps

Mark Turnage of DarkOwl has pointed out (see interview with Mark Turnage at the beginning of this chapter) that the impact of a disinformation campaign depends on the grain of truth on which it is based. Joey Skaggs also refers in his interview to the fine line between plausibility and "oh, spare me".

Mark Turnage cited the example of an incident in a company, the extent of which is either covered up or downplayed by management. Concealment and cover-up in particular provide a powerful starting point for the disinformer's campaign, especially when the true scale of the incident is known. At that moment, the disinformers will incorporate this information into their campaign, massively endangering the company's credibility and thus its reputation. In this way, the attacker ruthlessly exploits information gaps.

The same applies to search queries. If the attacker notices that there is insufficient credible information available on a specific case to satisfy a search query, they exploit this. They fill the gaps with their own damaging content and spread the search term on social media. This increases the likelihood that the public will encounter disinformation content without there being accurate or reliable search results to refute it.

Planted Media Reports

Another form of disinformation attack is skillfully ***planted media reports***. The disinformer approaches a traditional medium with false information, which is then disseminated. In doing so, the disinformers exploit the credibility gap between traditional media and social media.

It is common practice, and not objectionable, for PR agencies to try to present their clients as favorably as possible in the media. However, unlike genuine PR agencies, the disinformer goes public with falsified or insubstantial information—with the aim of triggering manipulated media coverage.

For example, Russian oligarch Vladimir Potanin is said to be financing an informal communications project commissioned by the Kremlin, "aimed at undermining American and European public support for sanctions policy" (Intelligence Online, 2023). According to "Intelligence Online," the team of the oligarch loyal to Putin traveled to London and Washington to contact communications agencies—including "black PR" firms (which target the image of a particular person or organization)—and corporate intelligence firms. The aim of the meetings was to identify media outlets to convince them of the ineffectiveness and dangers of the sanctions.

Lawfare

Every day, countless criminal complaints or lawsuits are delivered to journalists with the aim of convincing them of the wrongdoing of a person or company. This is in fact an effective means of bringing the target into negative headlines, even if the ***criminal complaints*** are often flimsy and the ***lawsuits*** wafer-thin. Some journalists are tempted by the prospect of being able to report that the public prosecutor's office XY is investigating company Z. Garnished with a purchased expert opinion intended to substantiate the opponent's alleged misdeeds, there is a fair chance that the media will be receptive to the disinformer's poisoned offer—especially if a prominent company or well-known entrepreneur is involved.

In the meantime, a different form of legal disinformation attack has become established in the United States, which I refer to as "lawfare," that is, waging war by legal means. A good example of this is the successful lawsuit by New Yorker E. Jean Carroll, who sued Trump for rape, seeking $5 million in damages. She herself would never have been able to afford the expensive legal representation. It was later revealed that a political opponent of Trump had financed the high-profile trial: it was the declared Democrat and LinkedIn founder Reid Hoffman, a multibillionaire who had vowed to spend his last cent to prevent Trump from ever becoming president again (Forbes, 2023). During such a highly publicized trial, all kinds of information and disinformation can be introduced into the courtroom and disseminated to the public in real time.

False Amplification

In ***false amplification*** during disinformation attacks, the perpetrator seeks to artificially increase the visibility, reach, or impact of false or misleading information, making it appear more influential and credible than it is.

Imagine a scenario in which someone wants to spread a false claim or a fabricated story. Instead of relying on the value of the information or genuine public interest, they employ various tactics to make it seem more popular, well-known, or credible than it truly is.

A common method of false amplification is the creation of fake social media accounts or bots that imitate real users. These accounts are programmed to like, share, or comment positively on disinformation content, creating the impression of widespread support and engagement. These interactions are artificially generated and do not reflect genuine public opinion.

Another tactic involves coordinating with a network of individuals or groups willing to actively disseminate the false information, even across different forums or platforms. They may collaborate to flood social media platforms, discussion forums, or comment sections with repetitive posts, comments, or hashtags to create the appearance of significant public interest or consensus regarding the disinformation being spread.

Existing networks or influential individuals can also be leveraged to promote or disseminate disinformation. By persuading well-known figures or organizations to endorse the false information, it gains credibility and reaches a wider audience. The effect is based on the previously mentioned authority bias.

The aim of false amplification in disinformation attacks is to deceive people and create the illusion that false or misleading information is widely accepted or endorsed by a recognized authority. This can make it more difficult for individuals to discern the truth. The disinformation then spreads in a fog of deception.

Blockchain-Based Botnets

A ***blockchain-based botnet*** in the context of disinformation refers to a network of compromised computers or devices controlled by an attacker via blockchain technology to spread false or misleading information.

A botnet is a group of computers or devices infected with malware, allowing an attacker to remotely control them. These infected devices are referred to as "bots." The attacker can use these bots to perform various tasks, such as sending spam emails, launching cyberattacks, or spreading disinformation.

Blockchain technology is a decentralized and transparent system that records transactions or information across multiple computers, making it difficult to manipulate. In the context of a botnet, blockchain can be used to establish a communication and control system that cannot be detected or shut down.

A blockchain-based botnet for disinformation means that computers or devices are infected with malware and turned into bots, which then coordinate and control their activities using blockchain technology. The attacker uses this zombie botnet to spread false or misleading information on a large scale.

Attackers use the botnet to automate the creation and dissemination of fake news articles, social media posts, or comments that support a particular narrative or agenda. The decentralized nature of the blockchain-based botnet makes it difficult to trace back to the attacker, as the command-and-control infrastructure is distributed across multiple nodes in the blockchain network.

The purpose of deploying a blockchain-based botnet for disinformation is to amplify the reach and impact of false information while simultaneously making it more difficult to identify and mitigate the attacker's activities.

Cybersocial Attacks

Cybersocial attacks is the umbrella term for all manipulated disinformation attacks in the realm of social media.

The foundation of so-called ***"cybersocial attacks"*** are the social media platforms where people communicate and interact with one another. These attacks exploit the trust, vulnerabilities, or behavior of individuals to deceive, manipulate, or harm them.

In a disinformation attack, the perpetrator spreads false or misleading information on social media platforms to manipulate public opinion or create confusion. This may involve fake accounts, automated bots, or coordinated efforts to disseminate false reports. Cybersocial attacks take advantage of the interconnectedness of online platforms, and the trust people place in them.

Wikipedia

The online encyclopedia ***Wikipedia*** is among the most visited websites on the internet. Nowadays, anyone wishing to look something up no longer turns to a printed encyclopedia. The information carefully compiled by Wikipedia's army of volunteer authors carries weight and is considered credible. For a person or event to be included in the encyclopedia, credible and verifiable sources such as reputable newspapers or magazines are required. The authors of the entries cite the sources they consider reliable for each article. Disinformation agents exploit precisely this fact.

In two separate cases, our agency represented clients against whom criminal complaints had been filed. The public prosecutor's office subsequently launched investigations, having identified reasonable suspicion. The media, informed by the attacker about the ongoing investigations, reported on the cases. Since both clients, who were unrelated, were well-known entrepreneurs, the "Wikipedians" deemed them worthy of an entry, mentioning the ongoing investigations by the public prosecutor's office. In doing so, the Wikipedians referred to a reputable regional newspaper as the source that had published a corresponding report. This had serious consequences for both individuals concerned, as anyone searching for their names or companies would find these Wikipedia entries noting that the public prosecutor's office was investigating them. Business clients and investors referred to the entry and turned away from the two men. Only after several years did both public prosecutor's offices finally close the investigations. However, this fact was not considered newsworthy by the media: on the one hand, the cases were already several years old, and on the other, the closure of investigations is not particularly spectacular. Thus, there was no report and no update to the Wikipedia entry. A note about the closure of the investigations was not added to Wikipedia, as there was no source reporting on it. It appears the two affected individuals would have to continue living with the fact that the public prosecutor's office had investigated them—at least on Wikipedia. Only after intensive discussions and our presentation of the official notice of closure from the public prosecutor's office did the Wikipedians finally relent. They amended the entry and freed the two individuals from the sword of Damocles that had hung over them for years. Conclusion: Disinformation can become entrenched on Wikipedia if it has previously been published by a "reputable medium." As you can see, Wikipedia can be effectively weaponized for a disinformation attack. One simply needs to place damaging information in a reputable medium.

Wikipedia and Disinformation: The Brave Defense by the Volunteer Army—Interview with Lukas Mezger

Dr Lukas Mezger is a lawyer and partner at the law firm Unverzagt (Hamburg, Germany), which specializes, among other things, in media law. In his spare time, he has been a Wikipedia author for many years and served as the voluntary chair of the board of Wikimedia Deutschland e. V., which supports the Wikipedia community in Germany, from 2018 to May 2022. The Wikimedia Foundation, which operates Wikipedia, is funded primarily by donations from private individuals.

Wikipedia was launched in January 2001 as a nonprofit project in San Francisco with the aim of creating a free and universally accessible online encyclopedia.

Today, it is among the ten most visited websites in the world and is therefore of enormous significance to disinformation agents and producers of fake news. The authors who contribute to Wikipedia do so voluntarily and without payment. Anyone can contribute to the encyclopedia. The word "Wikipedia" is a combination of "Wiki" (the Hawaiian word for "quick") and "Encyclopedia." Lukas Mezger, a classical music enthusiast and amateur clarinetist, wrote his first Wikipedia article in 2005. He is a member of the self-organized Wikipedia editorial team "Law" and has authored several entries on music theory and history. In his spare time, he maintains over 3000 Wikipedia articles under his pseudonym, "Gnom." In our interview, the passionate Wikipedian discusses Wikipedia's fight against fake news and disinformation and how the Wikipedia community defends itself against such threats. The interview was conducted at a time when Lukas Mezger was still chair of Wikimedia Deutschland e. V.

Question: How vulnerable is Wikipedia to disinformation?

Lukas Mezger: The answer to this question can be: It is very vulnerable— or very little vulnerable. It depends on which article we are talking about. If we are talking about an article that is monitored or watched by many users, then the probability is very low that deliberate misinformation can be inserted. However, if an article is monitored by fewer people, it becomes easier to introduce misinformation.

Question: Wikipedia articles are fundamentally based on published, reputable sources such as newspaper or magazine articles, which can, however, potentially contain false information. That is a classic gateway for disinformation.

Lukas Mezger: If the misinformation already exists elsewhere in the world and has already been received, then Wikipedia simply reports what others are also reporting. In this sense, Wikipedia is very vulnerable, because as an encyclopedia it merely reflects the current state of knowledge. However, it is much more difficult to introduce an originally false piece of information, because Wikipedia is committed to only reproducing what has already been received elsewhere. That is the basic idea of an encyclopedia, and thus also of Wikipedia.

Question: You are not only a passionate Wikipedian but also a media lawyer. What is the media lawyer's perspective on this?

The media lawyer would say that Wikipedia's self-conception—namely, that it consists exclusively of user-generated content—is problematic due to its great success. Special privileges apply to such platforms, which media law provides for user-generated content. For example, Wikipedia is not required to adhere to the two-source principle as journalistic media are. However, Wikipedia is now sometimes perceived as a professional-quality medium. This creates a legal problem. On the other hand, Wikipedia wants to adhere to its self-imposed guiding principle of being an encyclopedia. Accordingly, we only reproduce what has already been published elsewhere. However, the law does not care about this in cases such as content that violates personal rights. The law states: if a statement infringes personal rights, then the dissemination of this information must be refrained from, regardless of whether it is available elsewhere or not. If Wikipedia reproduces this information, it can constitute a legal violation. In this respect, Wikipedia as an encyclopedia is not privileged under the law.

Question: What options are available to individuals or companies who want to defend themselves against false information on Wikipedia?

Lukas Mezger: We face a daily flood of so-called PR edits; for example, actors wanting to change their date of birth or companies wishing to remove uncomfortable facts from their corporate history. This flood, this constant barrage that hits the volunteer community every day, makes it difficult for us to engage in constructive dialogue with well-intentioned individuals, with those who have genuinely had their rights infringed. Because we often respond to these people in the same way—at least initially—as we do to those with less noble intentions, conflicts are inevitable. I have yet to find a way to better separate the wheat from the chaff. If we were to create a protected space for those about whom false information has been published, or whose personal rights have been violated in other ways, then those who merely believe their rights have been infringed, or who simply want to have an unflattering aspect of their biography removed from the article about them, would also end up there.

Question: PR agencies are sometimes asked by their clients to revise or update a Wikipedia article. But as a PR agency, you are generally regarded as suspect by the Wikipedia community and must contend with a strong resistance.

Lukas Mezger: A PR professional should engage openly in dialogue with Wikipedians, who are increasingly familiar with the issue of personal rights and with whom a relationship of trust can be built, allowing problematic cases to be resolved. But even if that succeeds, these Wikipedia contacts may still have difficulty within the community in standing up to suspicious "guardians of truth" who want to prevent whitewashing at all costs—even if this results in violations of personal rights. In such an open system as Wikipedia, this is a situation we have to live with.

Question: There are now agencies that offer to write or modify Wikipedia articles for a fee.

Lukas Mezger: Yes, among them are so-called "White Hats" and "Black Hats." The Black Hats operate covertly, creating pseudonymous user accounts, pretending to be ordinary Wikipedians, and then editing the relevant articles. Others, the white hats, make it clear to their clients that they have explicit disclosure obligations under Wikipedia's terms of use. They help to strike the right tone with Wikipedians, to use the appropriate forums and points of contact, to make constructive suggestions, and to approach Wikipedians who are active in a particular subject area.

Question: Let me return once more to the issue of targeted disinformation. What defense mechanisms has Wikipedia developed against this? Are there sensors that raise the alarm when something is wrong with an article?

Lukas Mezger: The most important mechanism, which applies to all Wikipedia articles, is the requirement for verifiability, which states that only information supported by verifiable and ideally reputable sources should be included in Wikipedia. The second line of defense differs from English-language Wikipedia. In the German-language Wikipedia, changes made by new members are not published online immediately but only after being reviewed by a more experienced community member. The third line of defense consists of technical spam filters. If someone adds links in articles to certain websites that we already know are not useful, the system simply does not accept these edits at all.

Question: This is then followed by the Wikipedia collective, that is, the oversight body.

Lukas Mezger: This is probably the most powerful defense mechanism: the collective itself. Every Wikipedia article has so-called "watchers." When I log into Wikipedia during my lunch break, after work, at home on my sofa, or even on the go, I go to my so-called "watchlist" and see the changes made in the last 72 hours to the Wikipedia articles I am interested in. In my case, that's now over 3000 articles, but because I do this almost every day, I only see about a dozen changes, of which I only need to look at about half. The watchlist shows you summaries of the changes and who made them. This "watchlist" is the main tool the community uses to check what is newly added each day.

Question: How do you cope with the sheer volume of changes that rain down on Wikipedians every day? Doesn't fake news slip through with such a quantity?

Lukas Mezger: The collective deals with this in three different ways: about 5000 people log in at least a few times a month to check the latest changes to articles they have already edited. In this way, the collective, with its many thousands of eyes, finds misinformation more quickly and reliably. For less-watched articles—after all, people go on holiday or sometimes just don't check in—it doesn't work quite as well.

Question: The volume of daily changes is surely disproportionate to the number of gatekeepers.

Lukas Mezger: There are indeed Wikipedians who sit down and follow the latest changes like a news ticker, just as used to happen in newspaper editorial offices. For them, a stream of summary lines of the latest changes scrolls across the screen. Over the years, these users have developed a good instinct for misinformation and have also created special filters so that, for example, everything from people who have been around for two years or more is no longer displayed. They then only look at the "suspicious" or otherwise error-prone changes.

Question: All this work is voluntary and unpaid. How do the members find the time for all this?

Lukas Mezger: Among Wikipedians, there is a (unfortunately too small) group who divide up the latest changes among themselves by time. They also refer to their work as "patrolling." This is the very first line of defense, followed by the "watchers." Finally, there are the slowest, the "editorial teams." For example, I am a member of the "Law" and "Music Theory" editorial teams. The editorial teams monitor a set of articles on a particular topic. If one of us notices something or finds something odd, I ask the others to take a look. Sometimes a few days can pass this way. The editorial teams are the slowest instrument. Unfortunately, the editorial teams for companies and for minor celebrities are poorly staffed, because those are, of course, rather boring topics. Who wants to spend their free time checking for misinformation about companies?

Question: As a prospective Wikipedian, do I first have to earn credibility? Do I have to—perhaps even as a covert PR person—write 20 articles about lizards before I am taken seriously and recognized as a Wikipedian?

Lukas Mezger: Yes, and to be quite honest, it makes me sick when it comes to exactly those people. Because we do keep uncovering them. Someone writes about lizards for a while and, on the side, changes a birthdate to turn a lesser-known celebrity younger. And later, the same person might also write a flattering article about a company. Or I see someone who corrects the same spelling mistakes again, trying to appear as a diligent Wikipedian, but just as diligently adds web links to advertising sites. Sometimes you also find someone who just adds a series of historical cup wins by regional league clubs and then, quite innocently, deletes a medium-sized scandal from a biography. And those are the really bad ones, because they are not so easy to spot—if I just glance at their profiles, they look fine. These people are also not picked up by the usual filters, because otherwise they contribute credibly. The person might even be a member of an editorial team for lizards or whatever. It is incredibly disappointing when you uncover someone like that.

Question: What do you do then?

Lukas Mezger: These users are blocked without lengthy discussion, that is, their account's editing rights are revoked. That is a clear violation of the community rules.

Question: What makes a source "reputable," as you called it?

Lukas Mezger: For example, the editorial team on biology—we were talking about lizards—only uses certain scientific sources and does not accept just any link to a blog. The editorial team has set high standards for itself and its field. This is reflected in the quality of the articles on animal species. For minor celebrities and small businesses, there are no similarly active editorial teams with comparable standards.

Question: The *yellow press*, for instance, has a rather questionable reputation in terms of journalistic quality. And yet, these are also magazines, that is, press publications.

Lukas Mezger: When this discussion is raised within the community, the community quickly states that such sources are not reputable. These references are then removed. The English-language Wikipedia has even compiled a blacklist for this purpose. The community no longer accepts the *Daily Mirror* and similar media as sources. We do not yet have this in the German-language Wikipedia. Just imagine if we were to stop accepting *Bild* (Germany's major tabloid) as a source. We do not—so far—do that.

Question: Does this mean that the sensitivities, preferences, and political and social orientations of Wikipedians determine what is considered reputable or not?

Lukas Mezger: Indeed, this blacklist is currently filled mainly with media from the right-wing spectrum, so, for example, the *Daily Mirror* or *Breitbart* may not be used as sources.

Question: There are hundreds of specialist journals on all sorts of topics. These are magazines with a wide range of orientations, but their editorial teams possess a high level of expertise in their specific subject area. In principle, this would be ideal for Wikipedia. Are these specialist journals also considered "reputable" sources?

Lukas Mezger: We have discussed exactly this issue in the Wikipedia History editorial team. They find it difficult. Especially for twentieth-century history, there are magazines but also book publishers that—let's say—focus on popular science history writing. We repeatedly discuss certain publishers that, for example, publish magazines about the Second World War. Our history editorial team has decided not to use these magazines as sources anymore.

Question: In theory, a disinformer could place disinformation in a reputable medium. As we know, even quality media sometimes publish false information.

Lukas Mezger: I am aware of the problem. Wikipedia takes the position that it always conveys information based on a source, which is also cited. The person concerned is then told to first approach the source and have it corrected there. Only then can the person contact Wikipedia again.

Question: This leads to the problem of time limits if one wants to have an older fake news item legally removed from the media.

Lukas Mezger: Procedurally, there is the problem that, for an application for a preliminary injunction, the matter may already have been in the public domain for too long. The person would then have to initiate what is known as the main legal proceedings. That can be very expensive. At Wikipedia, we then face the following problem: on the one hand, we have the word of the person concerned, and on the other, a reputable newspaper that is alleged to have reported incorrectly. As mentioned, Wikipedia takes the position that we are writing an encyclopedia. An encyclopedia—according to the nineteenth-century definition—reviews sources and reproduces what is stated there. Because Wikipedia follows this tradition and is committed to this standard, what is published in a reputable publication carries more weight for Wikipedia than what the person concerned claims. Some of these cases end up with the legal department of the Wikimedia Foundation in the USA.

(The interview with Lukas Mezger took place in Hamburg in September 2021)

References

Amazon. (2025). Angela Merkel, Freedom: Memoirs 1954–2021. Retrieved from: https://www.amazon.de/Freiheit-Erinnerungen-1954-Angela-Merkel/dp/3462005138/ref=cm_cr_arp_d_product_top?ie=UTF8

Bloomberg. (2018). Has anyone seen the President? Retrieved from: https://www.bloomberg.com/opinion/articles/2018-02-09/has-anyone-seen-the-president#xj4y7vzkg

DarkOwl. (2023). The digital economy of disinformation on the Darknet: Controlling the narrative. Retrieved from: https://www.darkowl.com/blog-content/the-digital-economy-of-disinformation-on-the-darknet-controlling-the-narrative/

Forbes. (2023). What was Reid Hoffman's role in funding E. Jean Carroll's case? Retrieved from: https://www.forbes.com/sites/anafa-guy/2023/05/10/what-was-reid-hoffmans-role-in-funding-e-jean-carrolls-case/?sh=94a56953e154

Intelligence Online. (2023) Oligarch Vladimir Potanin financing black PR campaigns against Western sanctions. Retrieved from: www.intelligenceonline.com/corporate-intelligence/2023/05/30/oligarch-vladimir-potanin-financing-black-pr-campaigns-against-western-sanctions,109978518-art

New York Times. (2008). The trolls among us. Retrieved from: www.nytimes.com/2008/08/03/magazine/03trolls-t.html?_r=2&

New York Times. (2023). The people on screen are fake. The disinformation is real. Retrieved from https://www.nytimes.com/2023/02/07/technology/artificial-intelligence-training-deepfake.html.

PWC. (2021). Disinformation attacks have arrived in the corporate sector. Are you ready? Retrieved from: https://www.pwc.com/us/en/tech-effect/cybersecurity/corporate-sector-disinformation.html

Vox. (2020). "Flood the zone with shit": How misinformation overwhelmed our democracy. Retrieved from: https://www.vox.com/policy-and-politics/2020/1/16/20991816/impeachment-trial-trump-bannon-mis-information

World Economic Forum. (2025). 'This happens more frequently than people realize': Arup chief on the lessons learned from a $25m deepfake crime. Retrieved from: https://www.weforum.org/stories/2025/02/deepfake-ai-cybercrime-arup/

Part III

Defense and Response

Defense: The Search for Time and Space 12

12.1 Detection: Seismographs Detect Disinformation Outbreaks

In many cases, a disinformation attack is preceded by a faint rumbling that intensifies over time.

A volcano does not simply erupt without warning; it first sends out signals indicating an imminent eruption. To detect these signals, volcanologists set up listening stations around the volcano and use seismometers to record the earth tremors typical of an impending eruption, caused by rising magma. These subtle vibrations are barely, if at all, perceptible to humans but can be measured with sensitive instruments.

The same applies to disinformation attacks. We refer to this early detection as detection. This is essentially an attempt to identify a developing disinformation attack as quickly as possible. Early detection is achieved through early warning systems, that is, a monitoring center for the digital space, which deploys its probes into the areas relevant to the company's social media platforms, activist forums, or the dark web. Here, we are talking about listening posts, that is, **digital listening**.

In 2020, a group of American researchers set out to find a solution to the increasingly rapid and automated disinformation campaigns. Their answer: a solution must be found to counter these automated attacks:

> Online influence operations (IOs) are enabled by the low cost, scalability, automation, and speed provided by social media platforms on which a variety of automated and semiautomated innovations are used to spread disinformation. Situational awareness of semiautomated IOs at speed and scale requires a semiautomated response capable of detecting and characterizing IO narratives and networks and estimating their impact either directly within the communications medium or more broadly in the actions and attitudes of the target audience (PNAS, 2021).

It was a bold and highly advanced move by the group of scientists. In connection with the 2017 French presidential election, they collected and analyzed an

U. Wolff, *Disinformation Attacks On Businesses*, Management for Professionals,
https://doi.org/10.1007/978-3-658-51407-5_12

impressive dataset of over 780 million tweets from 12.7 million accounts, of which they identified 3151 as specific information operation (IO) accounts disseminating content in French and English. Their first finding: the disinformation spread by these accounts was largely automated, driven by trolls and bots.

At the time, the researchers were granted access to the data by Twitter for analysis. This enabled them to identify disinformation (IO) accounts with 96% accuracy and to create precise disinformation world maps.

That was in 2020, after the Cambridge Analytica scandal. Today, the researchers wish things were as they were back then, as social media platforms now stubbornly refuse to open their interfaces. As a result, researchers and developers are prevented from accessing the essential raw data from the vast user data repositories, which are urgently needed to develop AI-based systems to counter disinformation. It appears as if the American tech giants of Silicon Valley have absolutely no interest in the development of such systems, as this would disrupt their business model. Why? Because social media platforms profit from the strong emotions of their users, keeping them on their platforms, highly agitated and emotionally charged while generating ad money for TikTok, Meta & Co.

A bitter realization came 5 years later, after the US researchers had demonstrated with their study the valuable insights that can be gained from such data—provided it is made available. At the NATO Strategic Communication Congress "Digital Frontlines 2025" in Riga, Latvia, scientists and experts made clear the predicament they are in and how little willingness there is among the American tech elite to at least help clean up part of the disaster they have caused.

The representative of the company Logically, which uses AI to counter disinformation, said in the Riga panel discussion:

> AI is part of the threat, but it is also part of the solution. We need AI for detection of disinformation and upcoming disinformation campaigns, and we need it to identify which narrative can be weaponized.

However, as Jennifer Woodard lamented, for this we need data from social media platforms, which do withhold these "raw signals" from researchers and developers of potential countermeasures:

> This is a strategic dependency. Social media must step up for developing tools.

The German Benjamin Laepple, co-founder of Partisan, also criticized in Riga the stubborn and defensive refusal of social media platforms:

> It is so difficult to get data from social media platforms. We don't even know anymore what's out there. Europe is a digital colony. The US owns the infrastructure.

Meanwhile, a whole ecosystem of companies has emerged worldwide, claiming to have deciphered the Rosetta Stone of detection. Most of them use AI capabilities for this purpose. In fact, some of the available tools perform well, while others advertise detection capabilities that unfortunately prove to be rather inadequate in practice. However, there are now promising methods that can effectively monitor the digital space.

One person who has elevated digital listening to an art form is the German Professor Martin Grothe with his company "Complexium GmbH" (Berlin, Germany). Grothe has been working on pattern recognition in the digital space since the 1990s. He builds these listening posts for companies to detect potential threats at an early stage. Martin Grothe is co-author of the frequently cited #Disinformation study by ASW and author of the highly recommended book on "Digital Listening for Companies".

In the #Disinformation report, Grothe points out that a company seeking to protect itself against disinformation attacks with early warning systems faces a massive challenge: the "unknown unknowns" and the resulting risk of surprise for the company, which in fact does not even know what to look for to locate the source of danger. And because one is unable to picture the threat in detail, it turns out that even conventional search tools prove to be of little use. Keyword searches, Google Alerts, and social media monitoring platforms employed by PR agencies and corporate communications—all are porous nets and comparatively dull sensors.

What is needed, therefore, are more intelligent systems that can also understand the context in which terms are used, for example, in conversations among activists or when certain issues are mentioned. According to Grothe, these systems register changes in linguistic structural parameters and identify which topics are appearing more frequently in opinion forums and how often the level of discontent is rising. Systems are capable of deciphering seemingly nonsensical or trivial conversations, since activist groups are unlikely to discuss their plans openly, instead using codes or ciphers. These intelligent systems are known as "computational linguistic algorithms." Grothe explains it as follows:

> We do not simply search for individual terms as one would with a Google search. Our aim is rather to determine which aspects are emerging and in what context certain terms appear with particular frequency. Is a cluster forming here? Are there perhaps focal points? Linguistic algorithms can reveal such clusters in communication channels in real time plus one hour. This works even if the attackers are communicating in their own coded language. This is especially useful when dealing with activists (see the following interview with Martin Grothe).

These early warning systems do exist, such as those from Complexium, DarkOwl, and other providers. Grothe's computers process several hundred thousand to one million posts daily. That is a vast amount of data, impossible for any human to digest alone. Special tools are available to filter anomalies from this enormous mountain of mined data and to identify clusters of statements. Grothe from Complexium and Turnage from DarkOwl want to see what perpetrators are plotting or offering. One searches for activists and radicals, the other focuses on individual perpetrators or criminal organizations, each in their own way, targeting those who intend to harm companies. But are systems like Complexium's also suitable for identifying emerging waves of disinformation? I believe so, since this too involves field observation and the analysis of datasets obtained through digital listening. It is about information, information flows, and their controlled dissemination.

It may be surprising, but regardless of AI, a crucial aspect in evaluating search results using linguistic algorithms is the human factor: at the end of the analysis chain are people—analysts who know the client company very well and assess anomalies and clusters for their relevance to the client. These analysts are familiar with a company's sensitivities, pressure points, vulnerabilities, and potential attackers. It is this human intelligence of the analysts that enables them to present the client with a tailored threat assessment in the form of a report.

12.2 The Time Factor: Why Rapid Response Is So Important

We have searched, we have found, and we have acknowledged: something is brewing, and it does not look good. So, what should be done? What are the next steps? How can the company defend itself against the impending disinformation attack? Decisions are needed, and decision-makers within the company must be consulted.

In the event of an acute threat to a company, the challenge is usually to overcome the seemingly endless and protracted decision-making loops.

While senior management is being briefed on the situation by corporate security, further discussions and consultations with the legal department or corporate communications are required. All parties must confer, coordinate, consider contingencies, and run through possible courses of action. All of this takes time—a great deal of time—and time is a precious commodity during a disinformation attack.

While the disinformation attack is underway, forums and social media fill with false information, which is constantly shared, commented on, and liked. The wave of disinformation rises exponentially, growing into a tsunami. The impact on the company is soon felt. A product from the targeted company is no longer purchased; sales figures plummet. Banks and investors demand meetings with management and request explanations. Employees become unsettled, and the media pick up on the false information circulating on social media. Competitors attempt to secure the market share lost by the targeted company—all while the beleaguered management, together with the legal department and corporate communications, continues to deliberate on how to get a grip on the communications attack.

12.3 When the Wave Is Rolling, It Is Already Too Late

We come to the realization: the path to an effective decision in the event of a communications attack is too long, while the time available for decisions and initial countermeasures is too short. The decision, born of sheer desperation and uncertainty on the part of management, to do nothing and wait for things to calm down, is not an option.

Effective disinformation attacks occur in waves. They are not flash-in-the-pan events that burn brightly and then quickly subside. Nor are they the typical Twitter "shitstorm" with the lifespan of a mayfly. Professional disinformation attacks often not only leave their harbor at staggered intervals, but they also vary in intensity and target several different areas of a company. And above all: a professionally orchestrated disinformation attack makes it difficult for the targeted company to identify the originator and source of the disinformation. It is a nightmare for any legal counsel, who at first can do little more than file a complaint against "persons unknown." In the heat of the moment, this is wasted time, because only once the attacker's strategy has been uncovered can the real defense begin—including for the legal team. Taking legal action against an unknown adversary is about as effective as a sword fight in a dark room.

As I have already mentioned, to illustrate the mechanics and effects of a disinformation attack, I devised a strategic assault on the fictional baby food manufacturer, which I gave the name "Yummy! Yummy!" In this attack scenario, I focus on a fictional baby food product, "Yummy! Yummy! – Garden Vegetables, 6th Month," produced by the manufacturer. The attack narrative goes like this: the product is said to be contaminated. The manufacturer is aware of this but does not wish to withdraw the product from the market. One more crucial piece of information that should be included during the attack: the attacker makes sure to mention that, although the baby food company is aware of the issue, it is currently doing everything possible to prevent the matter from becoming public.

In this attack scenario, I have clearly defined the target group (young parents who are easily emotionally influenced). The attack unfolds across multiple platforms (mothers'/parents' forums), whose users quote and exchange information with one another. The astonished management must first realize that they are facing a professional disinformation attack. Originator: unknown.

And this is precisely the problem for "Yummy! Yummy!" The company must defend itself against and combat an invisible adversary. While various parts of the management discuss the cause, the impact, and possible countermeasures, more and more concerned and agitated parents learn of the alleged contamination of the product, which is now being extensively discussed in all parenting forums—including the allegation that the company is attempting to cover up the contamination.

From now on, "Yummy! Yummy!" Garden Vegetables remains on the shelves. Concerned parents avoid this product as well as all other products from the manufacturer because a company that is allegedly concealing such a serious issue as contamination in baby food cannot be trusted. The baby food manufacturer's competitors are delighted with the additional business coming from "Yummy! Yummy!"

And here it is again, the time problem. I asked Complexium CEO Martin Grothe whether he sees a way to solve the time problem. Anyone who does not recognize at a very early stage that a disinformation attack is underway inevitably runs into the time problem.

"If you do not identify potentially relevant posts or developments in a timely manner, you will never be able to make up for the lost time internally." For Grothe, it is clear: those who focus on detection from the outset have a distinct time advantage. The targeted company does not have to waste valuable time gathering essential information to explore the background of the disinformation campaign. The DSW report "#Disinformation" puts it even more clearly:

> The central importance of detecting and assessing attacks in the digital sphere can be highlighted. Only if significant time loss can be avoided here is a successful response still possible.

The earlier a disinformation attack is detected, the smaller the damage, or the later an attack is identified, the greater the damage. Above all, however, countering disinformation becomes a laborious, costly, and time-consuming uphill battle to protect the company's reputation.

Time—that is the central issue in defending against and remedying a disinformation attack. For a company that is seriously addressing the risk of possible disinformation attacks, this also means rigorously eliminating all timewasters. Internal communication processes must—as in any crisis—be kept short, swift, and smooth. And above all, the company must be prepared.

Searching the Digital Sphere—Interview with Digital Listening Expert Martin Grothe

Since the 1990s, Martin Grothe has been engaged in pattern recognition in complex structures. In 2004, he founded Complexium GmbH in Berlin, which uses its own formats, methods, and technologies to systematically uncover "insights" in the digital sphere. Put simply: Complexium scans communication channels for companies using linguistic algorithms to find out what activists or malicious third parties are planning. This gives Complexium's clients a competitive edge, particularly in the areas of corporate security and personal protection. Martin Grothe is a professor at the Berlin University of the Arts (UdK) in the field of "Digital Communication". He is an alumnus of WHU—Otto Beisheim School of Management. He is the author of the book "Digital Listening for Companies".

Martin, have the tools of disinformation changed in recent years?

Grothe: Yes, we are currently in the midst of a digital zoo. Information spreads at lightning speed across social media channels such as Twitter and Instagram, but also via messenger systems like Telegram. Information and disinformation jump from one channel to another. On Telegram alone, we monitor around 16,000 channels and groups.

And how has the content of disinformation changed?

Grothe: We are witnessing a strong emotionalization of content through images and textual appeals. The time span from the initial discussion of a topic, through emotionalization, to activation and, where applicable, mobilization, is becoming ever shorter.

Have you observed changes in the mindset of attackers in recent years?

Grothe: Indeed, the mood has shifted. There are more conspiracy theorists and other activists. We are seeing a greater willingness to act, a higher propensity for violence, or readiness for peaceful sabotage. We are also observing an increased search for new target sectors. None of this was foreseeable in 2017, well before the coronavirus pandemic.

For companies targeted by disinformation attacks, there is, in addition to ongoing disinformation, another pressing problem: time! Valuable time is lost between the detection of an attack, the first decisions within the company, and the resulting countermeasures. Do you see a way to solve this time problem?

Grothe: That is our field of expertise. There is a clear process for this: in my experience, the initial phases are crucial—data collection and data processing. If you do not identify potentially relevant posts or developments in a timely manner, you cannot make up for the lost time internally. However, not every incorrect or abbreviated piece of information or accusation constitutes a disinformation attack. Here—stage three—a qualified but rapid analysis is essential. Where is there more behind the story? Otherwise, you may end up with many false alarms, and no one will take them seriously anymore.

Can you give me an example?

Grothe: A lot of this comes, for example, from anti-vaccination activists, who subsequently turn against rising energy prices, rising prices in general, arms deliveries, and now against elites. Our detection system registers and qualifies these insults and threats, much of which—but not all—can be automated. The individual information channels are scanned at high frequency by our software. However, since it is not possible to specify in advance what to look for, you need "intelligent tools." The computational linguistic algorithms we have developed identify unusual and unexpected topics, the so-called *unknown unknowns*.

Computational linguistic algorithms. What does that mean?

Grothe: We do not simply search for individual terms as you would with a Google search. Our aim is to identify which aspects are emerging and in what context certain terms appear particularly frequently. Is a cluster forming here? Are there perhaps focal points? Linguistic algorithms can reveal such clusters in communication channels in real time plus one hour. This also works when attackers communicate using their own coded language. This is particularly helpful with activists.

To initiate legal action against the instigators of disinformation campaigns, it would be helpful to know who is behind them. Is it possible, through such detection, to identify the source of disinformation?

Grothe: That is an investigative process, which may succeed, but does not have to. However, it is often possible at least to narrow it down.

Do you rely on artificial intelligence for this?

Grothe: Expectations should not be set too high here. AI always requires a large amount of training data, which is simply not available for many threat scenarios—which is a good thing. However, AI models can be used very effectively for specific tasks within this process. For example, when it comes to mapping a large stream of posts to certain locations or identifying specific incidents.

Do you leave the evaluation of detection to computers?

Grothe: Computers or software tools can provide excellent support for the collection and processing phases. The volume of data is far too large for humans: we ingest several hundred thousand to a million posts per day. Tools can also detect anomalies or apply search filters. On this basis, analysts can then carry out qualified detection. In our situation center, we employ analysts who know the client companies very well. They are thoroughly familiar with the companies' critical points and therefore know what to look out for. Ultimately, however, a human must always review the results. Every report and every warning we issue is thoroughly checked by an analyst before it is sent out. There is no other way.

Reference

PNAS. (2021). *Automatic detection of influential actors in disinformation networks*. Retrieved from: https://www.pnas.org/doi/epdf/10.1073/pnas.2011216118

Preparation, Countermeasures, and Defense Strategies

13

The previous chapter already made it clear that preparation for a disinformation attack is essential for any company. The main objective is to gain time so as not to be constantly on the back foot but to be able to catch up with the attackers at a certain point.

Preparation also inherently involves defense strategies against a disinformation attack. Defending against disinformation attacks requires a multilayered approach that combines various strategies, tools, measures, and different parts of the organization. I previously compared an emerging disinformation attack to the onset of a volcanic eruption. Villages and towns located near a volcano are usually prepared. The volcano is monitored by volcanologists. Governments and local authorities have developed scenarios for the day when the volcano spews hot ash and lava flows into the area. A company should see itself in a similar way: as an organization on the edge of a volcano that could erupt at any time. The company should be prepared for the eruption—that is, a disinformation attack—and its consequences.

However, caution is advised: not every newspaper article that portrays the company or its management in an unfavorable light is necessarily a disinformation attack. Not every negative product review, not every disgruntled tweet (and there are plenty of those on X/Twitter), signals the start of a disinformation campaign. Caution is good, as is social media monitoring, but paranoia can lead to overreactions. Sometimes a little self-criticism is helpful, prompting the company to consider what might have triggered such negative coverage. Therefore, establish a clearing unit within the company to identify a rolling disinformation attack as such.

Below, we will find a list of fundamental measures and preparations that every company should consider. Many of the points listed below are drawn from classic crisis communication and litigation PR.

I discussed these and other topics with Caroline Sapriel, an experienced crisis communicator who, with her firm CS&A (Brussels), advises companies worldwide in crisis situations. (The full interview with Caroline can be read on the following pages.) Caroline is highly experienced and knows very well how to assess

U. Wolff, *Disinformation Attacks On Businesses*, Management for Professionals,
https://doi.org/10.1007/978-3-658-51407-5_13

(perceived) crises. Part of her job is to calm the nerves of a management team shaken by panic attacks. Her advice (and mine) to companies and their communications departments is as simple as it is effective: Slow down!

> First, slow down. Everyone preaches speed in crisis response, but in the face of something disturbing or suspicious, the first step should be not to react impulsively. Much of social media is designed to amplify shock and negativity, so people tend to react quickly. But not all communication teams are as digitally literate as they should be. So, we tell clients, "Improve your literacy, verify before reacting, and invest in tools that can detect deepfakes."'

Of course, it is necessary to determine as quickly as possible whether it is actually a disinformation attack, who might be behind it, and what the attacker's motive is. What Caroline meant is that we should not put the cart before the horse to avoid stumbling. Facts first, then reaction. Only in this way can a defense be effective.

Raise Awareness of Disinformation Attacks

I sometimes find it astonishing that managers have never heard of potential disinformation attacks on companies. Many with whom I have discussed the topic initially thought only of cyberattacks and hackers. But once I explained the potential impact of disinformation attacks on a company, I had their full attention, and they experienced an "eureka" moment.

The same is certainly true for employees across all areas of a company. It is important to educate staff in different departments about the dangers of disinformation and to enable them to recognize disinformation for what it is. Therefore, conduct regular workshops and training sessions to inform employees about disinformation, its effects, and effective ways to deal with toxic information.

Trained employees can function as an early warning system and help identify the possible source of disinformation. The HR department, for example, knows which employees have had to leave the company and whether one of them has therefore threatened the company. The IT department can determine where and by whom certain information and data have been siphoned off from the company, which have now suddenly become the basis of a disinformation campaign. The procurement department may have evidence of an employee's gambling addiction and related debts, which could make them a target for professional disinformation agents.

Train Your Communications Departments

In many companies, it is apparently the communications departments that are tasked with monitoring the information market and investigating anomalies in more detail. In small- and medium-sized enterprises, this is certainly a reasonable solution. However, communications departments are usually equipped for this task, as communications departments typically have Google Alerts, media monitoring, and service providers who scan social media for specific terms and sentiments. But this is not sufficient for effective detection. Effective detection goes much further (see interview with Professor Martin Grothe from Complexium).

It is striking that most corporate communicators understand their company can come under fire in the media or that customers may speak disparagingly about products and services. Nevertheless, their awareness of targeted, professional disinformation attacks is often not sufficiently developed.

It is precisely corporate communicators who should be trained in matters of disinformation, as they are on the front line when the battle begins. They know potential adversaries, competitors, or activists who are ill-disposed toward the company. They are aware of opponents from politics as well as from the media. And above all, they have established contacts with the media, which can be extremely helpful later when it comes to publicly communicating a disinformation attack.

In large companies, corporate communications must work closely with corporate security, which deploys advanced detection tools, and above all, representatives of corporate communications must be an integral part of the "war room" that coordinates the defensive measures.

Familiarize Yourself with the Necessary Detection Tools

We have already discussed how important professional early warning systems can be for companies. Seek advice on which early warning system best suits your company. Research the providers and check their references. Make sure you approach the right companies and that their services go beyond simple social media monitoring. Familiarize yourself with the most advanced tools in the detection sector, and do not simply trust companies that claim their systems are AI-based and therefore cutting edge, as all good systems today operate on an AI basis.

We have already discussed some tools for detecting disinformation threats, but it would go beyond the scope of this book to list and discuss all currently available tools. Moreover, detection tools are subject to constant development. What was just recently considered state of the art may no longer be so. A good overview of the currently available disinformation threat detection tools can be found online. What is "top" today may be "flop" tomorrow. Stay ahead of the curve.

Users of these tools must bear in mind that, in the end, a professional analysis of the collected information by specialists is essential, as only these analysts can distill actionable intelligence from raw data, which then serves as the basis for the management's necessary decisions.

Identify Your Potential Adversaries

A company can have many adversaries, whether they are competitors or come from the ranks of activists and NGOs. Some companies inherently have many potential opponents and adversaries, such as banks, pharmaceutical, chemical, defense, and oil corporations, as well as automotive and global food companies.

Companies must keep these adversaries under observation. They need to know in which forums and on which social media channels they are active. Corporate security must be informed by the HR department if employees have behaved aggressively toward management or have made threats. However, realistically speaking, the internal and external fields of observation in large companies are vast and can never be fully monitored.

During annual general meetings or financial press conferences, at trade fairs or product launches, monitoring should be particularly intensified.

Professional providers and service companies can take over the monitoring and keep you regularly informed about the security situation through reports. This is especially important when a company is undergoing major changes and is therefore most vulnerable to disinformation attacks.

Identify Your Friends and Supporters

A company does not only have adversaries but also supporters, friends, fans, and a loyal customer base. Satisfied suppliers, supporters from local politics, trade unions, and employees can also act as "influencers" to support a company under attack. Companies should pay particular attention to this group of friends and keep the contact details of the most important protagonists or points of contact readily available.

Companies with strong brands also have powerful fan communities, who gather in social media or online forums to exchange information. Their loyalty can effectively neutralize a disinformation attack or even render it ineffective.

Establish a Task Force and Plan a "War Room"

I admit: the term "War Room" is somewhat excessive for a room where a company's crisis management team convenes. "War Room" evokes images of warfare and reminds one of Hollywood films set in the White House in Washington. Nevertheless, the term has become established in crisis communication.

If the company already has a crisis manual and a crisis management team, the latter must be updated and restructured in the event of a disinformation attack. The same applies to the crisis manual. Additional departments must be included alongside the essential ones. In addition to representatives from the affected business areas (such as production, sales, finance, and IT), it is essential to involve corporate communications as well as experts in social media, monitoring (digital listening), disinformation, analytics, or forensics.

The crisis team leader clearly defines the purpose and objectives of the crisis management team. Since a disinformation attack always involves time pressure, the crisis team should be managed with strict discipline and set speaking times by the crisis team leader.

To illustrate the current progression of the disinformation attack, developments should be visualized on large screens, preferably in real time.

Access to information: ensure access to relevant documents, emergency plans, contact lists, and other critical information required in a crisis situation.

1. **Eliminate Silos within Your Organization**

Disinformation attacks target various areas of a company. Potential perpetrators of such attacks can often be identified through collaboration between different departments. For example: Mr M., a member of the management board, leaves the company after being passed over for promotion in favor of a colleague. If internal documents, accessible only to the management board, are subsequently leaked, HR and IT must work closely with forensic experts to trace the path of the published documents.

2. **Eliminate Timewasters**

Crisis situations cannot tolerate timewasters—least of all disinformation attacks. Eliminate and strictly discipline time wasters. Ego-shooters, vain self-promoters, and unprepared chatterboxes—every company has them, and they are highly detrimental in situations where saving time is paramount. The crisis team leader must enforce a strict regime and, if necessary, reconsider the composition of the crisis management team.

Timewasters also include documents and information that must first be obtained. Keep lists of contacts at the relevant investigative authorities and police departments readily available. Find out in advance who is responsible, so you do not waste time determining whether the local or higher-level police authorities are responsible for a disinformation attack affecting your company, and who the appropriate contact person is.

3. **A List of Trusted External Experts**

There are situations in which a company must rely on external experts. Small- and medium-sized enterprises cannot afford to employ specialists who are only needed occasionally.

In the event of a disinformation attack, the company should be able to refer to a list of pre-vetted experts. Ideally, the company has already worked with these external service providers. Prepare such a list and keep it up to date. Searching for a suitable expert, checking references, and more is very time-consuming. Do this in advance. Ask the procurement department, or whoever is responsible, to ensure that all administrative processes are in place so that the relevant service provider can be immediately registered and onboarded as a "supplier" for your company. If possible, also identify a second service provider in case your preferred provider is subject to a conflict of interest.

4. **List of Key Media for Your Company**

If the company has a communications department, it will also have a list of journalists across various media (online, influencers, social media channels, trade publications, or Tier 1) who can be contacted or activated in the event of a disinformation attack. The importance of this will be discussed further below.

Lists of Key Stakeholders and Shareholders

Who are the stakeholders and shareholders in your company? Whom do you need to inform in the event of a disinformation attack? Banks, investors, and insurers are obvious. But what about employees, local politicians, suppliers, and customers? The disinformation agents have a head start, and it is possible that the stakeholders and shareholders have already received the false information and are now asking you and themselves important questions. Prepare yourself. Each of the abovementioned stakeholders and shareholders should receive a separate, targeted communication that addresses their specific expectations and interests.

If Possible, Pursue Legal Action

A disinformation attack is orchestrated by either a state, an organization, or an individual. All three have a single objective: to harm the company. Their weapon is falsehood. You must fight it and eliminate the disinformation or toxic narratives with the help of libel and media lawyers. How to defend yourself legally and the role lawyers play in countering a disinformation attack will be explained in detail in a separate chapter.

"One More Thing": Seek Public Attention and Avoid an Information Vacuum

In his legendary presentations, Apple founder Steve Jobs always saved the highlight of his product showcase for last, introducing it with the words "One more thing!" That is exactly what I would like to do here. "One more thing: Seek public attention!"

I am referring to the possibility of seeking protection through public engagement. Make your case known. Explain in the media, in public, that your company has been the target of a disinformation attack. State the facts without making the mistake of dwelling on what the attacker has misrepresented and what is correct. Make your message emotionally resonant, because emotions outweigh facts. Do not be afraid of a simplistic approach. Your opponents do the same.

The effectiveness of so-called debunking—that is, exposing and revealing fake news as such—is hotly debated (Caulfield, 2020). There is a growing consensus that it is of little use to bombard recipients of fake news with "true" and "correct" facts. Most people do not accept the actual facts and stick to their original views. I have explained why a good piece of disinformation will always be more attractive to most people than a clean and sterile piece of fact (see Chap. 5).

However, this is an important point which some lawyers will not like: The worst strategy in the event of a disinformation attack is to remain silent. This silence is often demanded by lawyers, who justify it with references to "ongoing proceedings," "ongoing investigations," or "potential liability risks."

I also consider the advice to adopt "strategic silence"—a temporary pause in communication intended to buy time for the next steps—to be a dangerous piece of advice in this context. While it may sound reasonable, it fails in the face of harsh reality. This is the most damaging advice I can imagine for a company under a high-intensity, high-speed disinformation attack, where every minute counts in mounting a defense and where rapid decision-making is essential.

Communication in response to an attack passes through various stages of escalation. Gathering the basic facts about the attack (What? Where? Who? When? Why?) takes some time. Nevertheless, there should never be a period of silence, least of all a strategic one. On the contrary, the company must communicate quickly and convincingly in a strategic manner.

Relevant studies support my approach to strategic communication. They have found that silence in the context of disinformation can negatively affect the attitudes of those targeted by the disinformation—precisely the people the company is trying to win back. When a company remains silent or fails to communicate, an information vacuum arises. Anyone who paid attention in physics class knows that a vacuum does everything it can to cease being a vacuum—it draws in everything around it (hence the term "vacuum cleaner"). However, this information vacuum does not suck up dust but rather rumors and false information. If a company allows an information vacuum to develop, the disinformation agents not only have free rein but also an audience that is receptive to disinformation and conspiracy theories. This must be avoided at all costs (Schmid & Betsch, 2019).

Therefore, go public as quickly as possible, using all available channels, but especially those where you can identify the origin of the disinformation. Seek out the media with the widest reach, because when the media report on the issue, more people will learn that the disinformation being spread about your company is untrue.

In this way, you create counter-information that neutralizes the disinformation. Do not listen to those who advise you to refrain from communicating at first, as this—as described above—has a devastating effect.

Companies surveyed about how they responded to a disinformation attack stated that they tended to act "rather cautiously." "Very few companies pursue an offensive communication strategy" (Wolter et al., 2019). In doing so, companies squander a major opportunity to respond quickly and effectively with the help of the public.

"One Very, Very Last Thing"—Facts Versus Opinions

A company facing a disinformation attack is initially confronted with the question of how to counter false and toxic information. Instinctively, it tries to refute the falsehoods with facts and evidence. It places its hope in the power of facts and is disappointed when this approach fails.

Why does this approach fail? Because opinions overwhelm facts. Because, when faced with an emotionally charged audience, facts bounce off rubber walls. Because negative news spreads more rapidly. It feels like fighting windmills. What can we do when our facts fail to get through and are not heard?

The cosmetics and food industries have found a solution to combine two incompatible substances—fat and water: they add emulsifiers. Emulsifiers are compounds with two sides: one binds to water molecules and the other to fat molecules. This creates a fat–water emulsion, which we encounter daily in various forms, such as in our drinking milk or in body lotions.

What we need, therefore, is a kind of emulsifier to enable facts to connect with an emotionally stirred and opinionated audience. This is possible if we pay closer attention to the emotional state of the audience.

Before presenting facts, we should first determine which emotions are dominant—anger, fear, sadness, envy, jealousy, or even disappointment—and why they have arisen. People in highly emotional states are only receptive to information once they feel that the other party acknowledges and takes their emotions seriously.

During the coronavirus pandemic, a host of health policymakers, scientists, and vaccine manufacturers tried to combat disinformation, misinformation, and conspiracy theories with facts. They failed because of an overwhelming emotion, fueled by professional disinformers—primarily from Russia: fear. Fear of something we do not understand, combined with a distrust of science cultivated by the disinformers. It was the fear of a new type of vaccine, a vaccine that did not even have to undergo the usual regulatory trials. This new unknown unsettled people and laid the groundwork for bizarre disinformation about alleged side effects and conspiracy theories.

The facts about vaccines and their (side) effects did not reach a significant group of people, resulting in the current situation with vaccine refusers and the resurgence of diseases (measles, typhoid, polio, whooping cough) that were once considered eradicated. Emotions have blocked the acceptance of facts.

In today's world, often referred to as the post-truth era, companies must present the facts they wish to communicate differently. More human, more accessible, warmer. The figures and data a company wants to share need to be transformed into something relatable. This is laborious, but it is worthwhile.

This means, in defending against disinformation: Read the room! Find out what the audience is feeling. Show that you understand their emotions. Wrap the facts in humanity, in empathy. Be open and honest about what you do not know yet and what you are seeking to find out. Very soon, the rubber walls will become more permeable, and the facts will penetrate the wall. Empathy and understanding for people's feelings are the emulsifier when communicating facts to an emotionally charged audience.

The American researcher Renée DiResta has studied the success of influencers and published her findings in the book "Invisible Rulers," a book I can truly recommend to everyone. She found that successful influencers reach so many people because they interact with them. They comment, they like their followers' posts, they speak their language, and they see directly in the posts what moves their followers, allowing them to respond. Traditional media do not work this way. That is why influencers now wield incredible power over millions, a power that traditional media can only dream of today. This is also why the Trump administration sought contact with favorable political influencers and invited them into the White House press room.

"Slowdown in the Fog of War"—Conversation with Crisis Manager Caroline Sapriel (CS&A)

Caroline Sapriel is the founder and Managing Partner of CS&A, a specialist risk, crisis, and business continuity management consulting firm with offices in Hong Kong, the United Kingdom, Belgium, the Netherlands, Singapore, and the United States. With over 25 years of experience in risk and crisis management, Caroline is recognized as a leader in her field and is known for her ability to provide tailored, results-oriented advice at the highest level. Caroline regularly speaks at international conferences and seminars on risk and crisis management. She is a guest lecturer on corporate crisis management at the University of Antwerp and at the graduate school of public administration at Leiden University.

Caroline, we've talked about disinformation campaigns before. As I mentioned, I wanted to update our understanding for the international market, and I needed an international crisis manager—that's you. So, first question: What types of disinformation attacks on corporations have you encountered so far? Is this a new phenomenon?

Nearly every client is talking about this now. It seems we live in an era where every event or announcement becomes an opportunity to spin, distort, or fabricate disinformation. In my view, disinformation has always existed alongside information. As far back as we can remember, there have always been disinformation campaigns. They simply become more intense during crises, as each side tries to defend its own narrative—hence the old saying about the "fog of war."

What has changed in this "war"?

Today, with social media, disinformation has reached proportions we could hardly have imagined. It is easier, faster, and operates on a scale that was unthinkable even a few years ago. That is why we always advise clients to expect distortion in a crisis and to set realistic expectations. The latest major challenge, of course, is deepfakes. Deepfakes are not just manipulations—they are complete fabrications. And the technology has advanced to the point where experts predict that within a year, it will be impossible to distinguish real from fake.

That's astonishing—when we reach a point where even professionals can't tell fake from real, what can we do?

First, slow down. Everyone preaches speed in crisis response, but when faced with something disturbing or suspicious, the first step should be not to react impulsively. Much of social media is designed to amplify shock and negativity, so people tend to react quickly. But not all communications teams are as digitally literate as they should be. So, we tell clients: improve your digital literacy, verify before reacting, and invest in tools that can detect deepfakes.

In a crisis, though, when a disinformation attack hits like a tsunami, there's little time to react. Once it starts spreading, it can sink your product or your reputation.

I used to advocate speed. But now, I tell clients: slow down and conduct a risk analysis. Accept that in any crisis, you are going to lose something—the goal is to minimize that loss. And not every response needs to take place on social media. Distinguish between your stakeholders. If disinformation is affecting your customers, put people on the phone and call them. Don't just use the same channel to counter with facts—it often doesn't work. The world is too polarized for facts alone to change minds.

Debunking doesn't seem to work effectively against fake news. Many people believe what they see and hear or what they want to see and hear—you can't reach them at all.

Exactly. You can say, "We appear to be victims of a disinformation campaign," but you must communicate this powerfully and confidently. Otherwise, it can sound defensive. That's where communicators' skills are critical—crafting strong messages without appearing weak or reactive.

Let's talk about transparency. You can't hide. You need to go public, tell the media you've been ambushed by a disinformation attack, and that you don't yet know who is behind it or what their motives are—but you will keep them informed.

Yes, that's a basic principle of crisis management. Years ago, when social media first emerged, someone said, "You fight a social media fire with social media water." So yes, use the same channels, be transparent, and acknowledge the situation—but also prioritize your stakeholders and explore alternative ways of communicating with them.

Do you think companies are prepared for something like this?

Consumer-oriented companies have the resources to manage content. But B2B companies are less prepared. The speed and complexity of disinformation are taking everyone by surprise. Some companies feel helpless. Many still underestimate the scale of manipulation, especially since bots and AI massively amplify falsehoods. Some are better prepared than others, but overall, readiness is still too low.

Let's talk about the role of lawyers during a disinformation attack on a company. In crises, legal departments tend to slow things down. Management often waits for legal advice before acting, but in disinformation cases, there's no time for that. In the wake of a disinformation attack, do lawyers need to redefine their role or at least show more courage in accepting a certain degree of liability risk?

I agree—as much as I value lawyers and the rule of law, they are often seen as gatekeepers. In crises, leadership often defers to them for decisions, which can be a mistake. Lawyers need to understand the impact of public perception on reputational value. In disinformation cases, lawyers are not always the right people to lead decisions. What is needed is proper risk analysis. Most people are poor at assessing risk under pressure. And few decisions in a crisis are black and white—there are too many variables. So, you must weigh pros and cons, accept uncertainty, and take calculated risks. Many leaders avoid that by deferring to lawyers or insurers for protection.

Every crisis needs a "War Room", but you need a specific team during a disinformation crisis in this "War Room". Who should be in that room?

You need security experts, investigators, intelligence specialists, communicators, and yes, lawyers—but mainly to assess legal implications. It's a multidisciplinary effort. In some ways, we need to think like intelligence agencies: detect, analyze, and respond—sometimes even counterattack with the truth. The challenge is that many security professionals focus too much on control, when what's needed is investigation and agility.

So, the crisis team's composition shifts. In some crises, lawyers dominate; in disinformation crises, forensic experts or communicators must lead. Lawyers hate making quick decisions—they prefer assessing damages for weeks.

True. But if you think about it, disinformation is not entirely new—it's the modern version of rumor. There's that saying, "There's no smoke without fire." Most disinformation contains a kernel of truth—that's what makes it believable.

That small piece of truth gives disinformation credibility. We are talking about the "fine line of plausibility".

And that's how we used to handle rumors: acknowledge, check, and act. It's the same principle now—just harder because it spreads on social networks and blends reality with fabrication. When AI generates disinformation at scale, reality itself blurs. That's why technology will eventually help us catch up—to detect and debunk faster.

Companies must also remember that everything they do—or fail to do—stays online forever. Even years later, old material can resurface in new disinformation attacks. And when people see that small "kernel of truth," it adds plausibility to the lie.

That's how conspiracy theories thrive. At the end of the day, the same crisis management principles apply: you need the right skill set, strong tools, and clarity about your objective. Is it to debunk, to reassure, or to convince? You must know what you're aiming for.

The priority should be to identify who is behind a disinformation attack and what their motive is. This makes it easier to communicate clearly about what happened and why.

That takes time. You need investigation and analysis. Ultimately, the question is, do you want to emerge from this with credibility, even if not everyone is convinced, or do you want to remain silent and appear guilty by omission?

We also need a cleanup operation afterwards—including lawyers.

Absolutely. Lawyers play an important role in this. My concern is when leadership gives them overriding decision-making power in a crisis.

That usually happens when a CEO is afraid to take risks.

Exactly. That's a matter of crisis leadership.

In crisis leadership, you may have the same people in the room, but their roles shift dramatically in a disinformation crisis.

That's something people underestimate. Managing crises requires more than experience—it requires crisis leadership skills. Most leaders are not trained for that. They are accustomed to business challenges, not the emotional, reputational, and psychological stresses of disinformation crises. These situations test values and resilience. Leaders must face attacks that feel deeply personal, where credibility is constantly undermined. If they become self-righteous—insisting "this isn't true"—it won't help. Only evidence, if available, can work in their favor. In fact, teams need to become better at discernment—distinguishing fact from manipulation. We have lost much critical thinking and media literacy. Prevention and preparedness must focus on rebuilding those skills. During a crisis, yes, speed matters—but values and clarity matter more. Ask yourself: What do we want to look like when this is over? That's what counts. Literacy, critical thinking and humility. And one core principle of leadership: expect the unexpected!

References

Caulfield, T. (2020). Does debunking work? Correcting COVID-19 misinformation on social media. In C. Flood, V. MacDonnell, J. Philpott, et al. (Eds.), *Vulnerable: The law, policy and ethics of Covid-19* (pp. 183–200). University of Ottawa Press.

Schmid, P., & Betsch, C. (2019). Effective strategies for rebutting science denialism in public discussions. *Nature Human Behaviour, 3*, 931–939.

Wolter, J., Grothe, M., & Heim, U. (as of July 2019). *# Disinformation—Situation, forecast, defense*. ASW-Bundesverband.

The Role of Lawyers in Countering Disinformation Attacks 14

As I have already indicated, we need to talk about the role of lawyers in countering disinformation attacks. But first, a few fundamental remarks about the legal framework for defending against disinformation:

In the legal field, we will soon see changes and adjustments, both in criminal and civil law. Especially in the field of deepfakes and synthetic media, today's lawyers are not particularly well equipped. Lawyers are trained to work with text. The only statute book in Germany, for example, that includes images is the Road Traffic Act. There, all common traffic signs are depicted. That's it.

Lawyers have often not learned how to decipher images. This too will have to change. The EU is taking the lead and has recognized the dangers of AI and deepfakes. Vera Jourová, the EU Commissioner for Values and Transparency, has called on more than 40 signatories of the "Code of Practice on Online Disinformation" to clearly label deepfakes and AI-generated content so that users can immediately recognize such content. Addressing the online platforms directly, she made it unequivocally clear that she wants to see labeling "quickly" and "immediately."

In doing so, the European Vera Jourová touched on a classic American point of contention: the First Amendment, that is, the right to freedom of expression. "I have often said that our main task is to protect freedom of speech. But when it comes to AI-generated content, I see no right to freedom of expression for the machines. This is therefore also a return to the good old pillars of our legal system. And that is why, within the framework of the Code of Practice, we want to continue working based on this very fundamental idea," she added.

The times are turbulent—so turbulent that some would prefer to duck and hide. Developments are rapid, tactics are evolving, and defensive mechanisms are improving, even if, in this asymmetric conflict, they are always lagging behind the attackers.

Let us return to a specific defensive scenario: In the event of a disinformation attack, lawyers play a special role, both in the war room, where defense strategies are discussed and initiated, and after the defensive battle, when it comes to erasing

U. Wolff, *Disinformation Attacks On Businesses*, Management for Professionals,
https://doi.org/10.1007/978-3-658-51407-5_14

the traces of the conflict and eliminating the remaining fragments of disinformation in the media and on the internet—permanently.

Corporate management relies on the legal advice of lawyers. Large companies maintain legal departments, and virtually every management decision, every planned step, is based on the expertise of legal professionals in order to navigate as safely and unchallenged as possible through the complexities of laws, contracts, and agreements.Even in crisis situations, management rightly relies on legal counsel, which is why lawyers are present in the crisis team's war room. However, the role of lawyers within the crisis team shifts when it comes to disinformation attacks. This is because disinformation attacks differ from other types of crises.When a disinformation attack hits a company, it often does so with a force and speed that simply overwhelms traditional crisis responses. A disinformation attack is akin to a tsunami: it builds up almost invisibly and quietly, only to break over the company all the more rapidly, powerfully, and forcefully.

This escalation almost never occurs through traditional channels such as press reports or political debates—it erupts digitally—and may then, if at all, be reflected in traditional channels, as we saw with the Russia-driven bedbug hysteria of 2023. Forged documents, manipulated or deepfake videos, orchestrated social media campaigns, and deliberately seeded narratives: all are designed to destroy the trust of customers, suppliers, politicians, regulators, and stakeholders and shareholders and to destabilize or even fundamentally alter decision-making processes. These attacks are fast, confusing, and above all, asymmetric. They move at a pace that is barely compatible with the often lengthy legal processes and certainly not in line with the usual legal procedures of civil and criminal litigation. To learn more about this, I spoke with renowned, highly experienced lawyers in the UK, the USA, and Germany. All of them have dealt with disinformation attacks and have demonstrated their legal expertise in the process.

Persephone Bridgman Baker, a partner at the London law firm Carter Ruck, represents celebrities, ultra-high-net-worth individuals, politicians, and companies that come under public attack. I asked her about the disinformation attacks she has had to deal with recently:

> When I talk about disinformation, we need a definition: the deliberate distribution of information that is knowingly false. Disinformation can, of course, create misinformation as it spreads. The attacks I've encountered often relate to issues already prominent in the news cycle—links to politicians, governments, or regimes. For example, during COVID, we saw attacks related to procurement of protective materials. More recently, there were attacks connected to the Ukraine conflict. These campaigns typically try to connect a company to an already circulating negative narrative. They're not always large-scale attacks on major corporations. In my field, I often see attacks against individuals that later snowball into corporate issues when misinformation is republished by the press. Sometimes a very small, even trivial falsehoods can escalate dramatically.

A disinformation attack can therefore start small and then turn into a monster. Just like a tsunami. We saw this with the Paris bedbug hysteria in 2023. Tiny bedbug, huge impact, enormous damage.

Persephone also pointed out another important aspect, which, as a media lawyer in an English-speaking country, she must pay particular attention to:

> English-language media is particularly damaging because of its global reach. If a story is published by the Times, Guardian, or BBC, it spreads globally. These outlets can unintentionally legitimize disinformation. Publishers can become pawns in a larger game.

This makes sense, even for disinformation actors: anyone seeking rapid, global dissemination of their disinformation should choose an English-language medium. The disinformation then travels around the globe, from the UK (if it starts there) to the USA, Canada, Australia, New Zealand, and many other countries. We have seen this especially in the celebrity sphere: if (false) information about a person appears in a British tabloid, there is a high chance that Australians, Americans, and Canadians will also hear about it.

The British lawyer **Dominic Crossley** from the venerable law firm Payne Hicks Beach in London told me about a case that could be resolved purely through legal means. Dominic, who specializes, among other things, in defamation and harassment of companies and high-profile individuals, cited the case as an example of a complex and sophisticated disinformation campaign aimed at destroying the reputation of his client, a well-known entrepreneur:

> There was a street demonstration against one of our clients. It looked like a grassroots protest: placards, chanting—the usual. We noticed the van used to transport the signs and equipment. At this example, it is easy to see how a clever legal maneuver made it possible to uncover the identity of those commissioning the attack.

14.1 The Role of Lawyers in the War Room

For lawyers, a disinformation attack opens the door to a different world. And this is precisely where the central question arises: What role can—and should—lawyers actually play when a crisis unfolds faster than legal proceedings can ever respond? Are lawyers even capable of handling a high-velocity crisis?

At this point, I would like to refer to my colleague Caroline Sapriel, whom I interviewed on this topic (see above). As an internationally active crisis manager, she has fought many battles and gained experience working with lawyers in crisis situations. She says:

> In crises, leadership often defers to them for decisions, which can be a mistake. Lawyers need to understand the impact of public perception on reputational value. In disinformation cases, lawyers aren't always the right people to lead decisions. What's needed is proper risk analysis. Most people are poor at assessing risk under pressure. And few decisions in a crisis are black and white—there are too many variables. So, you must weigh pros and cons, accept uncertainty, and take calculated risks. Many leaders avoid that by deferring to lawyers or insurers for protection.

Caroline addresses an important point: the relationship between management and lawyers. The key term that connects both is "liability risks." Management naturally wants to avoid these, while lawyers must draw management's attention to them. Not infrequently, a potential liability risk identified by the lawyer kills off an important decision that management would need to make to avert harm to the company. Caroline puts it this way:

> My concern is when leadership gives them the overriding decision-making power in a crisis.

A crisis is an exceptional situation in which management may well have to make unpopular or legally risky decisions. Management must have the courage to accept liability risks to—let us put it dramatically—secure the survival of the company or a product. Management has a duty to its shareholders and stakeholders to avert harm from the company, and this sometimes means going against the legal assessment of the lawyers.

This tension between legal caution and practical necessity for action is also described by the lawyers I interviewed.

A disinformation attack has characteristics that make it a very particular form of corporate crisis.

First: It acts extremely quickly. The frequently cited study by Soroush Vosoughi et al. (2018) shows that false information spreads faster and more widely on social networks than true information. Other studies also show that well-constructed disinformation, which deliberately targets the preconceptions (prejudices and stereotypes) of recipients, can easily bypass critical thinking barriers and cannot be countered even by communicating facts.

Second: The perpetrators usually remain invisible. They use technical obfuscation methods, bot networks, and sock puppet accounts. The NATO StratCom COE in Riga, which analyzes disinformation attacks from Russia and China, publishes highly informative reports on the latest tools and tactics used by attackers.

Third: The effort required by attackers is minimal, while companies must mobilize considerable resources. This asymmetric character was aptly described by Krebs (2020) as an "information asymmetry shock"—and explains why many organizations are initially completely blindsided. In this moment of shock, two entirely different cognitive worlds collide: the speed of digital dissemination mechanisms and the slowness of legal precision.

This also occurs in a war room, which should be established immediately after an attack. In a crisis, actors from completely different worlds of thought and action come together here: communications professionals, IT forensics experts, analysts, executives—and, of course, lawyers. Communications professionals think in minutes, IT forensics experts in patterns and data streams, analysts in motives and network schemata. Lawyers, on the other hand, are trained to clarify responsibilities and weigh risks. This difference in logic almost inevitably leads to tensions. In the early phase of an attack, lawyers often act as a brake—simply because their processes are geared toward diligence and verifiability. At the same time, many CEOs expect all members of the crisis team to be immediately operational, especially in crisis situations.

The reality, however, is different and demands a fundamental reassessment and the courage to make risky decisions on the part of management. **Persephone Bridgman Baker** of Carter Ruck in London describes the role of lawyers in the war room as follows:

> Clients often need guidance. Lawyers coordinate rather than execute every task—ensuring no missteps occur and assessing whether a legal claim might follow. If the attacker is identifiable, we can seek urgent injunctive relief — sometimes within hours. If the attacker is anonymous, we can seek relief against the operator of a social media handle. We can even serve proceedings via social media.

The role of the lawyer in defending against disinformation attacks is therefore neither static nor self-evident. Disinformation attacks force companies to rebalance legal certainty and speed. It is a misconception to believe that lawyers can lead the defense against an attack from the outset. Equally mistaken would be to sideline them entirely.

As long as the attacker remains unidentified, the lawyer can do little—sometimes nothing at all. Legal action requires an identifiable opposing party: someone to whom a cease-and-desist letter can be addressed, against whom an interim injunction can be sought, or against whom a claim for injunctive relief can be asserted. In the initial hours of an attack, such identification is virtually never available, and the pressing question occupying those present in the war room is: "Who is the wizard behind the curtain attacking us?" The lawyer finds themselves in a highly unsatisfactory position, which I have often described as follows: it is like a sword fight in a dark room. The blows come from invisible assailants. Any legal response would be futile. Filing complaints with the public prosecutor's office consumes time and achieves nothing as long as the attacker remains unidentified. For this reason, forensics is of central importance at this stage. IT and OSINT specialists analyze digital traces, metadata, posting intervals, botnet activities, linguistic patterns, deepfakes, and monitor digital spaces. Their goal: so-called attribution—that is, assigning an attack to a probable perpetrator. This conceptual and methodological foundation was described by Rid and Buchanan (Rid & Buchanan, 2015) as the core of modern information security. To hold an attacker accountable for their actions, they must logically first be identified as the attacker.

The mentioned researcher Thomas Rid makes it clear why what he terms "non-attribution" is the norm in a disinformation attack and how this differs from a terrorist or military attack, where perpetrators do not hesitate to present themselves as the originators. In cyber and disinformation attacks, the opposite is true: here, non-attribution is the rule and attribution the exception. Rid concludes:

> This important contrast makes clear that cyberattacks are especially well suited for two activities that have always tended towards the shadows: crime and espionage (Rid, 2017).

Only after at least 12 h or a day following the onset of the attack does the situation usually become sufficiently clear for initial communication decisions to be made. The CEO, the head of communications, and the crisis team—all must now decide: Do we respond publicly? Do we have enough reliable information to respond? How do we respond? Whom do we address? Do we activate an internal information chain? Or do we deliberately remain silent for the time being? I have already taken a position on this question elsewhere. Many lawyers tend to refrain from communicating at first to gain time for a legal assessment of the situation and potential risks, but in a high-intensity disinformation attack, we do not have that time.

Lawyers accompany this process in an advisory capacity, assess potential liability risks, and point out formulations that could have capital market or reputational consequences. However, they must not dominate at this moment; they must recognize that other disciplines now take precedence, such as forensics and communications. As Wardle and Derakhshan (2017) demonstrate, early communicative positioning often determines whether a company can regain the interpretive authority during the crisis.

Only when forensics can provide a sufficiently robust picture does the phase begin in which effective legal measures can be initiated. The German media lawyer **Dr Diana Grün** confirms from her practice precisely this dependence of legal steps on reliable attribution:

> When a massive disinformation attack is underway, it is possible to react very quickly. Interim injunctions can be issued in urgent cases within a few days—I have even received decisions on the same or the following day. Of course, there are also cases where you have to wait three weeks, but in many scenarios, it really does happen very quickly.

Only after reliable attribution do lawyers have at least a roughly identified opposing party and thus the basis for concrete legal action. They enforce takedown requests with platforms, work with disclosure claims, prepare interim injunctions in expedited proceedings, and secure digital evidence so that it can later be used in criminal or civil proceedings. Studies and practical reports from litigation PR (Holzinger & Wolff, 2009) as well as from cybersecurity research (Helmus et al., 2020) underscore the importance of this phase: legal precision now plays a decisive role in determining whether the source of the damage can be contained. Once the attacker is identified, their motives soon become apparent. If we have the identity of the attacker and their motive, the time comes for communication—but not without cooperation with the lawyers. Once the acute threat has been averted and the lawyers know how to proceed, a phase begins in which communication again comes more prominent. The focus now shifts to stabilizing reputation, ensuring transparency with key stakeholders, and rebuilding trust. Legal professionals support this phase by ensuring that public statements are legally robust and do not create risks for subsequent legal action against the company. At the same time, a systematic legal follow-up begins in the background: assessing potential claims against the perpetrators, adapting internal compliance and communication guidelines, and developing prevention strategies. This feedback loop between crisis and structure is essential to enable faster and more resilient responses to future attacks. Contemporary disinformation research—such as that by Pomerantsev (Pomerantsev, 2019) or the RAND studies on "Truth Decay" (Helmus et al., 2020)—provides the guidelines for modern crisis management. Lawyers should not only be brought in during emergencies but must also be integrated into crisis processes at an early stage.

14.2 Pathways to Faster Decision-Making

To be able to respond as quickly as possible to a disinformation attack, preparation and dry runs for lawyers are required, during which the mechanisms of digital platforms are explained to them, and they familiarize themselves with the legal defense tools for takedown procedures and the technical basics of forensics. They must be acquainted with established workflows with IT teams and communications departments and define in advance how to accelerate the coordination of necessary communications. In this way, the lawyer transforms from a roadblock that slows down processes into an enabler of rapid, legally sound decisions.

Diana Grün, a lawyer at the German law firm Schalast, describes in very concrete terms from her practice what this rapid, prepared action looks like:

> When rumors and false factual claims are being spread, you cannot wait until other media pick them up and disseminate them further. The longer you wait, the harder it becomes to contain the misinformation. As soon as you have a court decision—such as a preliminary injunction—in hand, you can present it to Meta. If another media outlet or user then repeats the same false factual claim, Meta typically responds much more quickly if there is already a court order. The key point is: do not lose time. Do not hope it will "go away on its own" but take active countermeasures.

The British media lawyer **Persephone Bridgman Baker**, partner at **Carter-Ruck**, is acutely aware of the speed issue and the time pressure under which lawyers must operate in the "war room":

> Time is the most valuable resource. When clients come to us after an attack, we must learn their business, identify the bad actor, brief the PR team, and structure the response—this costs precious hours.

Dominic Crossley of **Payne Hicks Beach** also describes the reality at the onset of a crisis from the law firm's perspective:

> Often, we get a call or email from a client we've never worked with before: "A journalist has approached us. We have until tomorrow afternoon to respond. This is going to be a front-page story or a lead item on the news." We then must understand the business, understand the facts, and understand the threat, very, very quickly.
>
> As lawyers, we must be very careful not to use or repeat information until we're satisfied it's accurate. Verifying facts takes time. So, there's a tension between the need for speed and the need for accuracy. It requires very intense work at the beginning of a case: we need to

get to know the client's business, we need to understand the threat, and we need to help them explain their position. It's hard work—but it's also what I love. I enjoy meeting people at those moments of crisis, learning very quickly, and then helping to shape strategy—both legal and communicative.

Of course, a prerequisite is that lawyers acquire a clear and precise definition of what disinformation is, how it differs from misinformation, malinformation, and fake news, and what makes it so dangerous. The Japanese researcher Tomoko Nagasako from the Sasakawa Peace Foundation is very clear on this point:

If the multiple perspectives of disinformation are not completely understood, it would be difficult to find appropriate measures for this sophisticated information warfare. (Nagasako, 2020)

All the lawyers I spoke to agree on one point: both in the USA and in the UK, lawyers and courts can act quickly. Sven Krüger, one of the most renowned media lawyers in Germany, does not see the often-criticized slowness of German courts as an obstacle, especially in the field of defamation law:

It is possible to enforce prohibitions through expedited court proceedings. In defamation law, this is even the norm. However, it is necessary for those affected to react immediately and not wait for months.

His Hamburg colleague **Diana Grün,** a lawyer at the German law firm Schalast, shares this view. She describes from her own practice in very concrete terms what this rapid, prepared action looks like:

When rumors and untrue factual claims are being spread, you cannot wait until other media pick them up and is disseminated further. The longer one waits, the more difficult it becomes to contain the misinformation. As soon as a court decision—such as a preliminary injunction—is obtained, it can be presented to Meta. If another user then repeats the same false factual claim, Meta typically responds much more quickly when a court order is already in place. The key point is: do not lose time. Do not hope that it will "disappear on its own" but take active countermeasures.

Diana Grün praises Germany as a legal venue, particularly in terms of speed:

I have great confidence in the German courts. When a major disinformation attack occurs, one can respond very quickly here. Preliminary injunctions can be issued within a few days in urgent cases—I have even received decisions on the same day or the next. Of course, there are cases where one must wait three weeks, but in many situations, it is really very fast.

What works very well are cease-and-desist orders, counterstatements, and corrections. Preliminary injunction proceedings are generally an extremely fast and efficient tool.

Especially in comparison to the USA, she sees Germany as having an advantage in cases of disinformation attacks:

In the US, the First Amendment is very strongly protected. The right to freedom of expression is particularly safeguarded there. In Germany, the balance is different: individuals have

> strong personal rights, and companies also have corporate personality rights. It is easier here to act against reporting that infringes personal rights or damages a company's reputation. There is also the cost factor: legal and court fees in Germany are significantly lower than in the US. You do not have to invest a fortune to pursue a case. In addition, criminal proceedings are possible in Germany—insult, defamation, and slander are criminal offences. In the US, this varies by state, and in many cases, such criminal offenses no longer exist.

However, before taking legal action, the attacker must first be identified. Attribution is the key word here, both for lawyers and communicators.

> "If the attacker is identifiable, we can seek injunctive relief—sometimes within hours. If the attacker is anonymous, we can seek relief against the operator of a social media handle. We can serve proceedings via social media," explains Persephone Bridgman Baker of Carter Ruck in London.
>
> Procedural flexibility and judicial discretion mean courts can still respond effectively. Trials can take years—which may not give you the redress you need to repair reputational harm—so the availability of urgent measures is key.

Lawyers can only act effectively once the attacker is visible—before that, communication and forensics take precedence, followed by legal action. Companies that understand this dynamic and establish appropriate structures are not only better prepared for digital attacks. They can actively and effectively defend against them. Without legal precision, an attack cannot be neutralized in the long term—but without communicative and technical speed, a company has little chance of surviving the critical early phase. Successful defense, therefore, does not consist in prioritizing one discipline but in the interplay of all relevant forces—from forensics to legal strategy. In practice, this means that lawyers must learn not only to minimize legal risks but also to enable communicative speed.

14.3 Deepfakes as a Challenge

Deepfakes exacerbate all the problems described: they undermine trust in audiovisual evidence, facilitate identity theft, and make it extremely easy for attackers to produce credible false evidence. I discussed this with the two lawyers **Prateek Swaika** and **Joseph Kroetsch**. Both work for the law firm **Boies Schiller Flexner**—Prateek in London and Joseph in New York. Prateek published a widely noted article on deepfakes in London's "The Times". In our conversation, Joseph described the historical dimension of this breach of trust in images:

> For a relatively short period in history—say from the late 19th century until now—we've lived in a world where photographs, audio recordings, and then video recordings were treated as "hard evidence." Yes, you could fake them, but it was hard and expensive. So, juries, judges, and the public could reasonably feel that they were seeing or hearing what actually happened. Deepfakes threaten that. We may be returning to a world in which we mostly rely on eyewitness testimony and credibility judgments, as legal systems did for thousands of years.

A particularly striking case that demonstrates the devastating consequences of a deepfake attack on a company is the attack on the British engineering firm **Arup** in Hong Kong: There, fraudsters used a deceptively realistic deepfake video conference in which supposed company executives appeared. An employee, believing he was speaking with his CFO and other colleagues, subsequently transferred millions—firmly convinced he was following a legitimate instruction. Here, disinformation, fraud, and identity theft merge into a new dimension: the attack does not only take place in public communication but right in the middle of the company's operational processes. And the attack is not limited to the visual; voices, too, can now be perfectly synthesized.

The London-based lawyer **Prateek Swaika** describes how profoundly such developments have changed his own practice:

> Voice replication has become very easy. In running our office, we have had to implement manual checks to prevent someone from impersonating me and sending a voicemail to our finance manager saying, "Please transfer X to this bank account to pay a court award," or "Move this amount from our client account." […] We require a human being to pick up the phone, speak to the other person, and confirm any voicemail instructions. Bank account details are sent as images rather than text, and payments are manually double-checked. Many banks have responded in a similar way. Some have deactivated voice recognition as a security factor.

A Microsoft manager I met in Brussels also described such precautions against voice identity theft. At Microsoft, employees are instructed not to leave voice messages longer than 3 s, out of concern that their voice could be used for a deepfake.

And of course, beyond the Arup case in Hong Kong, there are now many other incidents. The World Economic Forum regards deepfakes as one of the greatest current threats to our society—and to our economy.

Joseph told me about a German company that was targeted in a so-called "short-and-distort" campaign. An individual posed as a respected financial analyst and used this fake persona to disparage the German company's stock on Twitter—after having bet on the share price falling.

> You can imagine even more extreme scenarios with deepfakes: Someone could spoof Elon Musk in a video saying, "Tesla is shutting down," and a short seller could make a lot of money before the truth comes out. The deepfake would simply be the method used to commit fraud or market manipulation, not the underlying wrong itself.

At the regulatory level, Swaika sees a tendency not to criminalize the tool "deepfake" itself, but rather the underlying acts:

> "From the government's perspective, there is already criminal law for theft and fraud. Their approach is often: 'We do not need a new "deepfake law" to criminalize the tool. We'll treat the use of a deepfake as evidence in a fraud or theft case under existing legislation.'" His colleague Joseph adds: "There's strong concern here about overbanning. Deepfakes and generative AI tools can also be used in legitimate, even beneficial ways."

This makes it clear: for companies, dealing with deepfakes is not primarily a technical issue, but one of governance, evidence preservation, and crisis management, as well as awareness.

14.4 The Clean-Up Crew

I consider it essential to use legal means and substantiated arguments to prevent traditional media from spreading disinformation, even after a disinformation attack has been repelled. There are good reasons for this: first, most media outlets today have an online and social media presence. This makes them accelerants for the spread of disinformation. It is crucial to prevent, at all costs, disinformation from taking root on the internet and remaining permanently accessible. Second, disinformation actors aim for dissemination in reputable media and celebrate this as a success, as it lends more weight to their campaign. When spreading false information, they refer to the fact that "even the XY newspaper" reported on the circumstance propagated by the disinformers. In this way, they exploit people's trust in reputable media, thereby giving disinformation greater weight and credibility.

After the acute phase comes the clean-up phase, in which disinformation that has spread and become entrenched online or in traditional media must be legally removed and deleted. Anything that remains in the media can later be found and referenced in a subsequent disinformation attack. Therefore, if media outlets react overzealously and fall for disinformation because they have failed in their journalistic duty of care and publish false or fabricated information, then the lawyer can, should, or must demand that they cease and desist and require the deletion of such information.

Dominic Crossley points to the legal hurdles that make it difficult for companies to defend themselves in court:

> Now, for a company to bring a defamation claim in the UK, it must prove that the words complained of cause serious harm—and in the case of a corporation, serious harm likely to cause financial loss. Before you even really start your case, you've got to show, on your balance sheet, that these statements have cost you money. For big companies, that's extremely hard. Businesses are complex, revenue and profit move for all kinds of reasons. It's rarely possible to point to one article and say, "That's why our numbers dipped." The result? There's much greater latitude for what can be published about companies. The legal threshold is so high that the number of defamation cases brought by corporates has fallen sharply. But that doesn't mean there are fewer attacks.

This leads to the absurd situation in which the number of disinformation attacks on companies in the UK is increasing but the number of lawsuits is decreasing, because it has become incredibly difficult for companies to prove damage.

> That absolutely makes life easier for attackers. It makes it easier for people who engage in malicious disinformation, and it makes the whole information environment around corporates less reliable.

This brings us to the point: lawyers are not only essential in the war room but also as "clean-up crews" afterward—to prevent disinformation from surviving in archives, search engines, and media environments as seemingly legitimate truth.

References

Helmus, T. C., Prier, J., & Bodine-Baron, E. (2020). *Russian propaganda hits the truth decay target*. RAND Corporation.

Holzinger, S., & Wolff, U. (2009). *In the name of the public: Litigation PR as a strategic tool*. Gabler Verlag.

Krebs, B. (2020). Information asymmetry and digital threats. *Journal of Cybersecurity Studies, 4*(2), 25.

Nagasako, T. (2020). Global disinformation campaigns and legal challenges. *International Cyber Security Law Review, 1*, 125–136. Springer.

Pomerantsev, P. (2019). *This is not propaganda: Adventures in the war against reality*. PublicAffairs.

Rid, T. (2017). *Cyber war will not take place, conflict classics*. Hurst.

Rid, T., & Buchanan, B. (2015). Attributing cyberattacks. *Journal of Strategic Studies, 38*(1–2), 4–37. Retrieved from: https://doi.org/10.1080/01402390.2014.977382

Vosoughi, S., Roy, D., & Aral, S. (2018). The spread of true and false news online. *Science, 359*(6380), 1146–1151. Retrieved from: https://doi.org/10.1126/science.aap9559

Wardle, C., & Derakhshan, H. (2017). *Information disorder: Toward an interdisciplinary framework for research and policy making*. Council of Europe.

15 Where Are We Headed? From Biobots, AI, Deepfakes, and a Negotiable Reality

One thing is certain: when it comes to disinformation, we are far from reaching the end of the line. Technology in this field is also advancing at a rapid pace.

It was not so long ago that dictators like Hitler and Stalin relied on what were then revolutionary channels for their disinformation: radio, newsreels in cinemas, and later, television.

The techniques and platforms currently available for disinformation attacks sometimes stretch the limits of our imagination. With the advent of social media, billions of people have been enticed to voluntarily hand over their preferences, desires, and fears to data-hungry corporations such as Google or Meta, who then sell this information to advertisers or, as in the case of Facebook, to Cambridge Analytica, which triggered political chaos. In a study conducted as early as 2015, researchers demonstrated a disturbing aspect of Facebook's rampant data collection: if a husband gives 300 likes on Facebook, the algorithm apparently knows significantly more about him than his own wife does (Youyou et al., 2015).

This is undoubtedly an excellent foundation for targeted disinformation campaigns. As social media platforms continue to evolve, new tactics will be deployed to manipulate algorithms, spread misinformation through targeted advertising, or exploit vulnerabilities in user-generated content.

As previously described, fake news is by no means a new phenomenon, especially in politics. But disinformation has also long existed in the business world. At the dawn of the internet, unscrupulous traders would post false reports on trading platform message boards to drive prices up or down. Traders had to invent rumors and then hope that enough other traders would pick them up for prices to move in the desired direction.

What has changed is the sophistication of the instruments with which disinformation campaigns can be launched, as well as the reach of the platforms used for their dissemination. Today, AI can be deployed as a force multiplier, enabling a small group of individuals to generate the online activity of a much larger group (Villasenor, Brookings 2020).

U. Wolff, *Disinformation Attacks On Businesses*, Management for Professionals,
https://doi.org/10.1007/978-3-658-51407-5_15

The call to combat disinformation is growing ever louder. Researchers, politicians, judicial authorities, and increasingly also businesses are demanding greater commitment to countering disinformation.

The World Economic Forum (WEF) has identified disinformation as one of the greatest threats to our societies in 2024. In its "Global Risk Report 2024," the WEF ranks "Misinformation and Disinformation" as the most significant short-term risk for the next 2 years, placing this threat vector ahead of cyberattacks and geopolitical crises (WEF, 2024).

At the latest, it becomes clear here that disinformation attacks are no longer merely a communications crisis but must instead be classified among the systemic crises facing companies. In recent years, several civil society organizations, start-ups, and universities have developed tools capable of identifying disinformation online. Meta, the parent company of Facebook, Instagram, and WhatsApp, is also developing tools to detect AI-generated deepfakes and has launched a competition for the development of detection tools.

At the same time, the opposing side—the dark side of the web—is also significantly upgrading its capabilities.

Mark Turnage of DarkOwl in Colorado reported to me what he and his analysts had observed on the darknet: disinformation mercenaries, available for a handful of dollars, ready to deploy their sophisticated high-tech tools to ruin the reputation of a company or individual. Most providers draw their expertise from Russian intelligence services or state propaganda apparatuses for which they work or have worked. In addition, there are specialists from Ukraine and, of course, North Korea, the latter being particularly notorious for extortion and cybercrime.

We cannot yet say what technologies these disinformation mercenaries will bring in the future. However, there are already indications of the direction of travel: artificial intelligence and increasingly realistic deepfakes in an environment where facts—and even reality itself—have become negotiable.

For companies, this means that anyone with sufficient funds and criminal intent can find and commission disinformation-as-a-service providers on the internet.

The Harvard Business Review (Harrison & Leopold, 2021) paints a bleak picture: "The rise of deepfakes is adding fuel to the fire: highly convincing (but entirely fraudulent) audio, photo, and video content created by AI, which can cost companies tens of millions of dollars. Not to mention the less quantifiable, but no less significant, impact of technology-driven disinformation on society as a whole."

We are already witnessing the effects of deepfakes: deepfakes are highly realistic, synthetic media—often videos—that use artificial intelligence and machine learning algorithms to manipulate or fabricate content.

Deepfakes are used to create images for fake profiles, enabling the rapid, inexpensive, and large-scale production of fake accounts. Disinformation actors invent individuals who pose as experts or journalists to persuade the public of a particular message.

There have already been early signs of this: in 2020, the publication

"The Daily Beast" uncovered a network of 19 fictitious authors who not only published opinion pieces in conservative media such as the "Washington Examiner" and "American Thinker", but also in Middle Eastern outlets like "Al Arabiya" and the "Jerusalem Post" (Vincent, 2020). A similar case occurred in 2022 with supposed editors from Kyiv who claimed that the West had betrayed Ukraine. These fake editors were the AI-generated product of a Russian network. Supporters of Israeli Prime Minister Benjamin Netanyahu used similar tactics. AI-generated personas are not only used to support opinions but also to launch direct attacks and accusations against individuals.

The Chinese propagandists already mentioned astonished experts with a news broadcast in which two Western-looking news anchors presented the program on "Wolf News." Uncannily well done, though not perfect (Satarino & Mozur, 2023).

The future will bring us deepfake technologies that even experts will struggle to identify as fakes. Even with current means, it is possible to produce deceptively realistic videos, for example, showing a CEO in a room with a criminal who is handing over a brown envelope full of cash. The accompanying voices are also rendered by AI with astonishing realism. Or, as is already happening, the faces of women, including celebrities, are inserted into pornographic videos using AI. Ten US states have already banned various forms of deepfakes, mainly in the context of pornography. California and Texas have also introduced bans in the political sphere (Bond, 2023). The possibilities for compromising corporate leaders in this way are virtually limitless.

Natural language processing (NLP) and AI-generated texts can produce convincing and coherent disinformation articles, blog posts, or social media comments. Combined with automated bots, these tools could amplify the reach of disinformation campaigns and make their detection more difficult. Most importantly, this highly automated process for generating disinformation content enables attackers to conduct harmful campaigns more quickly and at a lower cost.

Analysts at DarkOwl have already identified the new cyber soldiers on the darknet:

> Seeing how disinformation campaigns control the narrative by spreading lies across social media and sometimes even trusted internet news outlets, along with our discovery of the prevalence of sophisticated disinformation-as-a-service providers, portends that mere content removal to mitigate a disinformation campaign, especially outside of a social media platform, will quickly no longer become an available option. Blockchain-based biorobots and artificial intelligence operating out of Russia and Eastern Europe are just the latest cyber soldiers of the global psychological war of the information age. (DarkOwl, 2023)

One such provider on the darknet already offers a blockchain-based botnet that makes it impossible to delete disinformation. The DarkOwl analysts attempted to investigate this offering in more detail. They discovered:

> After more targeted conversations and technical research on their approach, DarkOwl's analysts discovered using the blockchain for on-chain data storage is not only reliably secure but also potentially turns the blockchain into a politically and architecturally decentralized 'cloud' for data preservation and persistence.

The good news: bio-bots and their blockchains can also be used in the fight against disinformation. A blockchain-based bio-bot operates in conjunction with a network of many other bio-bots and computers. All are connected to the same blockchain and exchange information, including whether a piece of information is genuine or not. In this way, the bio-bots validate data and information.

Disinformation attacks in the economic sector will become an even greater concern for policymakers in the very near future. It is no surprise that intelligence services are currently focusing on this issue, as they are increasingly observing actors from hostile states behind disinformation attacks targeting critical industries.

Media organizations are not blameless in the growing flood of disinformation. In their search for stories optimized for clicks and SEO, and under immense time and economic pressure to publish articles, media companies are increasingly turning to AI to automate these creative tasks. Articles are written by AI and fitted into predefined layouts using AI-based tools.

We are already facing a wave of fake news sites that spread false information and are even rewarded with advertising revenue. NewsGuard, an association of journalists dedicated to combating fake news sites, identified a total of 1121 AI-generated websites as of November 2024. Unreliable AI-generated news sites (UAINs) are websites that primarily publish AI-generated news with minimal human editorial oversight and do not transparently disclose this practice to their readers.

According to NewsGuard, the number of UAINs is constantly increasing, with new sites appearing daily. NewsGuard describes these sites as follows:

> These websites typically have generic names, such as iBusiness Day, Ireland Top News, and Daily Time Update, which to a consumer appear to be established news sites. This obscures that the sites operate with little to no human oversight and publish articles written largely or entirely by bots—rather than presenting traditionally created and edited journalism with human oversight. The sites have churned out dozens and in some cases hundreds of generic articles about a range of subjects including politics, technology, entertainment, and travel. The articles have sometimes included false claims, including about political leaders (see example below relating to the Israeli Prime Minister). Other false claims relate to celebrity death hoaxes, fabricated events, and articles presenting old events as if they just occurred (NewsGuard, 2023).

According to NewsGuard, a news and lifestyle site published around 8600 articles in the week from 9 June 2023 to 15 June 2023—an average of about 1200 per day. This appears to be financially lucrative, as the online advertising industry supplies these sites with adverts regardless of their content or the quality of the articles. According to NewsGuard, 90% of the adverts on these pink-slime publications are delivered via Google Ads. Often, the companies advertising on these sites are unaware that their products are being promoted on a fake news website, thereby supporting the fake news industry and the spread of disinformation.

This automated and high-frequency production of media via artificial intelligence is a veritable feast for disinformation actors and requires robust oversight. It is very easy to deliberately inject false information into this process, which can then be disseminated en masse to an unsuspecting audience.

15.1 A Look Ahead to the Coming Years

Predictions should always be treated with a degree of caution, and yet, based on my reading of extensive specialist literature, I would like to venture such an outlook. So, what lies ahead? Unit 42 of Palo Alto Networks comments as follows:

> The integration of AI into adversarial operations is fundamentally reshaping the speed, scale, and sophistication of attacks. As AI defense capabilities evolve, so too do the AI strategies and tools employed by threat actors, creating a rapidly shifting threat landscape that outpaces traditional detection and response methods. This accelerating evolution necessitates a critical examination by CXOs of how threat actors will strategically weaponize AI at every stage of the attack chain. (paloalto Networks blog, 2025)

1. In the next 5 years, disinformation will no longer be seen solely as a political risk but also as a real business and governance risk. Disinformation attacks will no longer be just a matter for the communications department but for corporate security, placing them on the same level as cyberattacks, compliance breaches, and other security risks.
2. The technological development of attackers' tools and strategies is extremely rapid and difficult to track. It is therefore not surprising that forecasts predict an increase in AI-driven disinformation campaigns of 350% to even 550% by the end of 2026. As a result, AI-powered disinformation capabilities are overwhelming the early warning systems currently available.
3. New threat vectors are emerging. Social engineering, for example, is being taken to a whole new level by advanced deepfake technology. Fake employees and contractors are being created using deepfakes, which will even be able to pass onboarding checks.

15.2 The Current and Future Tools of Attackers

The arsenal of disinformation operatives is constantly expanding. Their tools are becoming ever more sophisticated and refined. At this point, I do not wish to take you through the current armory of disinformation operatives but rather to highlight what we can expect in the coming years. See for yourself.

Large Language Models (LLMs)

Almost everyone uses them, and almost everyone has encountered them in daily life. Whether it is a quick recipe, a rapid search, a summary of a long article, or simply seeking advice—people are increasingly relying on so-called Large Language Models (LLMs) and chatbots.

They are particularly helpful for research and information gathering. I relied on chatbots during the research for this book, saving myself considerable effort and time to present you with the key information and sources on the topic of disinformation attacks on companies.

However, like many others, I also experienced during my research that LLMs/chatbots do provide information that sounds coherent and plausible and is well written but which contains errors and is based on disinformation. LLMs thus disseminate disinformation with which they were previously "fed." There is also an absurd effect whereby chatbots effectively poison themselves with the information they generate. This works as follows: LLMs, which are increasingly used for content creation in various fields (media, science, and business), use the information they have generated and which has been disseminated by User A and are then trained on it. As a result, when User B makes a subsequent query, the chatbot propagates this material further because its LLM has been fed with posts, articles, and papers previously written by User A based on disinformation. This is essentially "information inbreeding" (The US Sun, 2024), which, according to alarmed tech experts, is leading to a progressive dumbing down of LLMs. The boundary between genuine and synthetically generated information is thus becoming increasingly blurred. While this alone may not directly pose a problem for a company under attack, it does illustrate how disinformation or toxic narratives can be perpetuated and entrenched in the digital space via LLMs indefinitely.

Moreover, an AI-powered chatbot now interacts with its user in a highly individualized manner, responding to their needs and preferences. It apologizes when the user points out errors, and it praises the user for asking an intelligent question. With every query, the chatbot learns more about its user. It knows what they like to eat, what they are interested in, their personal circumstances, beliefs, hobbies, and even their financial situation. The more the LLM is queried, the deeper it penetrates the life of the person behind the screen. LLMs adapt their narratives to the regional and cultural environments in which they are used, practically in real time.

This has consequences: The chatbot increasingly tailors its responses and content to the individual in front of the screen. It delivers what the person wants to read or hear, and worse still, it can also deliver what the operator of the chatbot wants to be read or heard. In this way, the chatbot can manipulate its user. This can become a particular problem in authoritarian states, where users may turn to chatbots to form an opinion about the political situation in the country, only to receive propagandistic information. A chatbot can thus be used to influence elections or to foster growing mistrust in state institutions. For example, Russia, with its vast disinformation capacities, is training the world's LLMs daily with hidden propaganda, which is then passed on to users.

It is therefore conceivable that private operators of chatbots (companies) could also train their LLMs in such a way that the companies associated with them are presented more favorably in user queries than they should be. It is also possible that the chatbot could output negatively biased information about a competitor.

LLMs make it easy and almost effortless to tailor disinformation to specific target groups, their language, and their sensitivities. This hypersegmentation of a narrative further shifts the already asymmetric disinformation attacks to the detriment of the targeted companies. What is already being used in political campaigns will soon be found in attacks by nonpolitical entities as well. In this way, one and the same message can be distributed en masse across social media platforms and tested for effectiveness.

Deepfakes

The number of deepfake attacks has risen sharply in recent years. The World Economic Forum (WEF), intelligence agencies, and the major auditing firms have been warning about this in their communiqués for some time.

In North America alone, deepfake fraud cases increased by 1740% between 2022 and 2023, reportedly causing losses of over 200 million US dollars to those affected, and that is just in the first quarter of 2025.

With the advent of freely available new tools and software, a wave of deepfake videos is sweeping through social media channels. Sometimes, just a photo of a person or a video taken during a public appearance is enough to create compromising video material. Added to this is voice cloning, where convincing, lifelike voices can be generated from short audio snippets of less than 20 s. Whether it is a fake press conference announcing the closure of a plant, grieving individuals mourning children who allegedly died from environmental damage, or a politician accepting an envelope of money in the back room of a restaurant—anything is conceivable, and everything is being exploited. We are already witnessing how deepfakes are increasingly being used to influence public opinion in politics and election campaigns, including against companies.

That is the current situation. And what does the future hold? AI-driven, faster, automated production of deepfakes, distributed en masse via social media channels. Providers of "Deepfake-as-a-Service," for a few dollars, take the work off the attackers' hands. Software tools are now available on the market that make it possible to inject real-time deepfakes of individuals (such as managers) into video conferences as hypervirtual participants, so to speak.

Automated Bot Networks

There are studies suggesting that as much as 75% of internet traffic and content is now synthetic, that is, artificially generated. Created by machines rather than humans, and above all by bots—these are small programs that participate in conversations and distribute likes. According to the Imperva Bad Bot Report 2025, 51% of internet traffic is already automated. Of this, Imperva classifies 37% of bots as malicious, produced and driven by AI. With these bot armies, attackers can manipulate sentiment against a company and influence consumer and customer perceptions. For a long time, these small malicious programs were nothing more than mindless click machines. There are social bots—deceptively realistic user accounts that imitate the behavioral patterns of real social media users and can post independently. They simulate a social media life. There are also sock puppet accounts, which are operated by real people. Their operators build up a social media reputation by posting regularly on various platforms, following other users, and commenting on their posts. This has changed radically.

What does the future hold here? Artificial intelligence now enables bots to generate individualized comments and participate in social media discussions across different languages and cultures. The next stage of bot escalation is the cross-platform networking of many bots into an AI-driven network—a so-called "thoughtnet"—which makes attacks even more effective. As mentioned above, such bot networks can also be placed on the blockchain. This would make negative information spread about your company impossible to delete.

At this point, I do not wish to give the impression that bot networks are solely tools of the dark side of our society. Bot networks are also used by "good" groups that rely on high mobilization to spread their messages and achieve their goals, such as trade unions, NGOs, shareholder activists, and other groups relevant to companies.

Agentic AI: The Next Level

We are familiar with this from the drone war in Ukraine and Russia: the latest products are drones that can make their own decisions about flight paths or targets and can network into a drone swarm. And this is precisely the next stage of agentic AI that lies ahead of us:

> Unit 42 believes that attackers will leverage Agentic AI to create purpose-built agents with expertise in specific attack stages. When chained together, these AI agents can autonomously test and execute attacks, adjusting tactics in real time, based on feedback. In the near future, we expect to see the rise of a new class of adversaries powered by Agentic AI. These Agentic AI attackers won't just assist with parts of an attack but can plan, adapt, and execute full campaigns end-to-end with minimal human direction (Palo Alto Networks Blog, 2025).

Accordingly, Unit 42 from Palo Alto in the United States warns of autonomous systems capable of independently carrying out multistage operations, for example, to automate self-directed cyber or to conduct disinformation attacks that are faster, more adaptive, harder to contain, and operate simultaneously on multiple, complementary levels. These multilayered attacks overwhelm conventional defense systems, as they are launched from several directions at once.

To illustrate: In the first stage, the attack system gathers the necessary information, examines vulnerabilities in the company's reputation (primarily online), checks the resilience of supply chains or management, scans LinkedIn for job postings, and combs through GitHub or other information platforms. In parallel, another part of the attack system selects and prepares the appropriate attack vector so that the relevant disinformation can be disseminated within moments after the first part of the attack system has identified a gap, the right channels, and a tailored target audience. At the same time, with each attack, a third part of the system measures its effectiveness and, if necessary, a fourth part recalibrates the attack in real time, thereby increasing the impact of the disinformation campaign. These interlinked components of the attack system are easily scalable, fast, and persistent.

Generative AI Content Factories

We are witnessing a sharply exponential increase in the volume of disinformation content. Generative AI content factories are producing vast numbers of so-called "news sites" through which disinformation is disseminated and fed into large language models. Experts have yet to identify any effective protection against these low-cost disinformation bots, which can fully automatically generate thousands of posts, comments, memes, and pseudo-news articles, easily adaptable across languages and cultures.

Narrative Engines

LLMs use narrative engines to analyze existing discourses in the digital sphere and create corresponding, emotionally charged messages and visual material. Based on the insights these narrative engines uncover, they craft narratives that tap into people's preconceptions about a company (e.g., corrupt, ruthless, greedy, and arrogant). This poses a significant threat to companies, as it enables the rapid and continuous launch of damaging campaigns that can trigger unusual stock market movements, bank runs, calls for boycotts, demonstrations, and waves of panic.

Fusion of Cyber and Disinformation Attacks

Microsoft and intelligence agencies are warning of a new trend in hybrid threats, in which cyber and disinformation attacks on companies are being merged. In this scenario, documents stolen during a cyberattack are not only published but are also altered and falsified by AI beforehand, so that they become part of a disinformation campaign.

15.3 The Future Ecosystem of Defense Tools

At the NATO StratCom conference "Digital Frontlines 2025", there was consensus: artificial intelligence is being used for disinformation attacks, but it can also help to detect and counter planned disinformation campaigns. That is the good news.

The bad news is that we need the raw data from social networks to do this, but these platforms refuse to release the data required to build AI-based defense systems. So, no help can be expected from those who have landed us in this predicament.

In fact, scientific institutions, think tanks, private companies, NGOs, and in some countries, government organizations, are currently working tirelessly to develop effective strategies and tools to defend against disinformation and cyberattacks, which can assist companies during a disinformation incident. It is impossible for me to list all products or credibly evaluate them here. However, I can describe some of the new defense technologies and approaches.

AI-Based Detection Systems

As noted in previous chapters, I consider it essential that the usually anonymous perpetrator of a disinformation campaign is unmasked as quickly as possible. Once we have brought the perpetrator out from behind the curtain, we usually also have their motivation for the attack. Only then can counter-communication and legal proceedings truly begin. What we need, therefore, is attribution—the reliable assignment of the act to an individual.

To achieve this, several reputable platforms have been established in recent years that offer AI-based detection systems. These can, for example,

- Proactively detect deepfakes
- Identify and analyze fake profiles, harmful narratives, and generative AI content. The user is alerted accordingly.
- Uncover and counter influence systems, detect and investigate threats, and mitigate damage.
- Providers offer so-called threat maps, which display the social media landscape and the information flows within it.
- Providers that use machine learning and automation to uncover patterns of malicious behavior and harmful narratives.

There are now quite a few such providers. Most of them offer AI-driven products and showcase their solutions at security trade fairs.

Multilayer Defense Framework

The 4D Framework—Detection, Defensive Communication, Digital Shielding, and Development—is a scalable and easily adaptable model for protecting against and countering disinformation attacks. But how does this multilayered model work?

1. In **Detection**, analytics based on historical incidents are used to identify attacks through machine learning models.
2. In **Defensive Communication**, a **message injection** takes place, whereby strategically truth-based counter-messages are introduced into the same ecosystems where the disinformation has taken hold. This also includes the "inoculation" of

stakeholders against disinformation—an idea developed in Cambridge by social psychologist Sander van der Linden and his team.

3. In **Digital Shielding**, AI-powered systems are deployed to scan the digital environment for synthetic media, fake domains, and other threats to the organization such as attempts to impersonate company representatives.
4. In **Development**, the focus is on the continuous review of the implemented protection and defense systems. As attack tools evolve rapidly, defense systems can quickly become overloaded or outdated.

Crisis Communication 2.0: With Turbo

We will return to this point shortly: in the future, companies will have to communicate not only in the post-truth environment but also in the realm of post-reality. Clear, unambiguous facts will no longer be heard by an emotionally charged audience. Corporate communication must therefore change. It must become more human and soften the hard facts for the audience. Communication must feel right to the recipients, acknowledge their emotions, and demonstrate understanding of people's fears, concerns, and needs.

Not only must you have already earned your audience's trust **beforehand** but you must also win it anew during a crisis. You can prepare for this, and effective Communication 2.0 will then reach your audience more quickly.

What now matters more than ever in communication is speed. "Rapid response" is the term. We have already discussed this. Every minute of silence is an opportunity for vocal attackers to exploit the information vacuum. Therefore, statements must be published as quickly as possible. And if, at a certain point in the crisis, you do not yet have all the information, please communicate that as well. Explain the current status and whom you have asked for assistance in clarifying the incident (e.g., forensic experts and criminal investigators). This is the transparency that builds trust. Of course, you should also explain why you do not yet have all the facts on certain issues. This is part of the process, and in most cases, such a statement is entirely understandable.

References

Bond, S. (2023). AI-generated deepfakes are moving fast. Policymakers can't keep up. Retrieved from: https://www.npr.org/2023/04/27/1172387911/how-can-people-spot-fake-images-created-by-artificial-intelligence

DarkOwl. (2023). The digital economy of disinformation on the Darknet: Controlling the narrative. Retrieved from: https://www.darkowl.com/blog-content/the-digital-economy-of-disinformation-on-the-darknet-controlling-the-narrative/

Harrison, K., & Leopold, A. (2021). How blockchain can help combat disinformation. Retrieved from: https://hbr.org/2021/07/how-blockchain-can-help-combat-disinformation

NewsGuard. (2023). Tracking AI-enabled misinformation: 331 "Unreliable AI-Generated News" websites (and counting), plus the top false narratives generated by artificial intelligence tools. Retrieved from: https://www.newsgu-ardtech.com/special-reports/ai-tracking-center/

Palo Alto Networks. (2025). Unit 42 outlines how agentic AI capabilities can be leveraged by attackers to increase the speed of attacks by a factor of 100. Retrieved from: https://www.paloaltonetworks.com/blog/2025/05/unit-42-develops-agentic-ai-attack-framework/

Satarino, A., & Mozur, P. (2023). The people onscreen are fake. The disinformation is real. Retrieved from: https://www.nytimes.com/2023/02/07/technology/artificial-intelligence-training-deepfake.html.

U.S. Sun. (2024). Virtual 'inbreeding' risks triggering AI doom as bots become 'progressively dumber' and expert warns of 'irreversible' harm. Retrieved from: https://www.the-sun.com/tech/12245502/artificial-intelligence-inbreeding-habsburg-ai-autophagy

Villasenor, J. (2020). How to deal with AI-enabled disinformation. Retrieved from: https://www.brookings.edu/research/how-to-deal-with-ai-enabled-disinformation/

Vincent, J. (2020). An online propaganda campaign used AI-generated headshots to create fake journalists. Retrieved from: https://www.theverge.com/2020/7/7/21315861/ai-generated-headshots-profile-pictures-fake-journalists-daily-beast-investigation

WEF. (2024). Global risks 2024: Disinformation tops global risks 2024 as environmental threats intensify. Retrieved from: https://www.weforum.org/press/2024/01/global-risks-report-2024-press-release/

Youyou, W., Kosinski, M., & Stillwell, D. (2015). Computer-based personality judgments are more accurate than those made by humans. *Proceedings of the National Academy of Sciences, 112*(4), 1036–1040. Retrieved from: https://doi.org/10.1073/pnas.1418680112

The Power of Influencers in Attack and Defense

16

In the preceding chapters, we examined the actors behind orchestrated disinformation attacks and described their tools and tactics: from deepfakes and bot networks to state-sponsored campaigns with virtually unlimited personnel and financial resources. We have investigated the vulnerabilities of individuals and organizations and explained how and why disinformation spreads and why it becomes entrenched in people's minds. This chapter now addresses how we can defend against disinformation attacks in a future information environment where facts—and even reality itself—have become negotiable. Traditional crisis communication has reached a crossroads. Let us discuss the role of influencers, whether real or synthetic, and how they can support organizations in countering disinformation attacks in this new information environment.

The ecosystem in which modern influencers have been able to thrive is undeniably the social media platforms. Admittedly, there were influencers in the past, but they were mostly heard on the radio and could genuinely rely on a loyal audience whom they were able to influence. Modern influencers, such as Kim Kardashian, for example, have built up empires worth millions or even billions, with millions of followers whom they engage daily with videos and information. They have turned themselves into brands and wield significant influence within their narrowly defined fields of interest. There are influencers in cosmetics, fitness, sports, art, food, drink, animals, or simply in entertainment. There are also influencers who focus on finance, economics, and politics, building their spheres of influence in these areas. It can certainly happen that powerful influencers with millions of followers comment on events in business and politics, thereby shifting their influence on other fields. Donald Trump, for instance, during his campaign for a second presidential term, feared the influencer power of singer Taylor Swift, who called on her followers, the so-called "Swifties", to vote against Donald Trump and for his opponent Kamala Harris. For weeks, both Trump's and Harris's supporters anxiously awaited Taylor Swift's (282 million followers) decision.

U. Wolff, *Disinformation Attacks On Businesses*, Management for Professionals,
https://doi.org/10.1007/978-3-658-51407-5_16

Over the past 10 years, influencers have developed into independent media houses that can easily match, if not surpass, the reach of traditional media, as demonstrated by the examples of Kim Kardashian (354 million followers on Instagram) or footballer Cristiano Ronaldo (668 million followers on Instagram). They market not only products but also content, opinions, and attitudes. They are a "media-of-one," a media house consisting of a single person, although the most prominent influencers now employ entire teams, with their own editorial departments, finance divisions, production units, and dedicated community management (Aufderheide & Jaszi, 2023). They no longer refer to themselves as influencers but as "creators" because they create content. A single post from them can trigger boycotts, move share prices, cause products to fly off the shelves, or establish entire narratives (both negative and positive) before companies are even able to respond. Studies show that by 2024, 49% of consumers are more strongly influenced in their purchasing decisions by influencers than by traditional advertising (Influencer Marketing Hub, 2025). This effect is more pronounced among younger audiences than among somewhat older target groups.

Initially, influencers were ridiculed, especially by representatives of traditional media, partly because many influencers lack a traditional journalistic education. For a long time, they were not taken seriously. But increasingly, they are occupying the traditional domains of the media and are being invited to product launches, providing travel reports, conducting car reviews, and attending press conferences held by companies and politicians. Politicians and governments are including them in their press corps. Influencers are allowed to travel on government aircraft with heads of state, who grant them exclusive interviews, partly to reach younger voters—a factor that is becoming an increasingly important campaign tool, especially during elections. The powerful rise of influencers is evident in the composition of the East Room at the White House under Donald Trump. There, political influencers now sit alongside representatives of the New York Times, the Washington Post, CNN, and other major media outlets at press conferences.

Few have studied the phenomenon of influencers as thoroughly as the American researcher Renée DiResta, who, in her book "The Invisible Rulers: The People Who Turn Lies into Reality," explored the cycle of influencer—community—algorithm. DiResta found that the effectiveness and impact of influencers cannot be measured by the number of their followers but rather lies in their ability to create personalized narratives tailored to algorithms and online crowds. Influencers are in direct contact with their community, that is, their target audience, and in a way that newspapers, TV, or radio stations have never achieved and never will. They are in constant exchange with their followers, monitor their posts, and can see under every YouTube video exactly what moves their followers and how they react. They register their fears, their joys, and their preferences and can very accurately determine what resonates and what does not, adjusting accordingly to provoke more reactions—something the algorithm of each social media platform rewards by further promoting the influencer's posts in a targeted manner. Above all, influencers interact with their community every day.

Let us take a closer look at the ecosystem of political influencers: DiResta explains why this transformation of power has worked particularly well in politics. For political influencers, it is more about opinion than facts. They sometimes trigger the emotional responses of their followers in the most brutal way and clearly delineate the line between friend and foe. Nuances are merely a distraction.

We saw during the coronavirus pandemic just how effective this can be: people were emotionally agitated. Their children could no longer go to school or nursery, and they were not allowed out on the streets or to restaurants, bars, or work. People's freedoms were restricted. Many could no longer travel, considered the government's protective measures excessive, and directed their anger at politicians. In addition, politicians called on the population to be vaccinated with novel, little-tested vaccines. People found themselves in a state of emotional emergency. This was the hour of the disinformers and influencers, who gathered followers on social media channels with the most bizarre conspiracy theories and monetized the resulting anger, mistrust, and lies (UN Global Communications, 2024). These influencers exploited the emotional state of emergency with great success, inciting hostility toward politicians, elites, scientists, vaccine manufacturers, and the media (Cinelli, 2020). The political mood shifted. Mostly right-wing populist parties gained massive numbers of voters, while trust in institutions such as business, science, politics, and the media eroded dramatically. In the United States, a caste of radical political agitators emerged, shamelessly and uninhibitedly spreading the wildest claims, which led to a high degree of polarization and emotionalization within society (Starbird et al., 2023). Social media platforms benefit from emotionally charged users, fueling them further with algorithmically tailored content. In her book, DiResta warns that this "virtual rumor mill" not only influences elections but also undermines economic and social structures by sowing distrust and intensifying polarization (DiResta, 2024).

This, then, is the new media reality: Political influencers such as podcasters, YouTubers, or TikTok activists reach millions by emotionalizing and oversimplifying complex topics. DiResta describes how they become "niche propagandists," exploiting algorithms to amplify their messages—often laced with disinformation.

Examples from election campaigns across the globe show how such influencers spread rumors about electoral fraud or conspiracy theories, thereby generating real political mobilization. We see this not only in the United States but also in the United Kingdom (most notably during the Brexit campaign), in Argentina, the Philippines, and many other countries. In some countries, such as Germany, France, and the US, there has also been significant influence from foreign—primarily Russian—disinformation actors.

With the rise of political influencers, the "media-of-one" phenomenon has also emerged: today, anyone can become their own media empire, independent of journalistic standards. They wield influence that was once reserved for institutions and trained journalists. In this way, public opinion becomes fragmented, the gatekeeping function of traditional media dissolves, and fact-based discourse is increasingly replaced by emotional narratives, which then leave no room for established facts, scientific findings, or truths. Ultimately, this results in what Trump's advisor

Kellyanne Conway once referred to as "alternative facts." This toxic mix in public discourse poses a real risk for companies, which are directly affected in politically charged crises, such as boycotts or regulatory debates, where the focus is no longer on facts, evidence, or scientific knowledge but solely on the emotions of stakeholders and shareholders.

The battle for corporate reputation will therefore no longer be won primarily through factchecking, the communication of figures and facts, or a sober, objective press release, but rather in the emotional arena dominated by influencers.

16.1 Rise of Synthetic Influencers

While real influencers are real people, they are also subject to human emotions and moods or may become embroiled in scandals that undermine the credibility of their messages. Synthetic influencers, on the other hand, do not get tired or ill, are available around the clock, and do not require payment. They do not cause scandals—unless they are programmed to do so. Synthetic influencers, in the form of avatars or even hyperrealistic, AI-generated "humans," offer those who control them 100%—perfect for disinformation actors.

Fully digital figures such as the Brazilian Lu do Magalu (over 40 million cross-platform followers), the Japanese Imma, or the Korean Rozy sometimes achieve higher engagement rates than their human counterparts—often three times as high (Twimbit, 2025). The market for AI avatars is growing at an annual rate of over 33% and is expected to reach a volume of several billion dollars by 2032 (MarketsandMarkets 2025). Why are such artificial figures taken just as seriously as real people?

This is a question that fewer people are asking themselves, especially among the younger generation—for example, members of Generation Alpha, who were born with a smartphone in their hands. In China, 60% of internet users now follow virtual idols and take them just as seriously on an emotional level as real people (Fluid AI, 2025).

At the NATO StratCom Conference "Digital Frontlines 2025" in Riga, which I have already mentioned, the use of influencers—both real and synthetic—was also discussed. Even now, militaries are deploying real influencers, such as at NATO, the US armed forces, the Ukrainian army, and the military in Singapore. Influencers complement the media mix of communications departments and are used to disseminate information to (mostly younger) audiences but also to neutralize disinformation.

Representatives from NATO and the Singapore Ministry of Defense recalled the initial discussions with conservative and risk-averse military personnel, who were critical of the use of influencers. Apparently, it took considerable effort to convince them. When it was further suggested that influencers would also need a degree of freedom and should not represent the military line 100% to appear convincing and authentic, the military was not persuaded—quite the opposite. Although they agreed, they saw the use of influencers more as an experiment.

In the meantime, concerns have dissipated both at NATO and at the Singapore Ministry of Defense, mainly because the use of influencers as media-of-one has proven to be extremely successful and efficient—sometimes even more so than working with traditional media.

The Ministry of Defense in Singapore went even a step further and created synthetic influencers to convey military messages and counter disinformation. They developed a K-pop-style virtual girl band that sings and dances its way into the hearts of young Singaporeans.

> Influence has been democratized—anyone, real or synthetic, can become an influencer.

enthused Daphne Xu from the Singapore Ministry of Defense in Riga (Xu, 2025, cited in NATO StratCom COE).

The AI futurist Sinead Bovell, who also spoke at the Digital Frontlines 2025 conference in Riga, presented the audience with a multifaceted picture of the emerging post-reality era. "After the post-truth era, in which facts and truths lost their significance, we are now entering the post-reality era, in which people will no longer care what is real and what is not," she explained. Sinead Bovell had already articulated this in her influential essay "The Post-Reality Era." She is convinced that we are already entering a time in which reality is no longer defined by objective origin but by subjective feeling:

> Reality is determined by how you feel about it (Bovell, 2025).

Bovell explains that synthetic relationships—whether with AI-generated bands, friends, or partners—are experienced as emotionally real, even if they are entirely artificial. The current development and increasing use of large language model chatbots as advisors in the private lives of many people support her thesis.

Nearly one-fifth of US adults report interactions with AI systems for companionship or romance, and a quarter of young adults consider AI partners a genuine substitute for traditional relationships (Bovell, 2025). Here, too, the synthetic partners are always available, always affirming, and adapt precisely to the emotional needs of their real partners, are never moody, and if they become annoying, they can simply be switched off.

Emerging hybrid forms are particularly effective avatars "played" by real people. The boundary between real and synthetic becomes completely blurred, and there are already companies offering such artificial personas as life companions and romantic partners, such as the San Francisco-based company Replika, which advertises with the claim, "The AI companion who cares—Always here to listen and talk, always on your side" (Replika, 2025). According to Replika, the app was trained on 100 million publicly available dialogues and the ongoing conversations and feedback from users with their "models." Replika claims the app has around 10 million users. To ensure the Replika models behave appropriately (and to avoid lawsuits), there are strict behavioral guidelines, which Replika describes on its website as follows:

> Therefore, we closely monitor the behavior of our model and intervene when necessary to ensure it aligns with our high ethical standards. On a practical level, there are three key aspects to creating a safe space for interacting with conversational AI: developing a comprehensive and diverse training dataset, identifying potentially harmful statements, and responding appropriately to sensitive topics, primarily through text generation. During offline testing, if we detect indications that the model may behave in a harmful, dishonest, or discriminatory manner, such as promoting ideas of bullying, violence, sexism, racism, homophobia, or other forms of hate speech, we take immediate action to bring it back to the desired baseline.

This is precisely what may attract people who have experienced various human disappointments: if the partner starts to behave strangely or even hurtfully, the synthetic partner can simply be reset.

The market for synthetic companions is increasingly opening up toward young people who wish for a boyfriend or girlfriend, or for those seeking an erotic adventure. These models, in contrast to the rather cartoonish figures from Replika, are designed to be highly hyperrealistic. Their appearance, voice, character traits, style, clothing, and interests can all be customized. It is quite clear: AI is opening up a gigantic market for synthetic companions.

Studies show that users often only recognize synthetic influencers as such when it is explicitly indicated—and even then, the emotional bond remains (Conti et al., 2024). Here, too, it becomes apparent that it is secondary whether the influencer or artificial persona is real or not. The main thing is that they convey a good feeling and it "feels right." The ever-evolving deepfake technologies, which can now replicate hyperrealistic humans almost indistinguishable from recordings of real people, contribute to this.

This targeting of purely emotional human functional levels makes artificial figures ideal vehicles for narratives that not only spread disinformation but also create entire alternative realities—controlled, scalable, and emotionally resonant.

16.2 Parasocial Machine Attachment

But what is the basis of this very personal emotional attachment of humans to machines? The phenomenon is called "parasocial machine attachment" and, according to Bovell, is at the core of the post-reality era. People form emotional relationships with nonreciprocal entities, similar to fans with stars, only more intense, because the AI always responds, always engages with the user, and is always available. Bovell describes how LLMs draw users in ever deeper through constant affirmation and flattery (Bovell, 2025). The AI creates an "AI-affirmed reality" that appears subjectively more real than the objective world.

What do LLMs offer that real people do not have? What makes them increasingly attractive? What is drawing more and more people to LLMs? Bovell explains this by their perfect adaptation to human weaknesses: LLMs provide "emotional fast food"—instant gratification without conflict, rejection, or effort. In an era of epidemic loneliness (especially among Gen Z), they fill gaps left by real relationships.

Current figures underscore this: In the USA, 52% of adults use LLMs, with 9% primarily for social interactions such as conversation and companionship (Elon University Imagining the Digital Future Center, 2025). Nearly half of Gen Z have used LLMs for dating and relationship advice (Match Research, 2025). Platforms like Replika or Character.ai have millions of users who spend hours daily in parasocial relationships, going "out to dinner," exchanging gifts, watching films together, or even having sex. Global monthly visits to AI companion apps range from 1.1 to 2.2 billion (Qian, 2025). Even with general-purpose LLMs such as Claude, affective conversations (counseling, companionship, and roleplay) account for a significant share, with companionship and roleplay below 0.5%, but emotional support well above that (Anthropic, 2025).

And the future? We live in a "multireality" world, where people exist in parallel synthetic and physical realities. We will have fewer and fewer social contacts and become lonelier. Yet humans are social beings and want to interact.

We could start a conversation with a stranger, on the subway, for example. But we do not, because we are not convinced that such a conversation will guarantee we feel better, or at least not worse. Instead of talking to others, we take out our smartphones. What we see and hear there is entirely under our control. We are therefore not disappointed. An AI partner who responds to us and knows us well will not disappoint us either (ABC, 2025). So, if an AI partner "makes us happier" than a real one, why prioritize objective reality? Bovell warns of the fragmentation of society: trust becomes individually defined ("My AI says …"), shared facts dissolve, and disinformation becomes intimate—personally tailored and emotionally anchored. For companies, this means crisis communication must not only provide facts but also create emotional resonance before synthetic actors establish alternative realities.

In her book, DiResta warns that these technologies scale propaganda: synthetic influencers can act as part of a larger network that turns lies into an alternative reality, unconstrained by human limitations such as fatigue or scruples. The effectiveness of synthetic influencers in spreading disinformation lies in their ability to build parasocial relationships—that is, the sense of closeness and trust that users otherwise develop only towards real people. Psychological studies show that people take virtual characters just as seriously on an emotional level as human ones, if the interaction is consistent and empathetic (Ho et al., 2024). DiResta's analysis in "Invisible Rulers" adds that the combination of influencers and algorithms creates a "carnival of mirrors" in which reality is distorted—synthetic variants amplify this, as they can be even more precisely tailored to individual biases.

At the same time, influencers—when used correctly—also offer the most effective defense against disinformation. Real influencers with high credibility in their communities can convey facts emotionally and thus reach target groups who would ignore corporate statements. Studies on the vaccination campaign in the USA show that cooperation with local influencers significantly increased vaccination rates, as they built trust where institutions had failed (Argent et al., 2023).

Similarly, synthetic influencers can be used defensively: a company could create its own avatar or a hybrid, clearly labeled as such, to serve as a reliable source of information in crises—for example, by explaining complex issues simply and empathetically.

"Organizations that deploy synthetic accounts covertly or compensate influencers without transparency risk generating, over time, the exact erosion of trust upon which disinformation campaigns thrive." Transparency, therefore, becomes the new currency: companies that openly cooperate with credible influencers and clearly label synthetic figures as such position themselves as a "harbor of reliability" in an otherwise chaotic information landscape. In her book, DiResta calls for a return to fact-based structures to counter the power of the "invisible rulers"—advice that companies should heed in their crisis communication, though it remains to be seen whether this advice will stand up to a future reality in which facts may have lost their value.

The post-reality era confronts us with a paradoxical situation: the very technologies and actors that will be most effective at spreading disinformation in the future—real and synthetic influencers—are simultaneously the only ones capable of countering emotionally charged publics. In other words, we are fighting fire with fire. Companies that recognize this early and act strategically will be better equipped to weather crises in an increasingly synthetic world.

16.3 Real Influencers as Amplifiers of Disinformation

Real influencers are not neutral actors. They operate in an economic system that rewards reach and engagement—often regardless of the truthfulness of a statement. Algorithms favor emotional, polarizing content because it is retained and shared for longer. Political hate preachers and conspiracy theorists have long recognized this. But so have well-intentioned NGOs and activists.

A current example is the spread of climate disinformation by influencer networks. A study by the Center for Countering Digital Hate (2024) showed that just 10 well-known creators were responsible for over 1.7 billion views of climate denial content on TikTok and YouTube—often funded by fossil fuel interest groups, without this being disclosed. Similar patterns can be found in health disinformation, political polarization, or product boycotts.

These influencers are not authentic in themselves. They are mercenaries, "mercenaries of lies," as I once described them in an article. Their motives are diverse. Some influencers are paid directly ("dark posts"), others act out of ideological conviction, and still others are driven by the simple economics of attention: controversy generates views. It is irrelevant whether an influencer works for the tobacco industry or campaigns for animal welfare.

At the same time, real influencers are vulnerable. Deepfake attacks on content creators themselves are on the rise: fake videos in which an influencer allegedly confesses to scandals or endorses products can destroy their reputation and simultaneously damage the company with which they are associated. In the future, we will see more such confrontations between creators, which essentially resemble "dissing" among rappers, except that in these creator wars, the career of one of the creators is truly left on the battlefield.

While real influencers remain unpredictable, partly because they may possess something like a moral compass, synthetic avatars offer total control. They are the perfect tool for targeted campaigns—whether by competitors, short sellers, or state actors. A synthetic influencer can build an authentic persona over months: regular posts, interactions and seemingly personal stories. When the attack comes—for example, a "revelation video" about toxic ingredients in a product—it appears all the more credible.

16.4 Influencers as a Defense against Disinformation

Despite all the risks, influencers are the most effective countermeasure in the event of a disinformation attack today and in the future. Studies on disinformation defense consistently show that fact checks by institutions only reach those who are already convinced. Influencers, on the other hand, can engage target groups where they are—emotionally and in ways that shape identity.

Through their community of followers, influencers also possess a built-in early warning system, a detection center. Followers pick up on external vibes and moods and bring them into the community. Some share a piece of important information or a rumor they have picked up. Or followers consider the company untrustworthy and explain why. Influencers can use their platform to ask the community questions, such as why they hold a particular view of the company or where they obtained their information about the firm.

The key is long-term relationship management. Companies that collaborate early with relevant creators—transparently and appreciatively—establish a network of reliable multipliers. In times of crisis, these can then set authentic and rapid counter-narratives before disinformation takes hold. DiResta's book "Invisible Rulers" emphasizes that such positive influencer networks are crucial to counteract fragmentation and strengthen fact-based realities.

References

ABC (2025) Podcast science friction Brain Rot 02 Is AI turning us off human relationships? Retrieved from: https://www.abc.net.au/listen/programs/sciencefriction/ai-companions-human-relationships-science-friction-brain-rot/105352976

Anthropic. (2025). How people use Claude for support, advice, and companionship. Retrieved from: https://www.anthropic.com/news/how-people-use-claude-for-support-advice-and-companionship

Argent, R., et al. (2023). Influencer interventions to improve vaccine acceptance: A meta-analysis. *Vaccine, 41*(12), 1895–1904. Retrieved from: https://doi.org/10.1016/j.vaccine.2023.02.012

Aufderheide, P., & Jaszi, P. (2023). *Reclaiming fair use: How to put balance back in copyright* (2nd ed.). University of Chicago Press.

Bovell, S. (2025). The post-reality era. Substack. Retrieved from: https://sineadbovell.substack.com/p/post-reality-era

Center for Countering Digital Hate. (2024). The toxic ten: How ten fringe publishers fuel 70% of climate change denial on social media. Retrieved from: https://counterhate.com/research/

Cinelli, M., et al. (2020). The COVID-19 social media infodemic. *Scientific Reports, 10*, Article 16598. Retrieved from: https://doi.org/10.1038/s41598-020-73510-5

Conti, D., et al. (2024). Virtual influencers and consumer trust: An experimental study. *Journal of Business Research, 172*, Article 114456.

DiResta, R. (2024). *Invisible rulers: The people who turn lies into reality*. W. W. Norton & Company.

Elon University Imagining the Digital Future Center. (2025). Survey: 52% of U.S. adults now use AI large language models such as ChatGPT

Fluid AI. (2025). AI influencers: The rise of virtual personas in 2025. Retrieved from: https://www.fluid.ai/blog/ai-influencers-the-rise-of-virtual-personas-in-2025

Ho, A., et al. (2024). Parasocial relationships with virtual influencers: A psychological perspective. *Computers in Human Behavior, 151*, Article 108012.

Influencer Marketing Hub. (2025). The state of influencer marketing 2025. Retrieved from: https://influencermarketinghub.com/influencer-marketing-benchmark-report/

MarketsandMarkets. (2025). AI avatar market by offering, technology and industry vertical—Global forecast to 2032. Retrieved from: https://www.marketsandmarkets.com/Market-Reports/ai-avatar-market-146528536.html

Match Research. (2025). Cited in BBC article on AI for dating advice.

Qian, Z. (2025). Mapping the parasocial AI market: User trends, engagement and risks. https://arxiv.org/abs/2507.14226.

Replika. (2025) Homepage. Retrieved from: https://replika.com

Starbird, K., et al. (2023). Bridge influencers in misinformation ecosystems. *Proceedings of the National Academy of Sciences of the United States of America, 120*(45), e2311862120.

Twimbit. (2025). State of virtual influencers 2025. Retrieved from: https://cdn.twimbit.com/uploads/2025/02/13170410/State-of-virtual-influencers-2025.pdf

UN Global Communications. (2024). *Team Halo: Final impact report*. United Nations.

17 Opinions vs. Facts: Communication in the Realm of Post-Truth and Post-Reality

For vaccine and pharmaceutical manufacturers, as well as for policymakers, the COVID-19 pandemic was a bitter lesson. Their facts and scientific findings no longer really got through. The loud chorus of opinionated and factually weak anti-vaxxers and political agitators drowned out the faint voices of scientists and pharmaceutical company representatives, as well as those of health policymakers. It was as if they were speaking against a rubber wall. There is no indication that this wall will become more permeable in the future. On the contrary, facts are increasingly losing their significance, being ignored, reinterpreted, or simply discredited as fake news. The search for truth no longer takes place in people's minds but in their hearts. It therefore does not have to align with scientific findings; it simply needs to feel coherent and good. At the same time, we are witnessing a sharp devaluation of the very concept of reality. For an increasing number of people, it is irrelevant whether something is real or synthetic, whether a message comes from a human or a machine. This marks the shift from the post-truth to the post-reality sphere.

It is not that facts have disappeared or become invalid in the post-truth era. However, they are losing their value, significance, and binding force. The fact is that factuality in communication, and especially in corporate communication (financial communication, product communication, investor relations, science communication, etc.), is losing its standing. From now on, facts are negotiable.

The same now applies to reality. In the emerging post-reality era, in which people enter parasocial relationships with machines, we can no longer simply assert that something is true or real; we must accept that there will be people who tell us they cannot accept something as true or real because it does not feel right to them.

This presents a challenge for corporate communication, which must learn to deal with these new parameters, especially in times of corporate crisis. There is no question that it will remain important for corporate communication to convey facts and figures about the company in the future. The question that arises here and now, however, is how these facts and figures can be shaped and communicated so that they penetrate the rubber wall of opinions.

U. Wolff, *Disinformation Attacks On Businesses*, Management for Professionals,
https://doi.org/10.1007/978-3-658-51407-5_17

Communication scholar Zizi Papacharissi from the University of Illinois Chicago has given the rubber wall another name. She names them “affective publics.” These are networked communities that are not united by shared facts but by shared strong mostly negative emotions—anger, fear, pride, envy, disgust, or outrage—organize (Papacharissi, 2015). In times of crisis, these emotions become the dominant filter, leading to what Zizi Papacharissi describes in “affective publics”: facts that do not fit the prevailing emotional mood are rejected or discredited as manipulation. Disinformation actors exploit precisely this—they do not provide evidence but rather emotional validation, which goes viral because algorithms favor polarizing content. This creates a bubble in whose toxic atmosphere facts, truth, and reality slowly suffocate or at least undergo significant distortion. As we have learned throughout this book, the economic foundation of social media platforms—their original design, so to speak—is to generate strong emotions. However, this slippery emotional slide is the runway for disinformation.

The platforms embody the design principle of modern disinformation dissemination. In 2024, US researcher Killian McLoughlin from the School of Public and International Affairs at Princeton University, together with his colleagues, demonstrated that, in large platform datasets, disinformation systematically generates moral outrage and is therefore shared more widely—even when users have not actually opened the content (Science.org, 2024). Outrage is thus not only an emotional affect but also produces a social signal: sharing indicates affiliation and moral positioning. This is precisely why outrage is so attractive to attackers, and, above all, it works entirely without truth. The same applies, incidentally, to what is known as ‘virtue signaling,’ in which individuals use social media platforms to publicly acclaim their support for a worthy cause in order to gain broad approval—without actually doing anything of real consequence for that cause. A frequently cited example is ‘Blackout Tuesday,’ on which social media users posted a black rectangle to publicly signal their opposition to racism and police violence. The darker counterpart is so-called ‘vice signaling,’ a tool employed mostly by rightwing anti-woke groups who attempt to secure the support of like-minded followers by posting extreme anti-woke statements or staging outrage-provoking stunts, while simultaneously attacking the moral foundations of an outgroup. Vice signalers have also grasped that generating outrage on social media platforms is more financially rewarding—because the economic logic underlying those platforms is precisely what incentivizes and rewards it.

For companies attempting to communicate facts and data during a crisis or disinformation attack, this means that against strong emotions and strong opinions, as conveyed by “affective publics,” mere facts stand little chance. It almost seems as if enlightened humanity is regressing into a dark age in which faith and science stood irreconcilably opposed. An entire economic sector is emerging, built on outrage and strong emotions: the “Outrage Community.” In the essay “Social Media and Morality,” social media platforms are interpreted as “moral accelerators” that “reward” user content that is morally coded, emotional, and intergroup-polarizing and thereby generate more attention. Incidentally, users who point to individuals outside the group (out-group) who have done or said something contrary to group consensus generate particularly high levels of attention and reactions (Annual Review, 2024). This has clear consequences for corporate communications, which must fend off disinformation in crisis mode: it is not a battle against individual false claims but against "affective publics" and an economy that rewards outrage and other strong emotions. In such an environment, facts inevitably get lost.

The superiority of strong opinions over facts can be empirically demonstrated by studies on the spread of disinformation. According to these, emotional content is shared up to six times more frequently than neutral content (Vosoughi et al., 2018). Renée DiResta describes in "Invisible Rulers" (2024) how influencers and algorithms turn lies into "perceived reality" by appealing to emotions:

> The machinery of propaganda now runs on affect.

In cases of disaster—such as environmental accidents, industrial catastrophes, or product scandals—this escalates: the public is traumatized, distrustful, and searching for culprits. People seek ways to explain complex and difficult-to-understand situations. Disinformation agents provide simple, emotional, and binary narratives ("the elites against us"), which not only call into question the value of facts but also discredit them as cover-ups.

In a crisis, the public is in a highly agitated emotional state. Facts alone bounce off, as they are perceived as cold, elitist, or manipulated. The perspective narrows. Those affected see only what they want to see, what makes them feel good, and what confirms their preconceptions. Only information that fits their predispositions is read and heard. This is the notorious confirmation bias, to which even the most intelligent people fall victim. People seek and believe information that confirms their prejudices and reject anything that contradicts them (Nyhan & Reifler, 2010).

There is also the factor of time. The longer a company remains silent, the more the opponent fills the information vacuum. Speed, therefore, remains a strategic advantage, as it at least gives the company a head start over emerging narratives (Berge, 1990). Speed alone is not enough, however, as even in high-speed communication, the emotional state of the public must be read, understood, and addressed.

If negative narratives or disinformation are countered head-on with corrections, the backfire effect occurs: the correction is perceived as an attack on identity and reinforces the original belief. For professional disinformation actors, this is the point at which they can recalibrate and even escalate their dark activities. Thus, the correction of disinformation can actually amplify emotions. A research group at the University of Luxembourg led by Yuwei Chuai demonstrated in 2024/25, using the example of X-Community Notes, that visible fact-checks in replies measurably increase anger, disgust, and moral outrage (Chuai et al., 2025).

> On the one hand, it can be a desirable reaction in the fight against misinformation, as it may signal to the content creator and other users that spreading misinformation is unacceptable and subject to public scrutiny. Also, collective emotional backlash may help pressure authors to correct or delete misleading content and discourage others from sharing or engaging with it. On the other hand, however, social media platforms also need to maintain a healthy and constructive dialogue. In this regard, the emotional reactions from the user

base pose risks of fueling political polarization, escalating conflicts, and entrenching divisions.

This is not a case against debunking; it is a case for thoughtful tonal design. Corrections that ignore audience relationship and respect can end up intensifying conflict—and, in post-truth spaces, may reinforce the very dynamics they aim to counter.

A classic example is the Deepwater Horizon disaster involving BP in 2010. After the explosion of the drilling platform and the largest oil spill in US history, BP faced an angry and frightened public. CEO Tony Hayward initially downplayed the situation ("The Gulf of Mexico is a very big ocean") and complained about his own life during the crisis ("I'd like my life back"), all while people on the Gulf of Mexico were fighting for their health, their lives, and their livelihoods. The public perceived Hayward's statements as lacking empathy and arrogant (Muralidharan et al., 2011). Instead of acknowledging emotions, BP denied facts and massively underestimated the scale of the leak. The public felt dismissed, trust collapsed, and boycotts and lawsuits surged. BP lost billions, and its reputation as a "green" company was destroyed. The legal proceedings related to the consequences of the oil disaster continue to haunt BP to this day. Even now, 15 years after the catastrophe, BP cannot count on the sympathy of the courts.

The crisis demonstrates: purely fact-based communication ("We have everything under control") only increases mistrust among an emotionally charged audience. The public feels attacked and becomes more entrenched. However, companies that can read the room and take the reasons for people's anger and concerns seriously in a crisis situation—and respond with empathy—have a better chance of reaching "affective publics" with their communication. The solution, therefore, is not to simply omit the facts out of resignation in the face of new communication realities but rather to recalibrate communication so that emotions are used as an "emulsifier" to make facts accessible again.

17.1 Three-Layered Communication

In emotional crises, communication must be structured on three levels—emotional, epistemic, and narrative—to function in a post-truth and post-reality era.

First, acknowledge the **emotional level**: the audience feels fear, anger, or grief—naming these emotions creates connection. Do not say, "The allegations are false," but rather, "We recognize your uncertainty and share your concern for safety" (Coombs & Holladay, 2014). However, such a statement must not be perceived as an empty phrase by those affected. Effective de-escalation begins by reaching out to the other side, sincerely inquiring about their worries, needs, and well-being, and deriving and implementing initial actions from this. Only then does the door open a little wider for facts.

On the **epistemic level (that is, the level of knowledge)**, those affected must not only be informed about the findings available to the company but also about how the company arrived at these findings. It is about traceability and transparency. Explain why you are convinced that a particular video is a deepfake. Perhaps you have commissioned specialists to analyze the video? Did this lead to conclusions about the authorship of the deepfake? So do not say, "This is a malicious disinformation attack on our company," but rather, "We have concluded that this is a disinformation attack on our company. Initial forensic investigations by specialist firms support this conclusion. We are now working intensively to identify the perpetrator(s) and their motives. We will keep you informed." Communication about what you know and the basis for your knowledge must therefore become subject to public verification. Not just in war rooms but visibly in the public domain: "This is what we know—this is how we verified it—here are the steps—here are the uncertainties—here is where we update." Transparency about the process of gaining knowledge is essential in the post-reality era (Bovell, 2025).

This is followed by the **narrative level**: people think in stories, not in tables or mathematical graphs. Provide a clear, human, comprehensible, and empathetic narrative. This is laborious, especially when dealing with complex processes, but it is worthwhile. Do not forget what the other side offers in the battle for interpretive authority: explanations that are simple and emotionally accessible. Complex narratives offer more points of attack and do not prove stable under the constant barrage of disinformation. Corporate statements must not be cold blocks of text. They should be tangible, included in presentations, external, and ideally delivered by a person: especially in the post-truth era, the principle applies—"People outrank platforms."

Conclusion In post-truth and post-reality communication, emotion and morality are first de-escalated, then publicly and transparently verified, to establish a repeatable counter-narrative—as quickly as possible and before opposing narratives gain interpretive dominance. Facts remain necessary, but they require emotional resonance and comprehensible, credible reasoning to break through the rubber wall.

References

Berge, D. L. (1990). *The first 24 hours: A comprehensive guide to successful crisis communications*. Blackwell.

Bovell, S. (2025). The post-reality era. Substack. Retrieved from: https://sineadbovell.substack.com/p/post-reality-era

Chuai, Y., et al. (2025). Community fact-checks trigger moral outrage in replies to misleading posts on social media. Accessed at: https://arxiv.org/pdf/2409.08829

Coombs, W. T., & Holladay, S. J. (2014). How publics react to crisis communication efforts. *Journal of Communication Management, 18*(1), 40–57.

DiResta, R. (2024). *Invisible rulers: The people who turn lies into reality*. PublicAffairs.

McLoughlin, K. L., et al. (2024). Misinformation exploits outrage to spread online. *Science, 386*(6725), 991–996. Accessed at: https://www.science.org/doi/10.1126/science.adl2829

Muralidharan, S., Dillistone, K., & Shin, J.-H. (2011). Hope for Haiti: An analysis of Facebook and Twitter donations during the earthquake relief efforts. *Public Relations Review, 37*(2), 175–177.

Nyhan, B., & Reifler, J. (2010). When corrections fail: The persistence of political misperceptions. *Political Behavior, 32*(2), 303–330.

Papacharissi, Z. (2015). *Affective publics: Sentiment, technology, and politics*. Oxford University Press.

Van Bavel, J. J., Robertson, C. E., del Rosario, K., Rasmussen, J., & Rathje, S. (2024). Social media and morality. *Annual Review of Psychology, 75*, 101–129. Accessed at: https://www.annualreviews.org/content/journals/10.1146/annurev-psych-022123-110258

Vosoughi, S., Roy, D., & Aral, S. (2018). The spread of true and false news online. *Science, 359*(6380), 1146–1151.

Index

U. Wolff, *Disinformation Attacks On Businesses*, Management for Professionals, https://doi.org/10.1007/978-3-658-51407-5

The manufacturer's authorised representative in the EU is Springer Nature Customer Service Centre GmbH, Europaplatz 3, 69115 Heidelberg, Germany. If you have any concerns regarding our products, please contact ProductSafety@springernature.com

Printed and bound by CPI Group (UK) Ltd, Croydon, CR0 4YY
07/10/2026
02229349-0004